Music and Image in Concert

Music and Image in Concert

Using images in the
instrumental music concert

Meghan Stevens

Music and Media, Sydney

First published 2009
by Music and Media, Sydney, Australia
MusicandMedia.com.au

Cover and internal design by Meghan Stevens
Contact the author via the web site at: MeghanStevens.com

ISBN 978-0-9807326-0-3

About the author

Meghan Stevens is a writer, graphic designer and composer. She holds a Bachelor of Arts in Contemporary Music from Macquarie University, Sydney, and an Advanced Graphic Design Diploma, Northern Sydney Institute of Technical and Further Education. Meghan's composition, *Twilight*, written in the early 20th-century French symbolist style, has been recorded by Marshall McGuire, one of Australia's leading harpists, and played on ABC Classic FM Radio. She has co-authored two books on yoga philosophy, published in the USA. Meghan has had a life-long interest in the music-image relationship.

Dedication

This book is dedicated to Michel Chion whose work laid the foundations of audio-visual theory.

Acknowledgements

I would like to thank Lena Quinto and Natalie Lewandowski for their ideas and feedback on this book. My thanks also to Peter Rendle for his assistance with editing.

Contents

Table of figures

Performances reviewed

A Midsummer Night's Dream, Sydney Symphony Orchestra
Book of Longing, Philip Glass
Electro Kardiogramm, Kraftwerk
Luminous, Australian Chamber Orchestra
Man Machine, Kraftwerk
Music Non Stop, Kraftwerk
(Improvisation), The Necks
Neon Lights, Kraftwerk
Numbers, Kraftwerk
Planet of Visions, Kraftwerk
Pocket Calculator, Kraftwerk
Radioactivity, Kraftwerk
Rembrandt's World, Australian Brandenburg Orchestra
Sinfonia Antartica, Sydney Symphony Orchestra
The Arrival, Australian Chamber Orchestra
The Colour of Time, Sydney Symphony Orchestra
The Model, Kraftwerk
The Red Tree, Australian Chamber Orchestra
Tour de France, Kraftwerk
Wild Swans, Australian Ballet

As many performances are referred to a number of times, please see the index for page numbers.

Ours is a visual age.
We are bombarded with pictures from morning till night.

E. H. Gombrich, *The Image and the Eye*, 1982 p.137

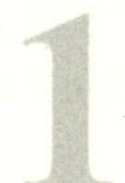

Music and image in concert

From the moment that flowers danced across the screen to Tchaikovsky's *Nutcracker Suite* in Walt Disney's *Fantasia*[1], I was entranced, and knew it was special. This childhood memory of a magical experience faded until, decades later, I attended a Christmas performance, *St Francis of Assisi,* at the University of New South Wales and again experienced the spelling-binding effect of integrated music and image. Projections of paintings and photographs of saints, stately cathedrals and lush Italian countryside accompanied musicians performing classical compositions on traditional instruments, with a commentary guiding us through a maze of image and music. This subtle but stunning performance was unique at the time.

Some twenty years later, it was with a feeling of expectancy, almost excitement, that I anticipated the Australian Chamber Orchestra's concert *Luminous*[2] that was to feature the work of Australian artist Bill Henson. A short time earlier, the New South Wales Art Gallery had featured Henson in a major retrospective. The first time I walked into this exhibition, I halted, stunned by a series of photographs of a young man, naked, beautiful and vulnerable. The images were entrancing but confronting, not due to the youth's nakedness, but because I had entered into his private world where his soul lay naked and exposed. I moved hesitantly around the gallery rooms. Photographs of naked grime-covered adolescents in barren outdoor environments were juxtaposed against rich interiors with brilliant chandeliers, gorgeous antiques and stately settings. These images were unsettling, even shocking, although it was not the nudity that was shocking but the realisation that this was the truth. The vast majority of the world's youth live in wretched circumstances while a privileged few live in opulence. It was with these images in my mind that I anticipated the *Luminous* concert.

The evening had arrived. It was April 2005 and I sat expectantly in my seat, tilting my head back to see the large blank screen that hovered above the orchestra like a monolith from the Stanley Kubrick film *2001: A Space Odyssey* (1968). Richard Tognetti, Lead Violin and Artistic Director of the Australian Chamber Orchestra is known for his innovative concerts but even so the program was surprising, ranging from classical through to pop classics that included a song *I've Been High* from the

[1] This was one of the early releases shown at a suburban movie theatre however I was too young to know the year of the release or the year it was shown.

[2] *Luminous* concert, Australian Chamber Orchestra, City Recital Hall, Sydney, April (2005).

group REM. The program notes stated that the performance was to start with a soundscape by Paul Healy, followed by the *Trio Sonata for Orchestra* by Alfred Schnittke, then *Corpus Christi Carol* by Benjamin Britten[1].

The concert began, images appeared and changed, music moved on, at times the images would stop completely and I would rest my neck but needed to look back in case I missed something. As the performance progressed I became more and more mystified. When it was over I walked out tired, disappointed, and my neck ached. The performance did not have the same impact I had experienced at the Henson exhibition or at previous concerts by the Australian Chamber Orchestra. Disappointment with the imagery might be explained to some extent by the works being filmed rather than original photographs, but that did not explain my disappointment with the music, which was expressive and perfectly performed. What had gone wrong? Why had the performance I had so looked forward to not met my expectations? Were those expectations unrealistic? Was I disappointed because I expected too much, or could each medium have detracted from the other? The thought, that this potentially rich partnership of music and image should be greater than the sum of the parts but was not, created questions that pervaded my days and nights for the next three years.

The answers to these questions are presented here as a group of theories on the concert music-image relationship. The term *instrumental music concert* indicates a performance where it is intended that the music remains dominant or at least maintains the same level of dominance as other **media** and where the music should at no stage in the performance be backgrounded by other media. These music-image concert theories are aimed at concerts where classical or contemporary instrumental music is performed live by an orchestra or band. They do not state how to turn such a performance into a pop concert but how to add images in such a way that attracts a wider audience, without alienating the traditional audience. Note that the term *classical* is used to refer to music from the baroque, classic and romantic periods, while *contemporary* is used to refer to music from the 20th century onwards such as jazz, minimalist, contemporary classical and **newstring music**[2] but excluding pop music and the various music forms that have developed from it.

[1] Full details of this program are provided in the section on the genre-style characteristic.

[2] Newstring music is a term coined by the author to describe original music that combines elements from classical, jazz and varying types of popular music, and is played on a combination of modern and classical instruments. See more details in glossary.

The aim of adding images to concert is to replace the more intimate visual aspect lost from music performance since the late nineteenth century due to large concert halls, for an audience that has become image-focused due to film, television and the Internet. Given that a strong visual component is now considered a normal part of entertainment, it is likely that younger generations would find the traditional instrumental music concert deficient in imagery, even in smaller venues where the musicians can be clearly seen. While the theories are aimed at live concert, many can be applied to any music-image performance where the music should not be backgrounded by added image, such as music performance on television and the Internet.

The theories can rightly be criticised as being created from limited evidence. I make no apologies for this for a number of reasons. Firstly, there is little written or researched that is directly applicable to the instrumental music concert. Secondly, this book is meant to provide a starting point for music-image concert theory. Thirdly, the proposals are supported by film theory, music-video theory, **multimedia** theory and cognitive psychology research, as well as actual concert situations, and all are discussed in detail. And finally, adding image to music is an art rather than a science, and the most effective way to determine what works is likely to be a trial and error approach.

Alternative arguments and research that disagrees with that referenced here have not been included. However it should be noted that there appears to be no literature opposing any of the audio-visual theories of the French composer-filmmaker, Michel Chion. Alternative arguments have not been presented because this is not meant to be an academic publication. It is intended as a guide for artistic directors and image creators to implement image in the instrumental music concert.

History of the visual aspect of concert

Pre 18th century

In the middle ages the public music concert was unknown and music was primarily an accompaniment for other activities such as social and religious events[1]. Music fell into three categories: sacred music, music of the aristocracy, and music of the peasants. In all these musical environments, visuals played a dominant role. In churches, if the singers were not visible then religious icons filled the gaze. At social events, the musicians and other artists were close to their audience. When performing in the

[1] Weber, W., Concert (ii), *Grove Music Online* (2007).

residences of the aristocracy, the audience and musicians were in a private salon allowing observation of the musician's every expression and movement. The visual component was an integral part of the music experience.

This intimacy between musician and audience continued in the Renaissance. Taverns provided music to peasants, while music became increasingly important in the courts of the nobility[1]. The church often provided strictly controlled music performances following religious services[2]. All venues had a strong visual component: taverns and private concerts were small and intimate, while imagery covered church walls. This continued into the baroque era.

Classical era

Throughout the classical era, the music concert became an increasingly popular event. The emerging middle class in the 18th century provided the opportunity for composers to become financially independent of churches and wealthy patrons by offering public performances. Concert halls of the eighteenth century were multi-purpose venues that normally accommodated no more than 300 people[3]. Secular concert performances were informal events with audiences of the classical period often conversing, eating and drinking throughout, all to the detriment of the performance. There was much to see in this environment, not only the performers but the social activities of the other patrons. Dramatic opening phrases were essential to catch audience attention, and were much like today's television theme tune that alerts the viewer that a program is about to start.

Romantic era

Throughout the romantic period an informal concert atmosphere continued. Audiences often freely expressed their reactions and it was not uncommon for members of the audience to shout insults at the musicians and conductor. It was also during this period that the instrumental soloist emerged with a popularity rivalling today's pop music stars. Liszt initiated the solo recital in the late 1830s and played to frenzied audiences[4]. The increasing popularity of the virtuoso performance of the nineteenth century resulted in the building of ever larger concert halls and this culminated with Royal Albert Hall being built in 1871 to seat an audience of six thousand; in parallel with concert hall expansion, professional orches-

---

[1] Kamien, R., *Music an Appreciation*, McGraw Hill (2000) 113.

[2] Weber, W., Concert (ii), *Grove Music Online* (2007).

[3] Weber, W., Concert (ii), *Grove Music Online* (2007).

[4] Schoenberg, H., *The lives of the great composers*, Davis-Poynter (1971) 181.

tras were founded[1]. At this time concerts became one of the main social activities in cities and now included middle and working class citizens. The intimacy of previous eras, where audiences could observe even the smallest musical gesture, had been lost.

20th Century

The concert hall developments in the twentieth century created a different social space that is unlike many other forms of entertainment. Described as an unnatural environment, the concert hall can be somewhat likened to a museum space with a rarefied atmosphere that creates a divide between musician and audience. The classical music concert has become a concentrated and extreme event where creativity has been stifled and audience needs subordinated. Today's classical concert places an unrelaxed emotional pressure on audiences that is far removed from the composing, improvisation and performance traditions of Bach, Handel, Mozart, Beethoven, Liszt and Busoni. This has imposed an artificial boundary that is restrictive and results in a performance that is constricted and concentrated.[2]

It was not until the instrumental concert became fully established that modern concert etiquette emerged with listeners expected to remain silently, almost piously, in their allotted seat for the duration[3]. This twentieth century protocol, combined with the concert hall size, created an impersonal, image-poor event for a large part of the audience. The belief that the classical concert atmosphere stifles musicians and audiences is widely supported. It is claimed that the current format reduces audience enjoyment due to the requirement to sit still for extended periods, clap at specific times and be attentive throughout the performance[4]. The large concert hall has been attributed to causing artistic asphyxiation and the effective demise of artistic creativity[5] with the music likened to museum art objects[6].

This concert hall environment may be responsible for the different attendance levels between classical music concerts, opera and ballet. Over time classical music attendances have decreased while opera and ballet attendances have increased[7]. One proposal for this discrepancy is that opera and ballet performances are often in smaller venues that allow a

[1] Weber, W., Concert (ii), *Grove Music Online* (2007).

[2] Said, E., *Musical Elaborations*, Columbia (1991) xix, 2-3, 5, 11, 20-21.

[3] Weber, W., Concert (ii), *Grove Music Online* (2007).

[4] Stockhammer, J., Morning Interview, *ABC Classic FM radio*, 7th March (2008).

[5] Cook, N., *Analysing musical multimedia*, Oxford University Press (1998) vii.

[6] Alperson, P., The Instrumentality of Music, (2008) 44.

[7] Hocking, R. & Letts, R., International classical music audience attendance trends 1990-2005, *Music Council of Australia* (2008).

more intimate relationship between performers and audience, and allow the performer to be more visible than musicians in large concert halls. Richard Gill, the music director of Victorian Opera, stated that when they have used small venues, audiences have expressed their pleasure at being in these intimate spaces[1].

The instrumental music concert as we know it today is a phenomenon of the last hundred years, and unless the performance environment changes, classical and contemporary concert may not last another hundred years.

Role of the musician in concert

Musicians playing instruments are the core of the music concert, and the relationship between body and instrument is of extraordinary importance, so much so, that at times the body-instrument connection becomes seamless[2]. At these times the body and its actions are part of the performance. Thus the animate and the inanimate come together to create music, and the sight of the musician is an important part of the performance. This is supported by cognitive psychology research that suggests that musicians express their musical intentions through their bodies; these intentions are perceived by the audience and affect the audience interpretation of the music[3]. Not only do these expressions, gestures and movements of the artists communicate their emotions during performance, they can be contagious, spreading through the audience during a concert[4]. Lucinda Moon, first violin and concertmaster of the Australian Brandenburg Orchestra, created this effect during her performance of Vivaldi's *Four Seasons* (2005). It was a very special experience for the audience. Her slim, lithe swaying body was one with the violin, like a nature spirit swaying in the breeze while conjuring music from the elements. The entire audience was entranced. When the performance finished there was absolute silence for many moments, the audience was literally spellbound.

While some musicians have the ability to communicate using their entire body, in classical and contemporary music most communicate through expressions and small gestures. These can be difficult to discriminate at the distances involved with large concert halls. As we tend to think of sound as an attribute of a visible object[5], in a live situation at least un-

---

[1] Nicolson, M., Weekend Life, *ABC Classic FM radio* 30th August (2008).

[2] Alperson, P., The Instrumentality of Music, *Aesthetics and Art Criticism* 66/1 (2008) 37, 40, 44, 47.

[3] Davison, J., Visual Perception of Performance Manner in the Movements of Solo Musicians, *Psychology of Music* 21 (1993) 103-113; Thompson, W., Graham, P. & Russo, F.,Seeing music performance: Visual influences on perception and experience, *Semiotica* 156/1-4 (2005).

[4] Gombrich, E. H., *Four Theories of Artistic Expression*, Manchester University (1996) 150.

[5] Metz, C. & Gurrieri, G., Aural Objects, *Yale French Studies* 60 (1980) 30.

consciously, we expect to see the source of the music, and much of the 'realness' of performance comes from seeing the musicians. If their facial expressions and gestures cannot be seen it may result in a lesser experience.

Recording and Broadcasting

In the late nineteenth and early twentieth centuries, the development of recording technology and radio broadcasting removed image completely from much music listening. However there is a growing body of evidence to show that visual information plays an important role in the understanding and interpretation of music[1]. Visual information, such as facial expressions and body movements, influence and can actually change what is heard[2]. Given that musicians' facial expressions and movements can literally change what we hear, it can be argued that recorded music is not authentic. At the same time as we are experiencing this loss of image with classical music, image dominates leisure in the Western world through television, film and the Internet. In 2006 the average amount of television watched by each American was 4 hours and 35 minutes a day[3]. While the visual aspect has been reduced or removed from music, there has been an increase in audience desire for image with "evidence that society is in a cultural bulimia that ravenously devours and regurgitates images at random"[4].

A solution might appear to be televised classical music, but this has a number of negatives including degradation of subtle acoustics, the loss of atmosphere, the forced focus of the close-up that removes choice, and the unnatural super close-ups of performers that force the viewer to observe every bead of sweat and imperfection in the musician's appearance and performance. If the musician is stressed by the difficulty of the performance, extreme close-ups that highlight the difficulties they are having can detract from the pleasure of watching the performance. If the music is played on acoustic instruments then a recording or broadcast does not have the harmonic complexity of a live performance. "It is only in live performance, offering 'real' sound and a balance of the expected with the unexpected, that the capacity for plenitude in human musical experience can be fully satisfied"[5].

---

[1] Cohen, A., Film Music: Perspectives from Cognitive Psychology, *Music and Cinema*, Buhler, Flinn & Neumeyer eds Wesleyan (2000).

[2] Thompson, W., Graham, P. & Russo, F., Seeing music performance (2005) 203-4.

[3] Nielsen Research, *Television's Popularity is Still Growing*, Nielsen Media Research (2006).

[4] Jones, S., Cohesive But Not Coherent: Music Videos, *Popular Music and Society*, 12/4 (1998) 15.

[5] Dunsby, J., Performance, *Grove Music Online* (2007).

Audio-visual performances

In most situations, past and present, when music is combined with other media it plays a supporting role; the pop concert has been an exception to this tradition and it has long been claimed that the pop concert is an audiovisual phenomenon[1]. The pop concert, as a music-image event, started in the sixties. In 1966, Pink Floyd extended stage lighting by projecting image slides onto band members, with the results described as colourful, frightening, grotesque and beautiful[2]. Image accompaniment for the pop concert continued to develop throughout the late twentieth century with current pop concerts, such as those of Kylie Minogue, approaching the sophistication of the stage musical.

While the orchestral concert has distanced the audience from the musicians, the pop concert has brought the audience closer to the performers. Even though pop concerts are often in larger venues, the use of real-time video screens and close-up shots allow the audience to see the musicians' smallest gestures, while at the same time experiencing the heightened atmosphere of being at a live performance that cannot be experienced watching television. Attendance at a pop concert does not demand quietness and stillness and audiences freely express themselves. This is not to suggest that the pop concert format would be acceptable to classical and contemporary music concert audiences, but shows how wide the gap between the two has become. Today, to attract a wider audience, the classical music concert has started to follow the lead of the pop concert, and in some performances, is using image to support music. This need to attract a wider audience has been necessary due to the declining popularity of classical music as well as its aging patrons who are not being replaced by a younger audience[3].

André Rieu has addressed the issue of declining classical music audiences by creating spectacle and audience involvement. However, shrouding musicians with mist, decorating a venue with balloons, and using whistles to accompany the music does nothing to enhance the music itself. Audience participation such as clapping, singing, and in one concert, gargling water to create sound effects, creates involvement but not the kind normally expected at an instrumental music concert. Such activities distract from the music and are likely to alienate the traditional concert goer. This is not to criticise Rieu's approach. His aim is to introduce classical music to a new audience by removing the solemn

---

[1] Björnberg, A., Structural Relationships of Music and Images in Music Video, *Popular Music* 13/1 (1994) 53.

[2] Mason, N., *Inside Out: A Personal History of Pink Floyd*, Chronicle Books (2004) 40.

[3] Hindson, M., The Future of Classical Music, *2MBS FM Fine Music* [magazine], May (2005).

atmosphere normally found in the concert hall and by making classical music accessible for everyone[1] and he has achieved this aim. His extravaganzas are a valid form of entertainment but should not to be confused with the music concert where it is expected that the audience will remain quiet and the music will remain dominant. However Rieu does at times create a more traditional performance, as with his interpretation of *Air from Suite No. 3* by Johann Sebastian Bach[2], with the visual aspect enhanced with an unusual arrangement of the musicians in an interesting setting.

Regardless of the problems of the concert hall and the restrictions classical music performances place on their audiences, many people believe the classical music concert is an important event worth preserving. In this twenty-first century the "distinctions between foreground and background sound are slowly disappearing and, with them, the distinctions among noise, sound and music"[3]. We are surrounded continually by noise pollution that includes a constant 'backgroundization' of music in shops, offices and public places, and this backgroundization of music also occurs through radio and television in the home[4]. The instrumental music concert fulfils an increasingly rare and important function by being presented in an environment where all sounds other than the instrumental music itself, are minimized. This environment prohibits interruptions, allowing the audience to truly focus on the music. In such a performance it is expected that the music should remain the dominant media. However, preserving the dominance of the music while at the same time introducing image is a more complex task than it might initially appear. Even so, the effort involved in adding image to music is worthwhile if it halts the decline in instrumental music audiences and this decline is significant. In the nineteenth and early twentieth century, the music concert was a major form of entertainment. Today the music concert plays a minor role in the entertainment spectrum.

Current audio-visual thinking

Although there is little written on the audio-visual relationship for the music concert, much has been written about the combination in a number of fields including education, film, music-video, multimedia, cognitive psychology, psychomusicology and music philosophy. In music philoso-

[1] Rieu, A., *Sunday Arts,* ABC1 [television], 12 October (2008); André Rieu www.andrerieu.com

[2] Rieu, A., *Australia Bound* [promotional DVD] track 6 (2007).

[3] Kassabian, A., The Sound of a New Film Form, *Popular Music and Film*, Wallflower (2003) 91.

[4] Said, E., *Musical Elaborations*, (1991) 96.

phy, symbolism in music is widely discussed often quoting philosopher Susan Langer's statement that music is an "unconsummated symbol"[1]. She suggests that music is symbolic of something but it is difficult to define exactly what that something is. Discussions of the meaning of music are so extensive and varied that they do little to clarify anything at all. Research on musical emotions is no less confusing and includes a wide variety of conflicting views[2]. Cognitive psychology experiments provide useful information about the combined effects of music and image[3], while the field of music education discusses the use of image to improve the music learning experience[4].

Audio-visual theory for film discusses music as a supporting medium or an equal partner. Possibly the most important audio-visual film theorist is French composer and filmmaker Michel Chion. His book *Audio-Vision: Sound on Screen* (1994) provides a basis for understanding the music-image relationship. Chion's theory of ***Added Value*** states that one sensory perception influences another and transforms it, resulting in us not seeing the same thing when we are listening, and not hearing the same thing when we are seeing[5]. In other words, if we look at something while listening to music, whatever we see may influence and may change what we hear. In the same way if we hear something while we are looking at an object, a scene or a film, what we hear may change our interpretation of what we see and we may see something different. The two senses can combine to create a different experience to what we would have seen or heard had each sense been experienced without the other. Cognitive psychology experiments support this claim and show that when we receive information from multiple senses, the information from one sense can distort the information received from another and the combined result may not accurately reflect either[6].

Discussions of the concert video are limited but there is much written on the music-video, even though it is often seen primarily as a promotional tool. Carol Vernallis in her book *Experiencing Music Video* (2004) presents a serious analysis that discusses the music-image relationship at

[1] Langer, S., *Philosophy in a new key: a study in the symbolism of reason, rite, and art*, Harvard (1960) 241.

[2] Juslin, P. & Västfjäll, D.,Emotional Responses to Music: The Need to Consider Underlying Mechanisms, *Behavioral and Brain Sciences* 31/5 (Oct 2008) 559-575.

[3] Cohen, A., Film Music: Perspectives from Cognitive Psychology (2000); Music Cognition and the Cognitive Psychology of Film Structure, *Canadian Psychology* 43/4 (2002) 215–232.

[4] Geringer, J., Cassidy, J. & Byo, J., Effects of Music with Video on Responses of Nonmusic Majors: An Exploratory Study, *Research in Music Education* 44/3 (1996) 240-251.

[5] Chion, M., *Audio-Vision: Sound on Screen,* Columbia (1994) 5.

[6] Cohen, A., Film Music: Perspectives from Cognitive Psychology (2000), McGurk, H. & MacDonald, J., Hearing lips and seeing voices, *Nature* 264 (1976) 746 - 748; Calvert, G., Brammer, M. & Iversen, S., Crossmodal identification, *Trends in Cognitive Sciences* 2/7 (1998) 247-253.

length. The book provides useful insights that, in many cases, can be applied to the use of image in concert. Works on multimedia are less common than on film or music-video but provide useful information that can be applied to the music concert. Multimedia is different to the instrumental music concert because in multimedia the dominance moves from one media to another. *Analysing Musical Multimedia* (1998) by Nicholas Cook proposes three models of multimedia[1] and these models provide valuable insights into the music-image relationship.

It appears that there have been no previous theories developed for the music-image relationship in the acoustic instrumental music concert, at least in English. However, a number of articles have been written for the use of image to accompany electronic music[2] and audio-visual combinations as an art form[3].

How the book is organised

This chapter discusses the motivation for this book; current audio-visual thinking; the background of the instrumental music concert; the classical music concert today; the role of musicians in concert; the impact of large concert venues; the impact of technology; and how to use this book. The following chapters, except for the last, propose a number of music-image concert theories, followed by reviews of performances showing the practical application of these theories. While the various theories are interrelated, they have been discussed separately for clarity. Regardless, there are a great many factors that jointly influence the music-image relationship, and how that relationship best meets the requirements of the instrumental music concert.

It appears that the most important aspect of the music-image relationship is the degree of **congruency** between music and image. However congruency is complex and includes congruency of **narrative**, congruency of **synchronisation**, congruency of **tempo**, and so on. Congruency also depends on the interpretation of music and image that is influenced by audience experience and education. Therefore congruency is discussed first as a general principle and then specific congruency concepts are expanded in subsequent chapters.

The final chapter discusses the importance of adding image to the instrumental music concert, how looking at the problems of early cinema

---

[1] Cook, N., *Analysing musical multimedia,* (1998) chapter 3 describes the multimedia models 'conformance', 'complementation' and 'contest'.

[2] Rantzen, A., *Audio Visual Synthesis,* (2005).

[3] Föllmer, G. & Gerlach, J., Audiovisions: Music as an Intermedia Art Form, *Media Art Net* (2004).

can help avoid similar mistakes, and how new technologies can be applied.

Application of the proposed theories

The theories in the following chapters have been developed specifically for the instrumental music concert, for a Western audience, and for various music genres including contemporary classical, jazz and new genres of music that span the classical-pop gap such as newstring music. These theories aim to prevent the concert becoming a multimedia event and to ensure that images support the music by assisting the audience to focus on the music.

Examples

A number of the discussions refer to Kraftwerk concerts on the DVD *Minimum-Maximum* (2005) because these provide clear examples of the theories and because Kraftwerk is an avant-garde cross between classical and pop music. A number of Kraftwerk songs have been arranged for classical instrumental performances and this highlights the inherent classical elements of much of their material[1]. These are not on the DVD. The music of Kraftwerk was leading edge in the 1970s and their latest series of concerts are leading edge today in their utilisation of image to accompany music. Their performances, as presented on the *Minimum-Maximum* DVD, appear to be unique in the development of the concert music-image relationship, showing that image can support music and assist the audience to focus on the music.

Kraftwerk have released up to eleven versions of some songs and every performance is different even on the same tour. It is likely that the Internet, as well as being low visual quality, will not show the performance discussed, and this will undermine much of what is suggested. It is not necessary to watch these performances. Reading the descriptions without visuals is no different to reading the descriptions of live concerts without seeing the performance. If you do watch performances on the Internet then expect to be disappointed.

References and formatting

If a reference is positioned at the end of a paragraph after the period, the entire paragraph is attributed to that reference. If several sentences are connected by semi-colons with a reference at the end before the period, all of those sentences are attributed to the reference.

The first time a word from the glossary is used it is in bold.

---

[1] Bussy, P., *Kraftwerk: Man, Machine and Music*, SAF (2005) 187.

2 Congruency of music-image characteristics

This chapter discusses the **characteristics** that create and influence the music-image combination, the issues of congruency and **incongruency** in the music-image combination, and it provides examples of various levels of congruency and incongruency in concerts where images accompany music.

Congruency

Congruency between music and image in the music concert is essential to maintain focus on the music. The degree of congruency between music and image influences how, and to what extent the music appears unchanged to the audience. However congruency, at least to some extent, is in the mind of the beholder.

Definitions

The meaning of congruency as it is used here is the common meaning found in most dictionaries, which is 'agreement, harmony and appropriateness'. The term congruency is used here to define a relationship where the characteristics of the image match the music, and vice versa. This match may be an actual objective match, or the music and image may be subjectively perceived as generally agreeing. It may also occur when music and image appear to coincide such as in synchronisation.

The term 'congruency' is at times used in audio-visual film theory to refer to music and image where these media are said to have the two relationships, congruency and incongruency, and this is sometimes related to counterpoint in music. However the concept of two relationships is simplistic and inadequate to describe the complex music-image combination.

The term **music-image characteristic** applies to two different types of characteristics. The first type consists of those characteristic that make up the music-image combination. These are: **narrative**, **synchronisation**, **rhythm**, **tempo-pace**, meaning, emotion, structure and genre-style. The following diagram shows the characteristics that form the music-image combination.

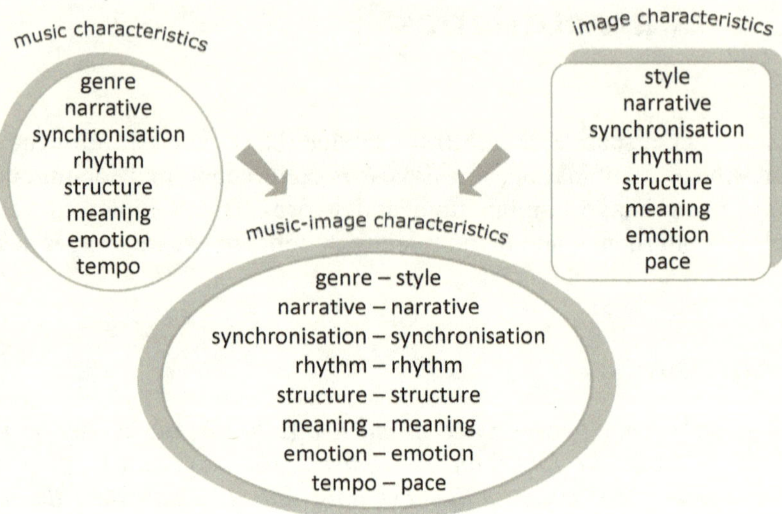

Figure 1 Music-image characteristics

The second type of characteristic influences the music-image relationship but is not part of it. These influences are: the voice as sung or spoken; text as written words; integration of the performance components; and, the musical interpretation by the musician or conductor. The following diagram shows both the characteristics that form the music-image combination, and the characteristics that influence it.

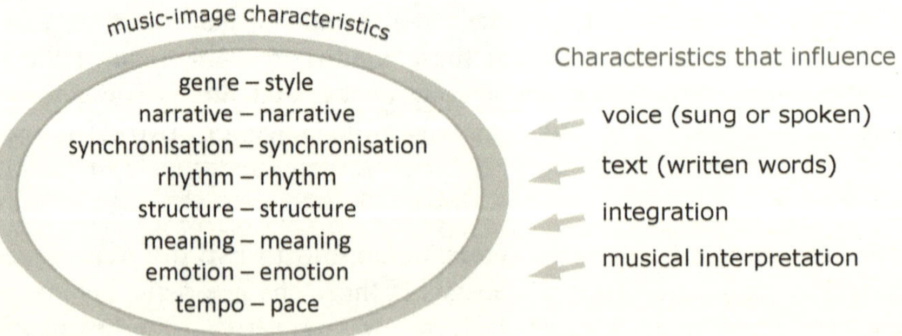

Figure 2 Music-image influences

Effect of image on music

It is known that music is judged more accurately and with greater concentration when not accompanied by image. This is shown in experiments where listeners evaluated sound quality with and without accompanying image. Sound was evaluated accurately when it was not accompanied by video but when video was added and sound quality reduced, the decrease in quality was not noticed. It appears that the addition of video decreased auditory sensitivity, allowing visual information to compensate for poor sound quality. However the reverse did not occur. When visual quality was reduced, the addition of sound did not compensate the loss of visual quality. In summary, the reduced sound quality was compensated for by the addition of visuals but the reduced visual quality was not compensated for by the addition of sound.[1]

Very different research shows that the brain can become overloaded when processing multiple media, and vision can cause loss of information if the brain's speed of processing the information is lower than the speed the information is presented[2]. This might occur in a learning situation where images accompany a talk. If the images are presented more quickly than the audience can process them, such as might occur with a video, the overload will distract attention from the speaker and the audience will miss at least some of the verbal information presented.

The claim that music is backgrounded by incongruent image is further supported by experiments with lights and tones. This research indicates that visual dominance becomes overwhelming when there is a conflict between image and sound[3]. Visual dominance may become so pronounced that vision may completely block other senses[4].

The conclusion that can be drawn from the previously described experiments and research is that visual information will at least to some extent distract attention from music. This will not surprise those music lovers who claim they hear better with their eyes closed. Even though music might be heard more accurately and some people prefer to close their eyes to experience this clarity and focus, the majority of the audience do not close their eyes, indicating that for most people a performance that includes the visual sense is more enjoyable.

---

[1] Iwamiya, S., Interaction Between Auditory and Visual Processing When Listening to Music in an Audio Visual Context: 1. Matching 2. Audio Quality, *Psychomusicology* 13 (1994) 152.

[2] Kozma, R., Learning with Media, *Review of Educational Research*, 61/ 2 (1991) 194-5.

[3] Colavita, F. & Weisberg, D., A further investigation of visual dominance (1979) 345, 347.

[4] Posner, M., Nissen, M. & Klein, R., Visual dominance (1976) 170.

Congruency versus incongruency

It is known that congruency between media leads to more accurate judgements than incongruency. A series of cognitive psychology experiments using different pitch and tempo in music (a simple melody) and different height and speed in image (a bouncing ball) measured the response to different combinations of the music and image. The music and image were evaluated separately with various types of bouncing ball and the music judged as happy or sad. Then different variations of the melody were combined with different variations of a bouncing ball. The results showed that when music and image were experienced separately, judgement was accurate and as predicted. When congruent music and image were combined, such as a high bouncing ball with high pitched music (happy-happy), judgement also accurately reflected the music and image. However when incongruent media were shown together, such as a high pitched melody with a low bouncing ball (happy-sad) neither media was judged accurately and the result was more like a compromise, even when subjects were asked to focus on specific media. The results were consistent over various combinations of music and image. These experiments indicate that congruency is required to accurately perceive music and image when they are combined.[1]

Further, when congruent music was added to image, the combination increased the audience's perception of reality, so that a congruent music-image combination created a heightened sense of reality that the images alone did not have. Thus image can be made to seem more real by the addition of congruent music. In summary: when incongruent music and image are shown together neither is judged accurately; when congruent music and image are shown together both are judged accurately; and when congruent music is added to image, the perception of reality is increased.[2]

The above experiments indicate that both music and image are perceived differently when they are combined. This claim is also made in audio-visual film theory[3]. If images are to be added to the instrumental music concert, it is essential to understand how the combination, particularly the congruency-incongruency aspect, will affect the music and under what circumstances the music will be backgrounded.

---

[1] Cohen, A., Associationsim and musical soundtrack phenomena, *Contemporary Music Review* 9 /1 & 2 (1993) 168-170.

[2] Cohen, A., Film Music: Perspectives from Cognitive Psychology (2000) 362-367.

[3] Chion, M., *Audio-Vision: Sound on Screen,* Columbia (1994) 5.

Determining Congruency

Music and image are very different media comprised of different elements with the possible result that the decision on what is congruent may vary from one person to another. Even so, there are three factors that will create similar associations of music and image between different people. These are: our cultural and educational background, learned associations, and the context in which the music and image are presented. We all listen to music through a cultural and experiential filter that affects how we interpret the meaning[1]. We attribute meanings such as tones being characterised by the physical characteristics of light or dark, high or low, rough or smooth, and piecing or round; certain characteristics are linked, such as 'large' associated with a 'low' tone; musical instruments often have specific associations such as the organ is often associated with the church and the gong is linked to the Orient and the exotic[2]. This information about music is transmitted and reinforced through discussions, reviews and program notes, which normally provide a consistent view of composers and their works. This consistency occurs because those experienced and educated in the arts are likely to coincide in their judgments of artistic works[3], and this is probably due to education transmitting culturally determined norms[4].

The second factor, learned associations between music and images or events, results in music reflecting a single congruent concept. For example the music of a Christmas carol will normally be associated with the festival. Another example is the actual title of music or its movements, such as *Requiem,* which by its meaning creates a specific association of music and function. The last factor, context, results in music meaning many things depending on the context in which it is performed, and to some extent music will take on the characteristics of any image that accompanies it[5].

Congruency is, to a large extent, in the mind of the beholder because the same music can mean different things to different people and indeed different things to the same people at different times. Opinion at a particular time and place can be influenced by current emotional state and expectations of the performance. Even so, to a large extent the interpretation of whether congruency is achieved between music and image depends on the cultural background, education and experience of the audience.

---

[1] Feld, S., Communication, Music, and Speech about Music, *Yearbook for Traditional Music* 16 (1984) 6-8.

[2] Meyer, L., *Emotion and Meaning in Music*, University of Chicago (1956) 259, 261.

[3] Pickford, R., *Psychology and Visual Aesthetics,* Hutchinson Educational (1972) 250.

[4] Iliffe, A. H., A study of preferences in feminine beauty, *British Journal of Psychology* (1960) 272.

[5] Cook, N., *Analysing musical multimedia* (1998) 22-3.

Congruency within a single characteristic

Each individual music-image characteristic has a level of congruency. While theoretically the congruency can be a continuum, this would be difficult to discuss. The diagram below shows the three types of relationships that are used to discuss a single music-image characteristic. These are congruent, neutral and incongruent[1].

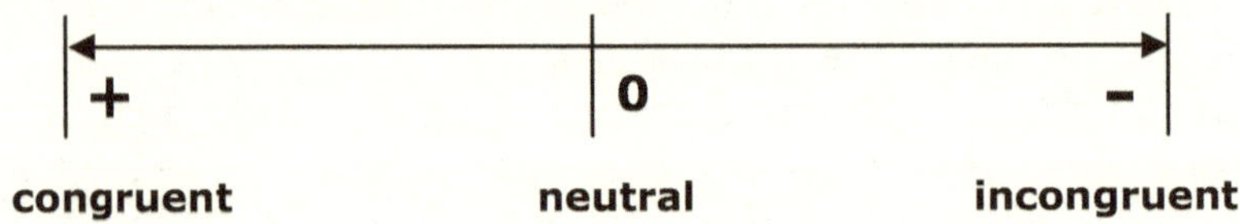

Figure 3 Congruency types for a characteristic

The congruent relationship is a match between the music and image and this is positive for focusing attention on the music. The neutral relationship is where there is neither match nor mismatch and this is neither positive nor negative. The incongruent relationship is a mismatch between the music and image, which is negative and distracts attention from the music. These three relationships exist between the music and the image for each characteristic within the music-image relationship.

The following diagram shows three different relationships of the genre-style characteristic. A single genre of music is combined with three different styles of image.

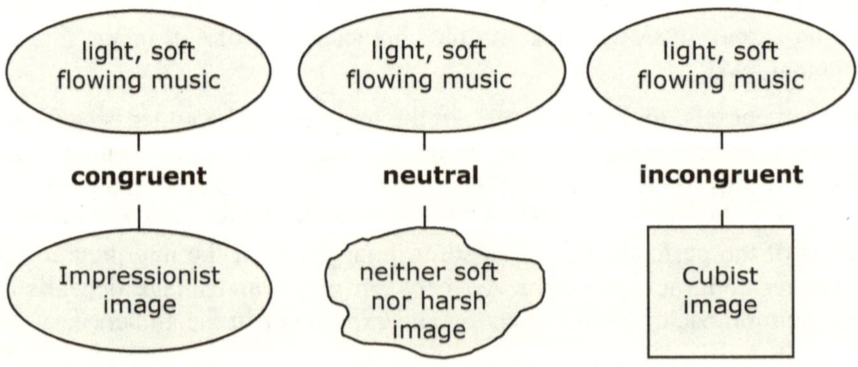

Figure 4 Relationships in the genre-style characteristic

---

[1] These relationships are similar to Cook's multimedia models: 'conformance', 'complementation' and 'contest', in Cook, N. *Analysing musical multimedia* (1998) 98-106.

An Impressionist image creates a congruent relationship with light, soft, flowing music. An image that is neither soft nor harsh creates a neutral relationship. A Cubist image creates an incongruent relationship with this light, soft, flowing music because Cubism has harsh, pointed edges

Overall music-image relationship

The overall music-image relationship is determined by the combination of all music-image characteristics. This overall music-image relationship is a continuum (as occurs with individual characteristics). The continuum of the overall relationship ranges from **full congruency** with the music and image of all characteristics matching, through to full incongruency, which is a mismatch within each and every characteristic. As previously stated, while congruency is a continuum, this would be difficult to discuss. The overall music-image relationship is discussed as having four relationships: full congruency, **partial congruency**, **neutral congruency** and incongruency.

Full congruency is where all characteristics are congruent. Partial congruency is a combination of congruent and neutral characteristics but no incongruent characteristics. Neutral congruency is where all characteristics are neutral; there is neither a match nor a mismatch between the music and image of any characteristic; they are not congruent but neither are they incongruent. Incongruency is where one or more characteristics are incongruent and this creates conflict, taking the focus away from the music. If even one characteristic has an incongruent music-image relationship, it is likely to create a negative impact therefore partial incongruency is likely to be just as negative as full incongruency. This being the case, the term 'incongruency' is used regardless of whether it is partial or full incongruency.

In summary, each individual characteristic is discussed as having three relationships: congruent, neutral, and incongruent. The overall music-image relationship is discussed as having four relationships: full congruency, partial congruency, neutral congruency and incongruency. These four relationships are shown in the diagram below. The term 'positive' means that audience focus will be maintained on the music or the music-image combination, whereas the term 'negative' means the focus is taken away from the music.

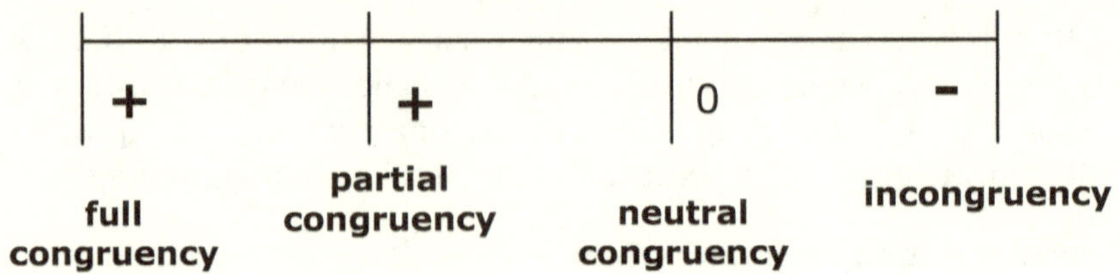

Figure 5 Types of overall congruency

The overall music-image relationship is more complex than it first appears. The music-image relationship is not necessarily stable and may change from moment to moment[1]. This may occur due to a change in any of the characteristics. This possibility for moment to moment changes makes the music-image relationship complex because it involves many different characteristics and each may have a different music-image relationship at any one time. However the overall music-image relationship can only be congruent when at least one of the characteristics is congruent and none are incongruent. To create full congruency over the entire music-image relationship involves every characteristic being congruent. This may be difficult to achieve and it is more likely that only some characteristics will be congruent. When only some characteristics are congruent, the ones that are not congruent become important in determining whether the overall relationship is congruent or incongruent.

Multimedia

The relationships of congruency, neutral congruency, and incongruency can be likened to multimedia models[2]. It is useful to draw on multimedia for working models in the music-image relationship, but the music concert has different aims to multimedia and adding image to the music concert should not create multimedia. In multimedia the dominance will pass to different media at different times, whereas in the music concert, the music should remain dominant, or at least the music should maintain equal dominance with the other media. An example of a multimedia performance is the Philip Glass *Book of Longing,* which is discussed in detail in the section on voice and text.

Incongruency is a normal part of multimedia but maintaining focus on the music requires congruency. Incongruency of music and image distracts from the music and can be likened to dissonance in music that distracts from the dominance of the melody. Once the dissonance is re-

[1] Cook, N. *Analysing musical multimedia,* (1998) 113.

[2] Nicholas Cook developed the multimedia models 'conformance', 'complementation' and 'contest', Cook, N., *Analysing musical multimedia* (1998) 98-106.

solved the dominance returns to the melody but this does not occur with incongruency because once attention focuses on the image it tends to stay on the image. This is not to suggest that multimedia is in any way inferior. Multimedia may draw new audiences but it is unlikely to satisfy the music-lover who wants to focus on the music.

Full congruency

Congruency across all characteristics of the music-image relationship normally maintains focus on the music-image combination, however full congruency must be handled carefully as it can produce unintentional results such as humour.

Full congruency occurs when there appears to be a match across all characteristics of the music-image relationship, as far as can be achieved with different media. The following diagram shows that to achieve full congruency, all characteristics must be congruent and none can be neutral or incongruent.

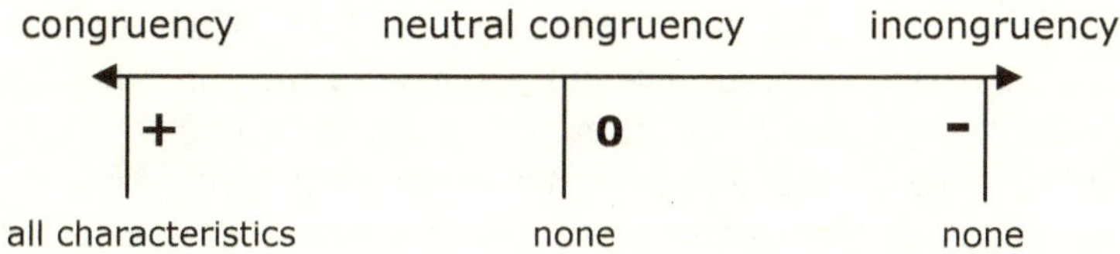

Figure 6 Full congruency

When there is congruency between visual and auditory information, attention and memory are high[1] and this congruency is one of the methods that can be used to focus increased attention on music in film[2] (normally music is backgrounded in film). The result of high levels of congruency is that it normally causes attention and focus to be on the composite rather than on the individual media[3]. Therefore when music and image are fully congruent there is a high degree of focus on the music-image

[1] Grimes, T., Audio-Video Correspondence and Its Role in Attention and Memory, in *Educational Technology Research and Development* 38/3 (1990) 15, 23-24.

[2] Kassabian, A., *Hearing Film: Tracking Identification in Contemporary Hollywood Film Music*, Routledge (2001) 53.

[3] Lipscomb, S. & Kendall, R., Perceptual Judgement of the Relationship between Musical and Visual Components in Film, *Psychomusicology*, 13 (1994) 91.

combination and the music is not backgrounded as normally occurs in film, but neither is it foregrounded.

Apparent congruency

Congruency can be an apparent music-image match. Apparent congruency depends on perception and interpretation. For instance, there may not be an actual match if the relationship was analysed exactly, as a computer might judge such characteristics as synchronisation and tempo. However, it is irrelevant whether the match is exact because congruency depends on interpretation and interpretation is often a subjective decision. Congruency is achieved if the music and image appear to be congruent. While this further complicates the relationship, it does not necessarily make congruency more difficult to achieve and may even make it easier to achieve. The decision as to whether the music and image appear congruent or otherwise requires an understanding of how audiences are likely to interpret the music-image characteristics.

Issues with full congruency

Full congruency can produce unintentional results such as humour and this is discussed further in the section on mickey-mousing. Cartoons often appear to have full congruency due to tight synchronisation that reinforces actions. There are normally some conflicts in other characteristics even though these are often not noticeable due to the humour. Humour may be an exception to the congruency rule because even if there is congruency in all music-image characteristics, in a humorous performance, the humour is likely to be forceful enough to background the music. This is discussed further in the section on **humorous narrative**. Another problem that can occur with full congruency is that something expected often creates little interest[1] but a combination of expected and unexpected, adds richness to performance[2]. This suggests that full congruency has the potential to be uninteresting but this need not be the case. Creating an exciting, fully congruent music-image relationship is far from impossible as was shown with *The Red Tree* (2008). *The Red Tree* (2008) was a classical concert that combined music, image and song, and was probably as close to full congruency as any classical music concert can achieve, while at the same time being a fascinating and inspiring performance.

The following two discussions of concerts are examples of full congruency. Individual characteristics are briefly discussed here as part of

[1] Boltz, M., Schulkind, M. & Kantra, S., Effects of background music on the remembering of filmed events, *Memory and Cognition* 19/6 (1991) 601.

[2] Dunsby, J., Performance (2007).

congruency but are discussed in more detail in the chapter on that characteristic.

The Red Tree

The Red Tree was performed by the Australian Chamber Orchestra and the Gondwana Voices children's choir in 2008. It combined the images and text from Shaun Tan's award winning children's book of the same name, with music (in seven movements) and lyrics created to accompany the book's images[1]. *The Red Tree* was successful for many reasons including congruency, which was achieved, as far as it can be achieved in classical music, across all characteristics. The success was also due to the style of narrative, which is discussed in the section on open narrative.

The words from the book were used during the silence between movements. Silence allows time for the music to breathe and time for audience contemplation. Silence is not neutral; it is the opposite of just heard sound and it creates contrast[2]. If badly handled the contrast created by silence becomes incongruency. Displaying text on the screen during the silent pauses at the beginning of the music and between movements is an ideal way of matching sound silence and image 'silence', creating congruency between music and image. Further, by adding text we force the audience to impose an internal sound, filling the silence[3].

The Red Tree book is about a little red haired girl and her feelings and reactions as she goes about her daily life. The story starts in the girl's bedroom, which is waist-deep in dried leaves. The music's first movement, *Black Leaves*, reflects the uncertain emotion but 'strangely familiar' feeling that the composer found in the images, and which he tried to replicate by creating a composition that was inspired by folk music and Gregorian chant[4]. This strangely familiar music is congruent with the images (bedroom and leaves), whose familiarity is made strange by their combination.

The words 'Darkness overcomes you' lead into a movement that shows an image of the girl walking along a street under the shadow of a huge open-mouthed fish with other people going about their daily lives apparently unaware of this aberration. This is followed by a very different setting, a lonely beach with the little girl in a diving bell helmet, sitting quietly inside a partially water-filled bottle that has been washed up on the pebbles under a dark sky that is clearing in the distance. The scenes,

---

[1] *The Red Tree* music was composed by Michael Yezerski and Richard Tognetti with lyrics created by Michael Yezerski, and image designed by Andrew Walsh,

[2] Chion, M., *Audio-Vision* (1994) 57.

[3] Quinto, L., personal conversation, 17 March (2009).

[4] *The Red Tree* program notes (2008).

the street in shadow and sitting passively inside the bottle but with a clearing sky, are open to an interpretation based around current problems that resolve, and this is reflected in the strange gentle beauty of the music, creating congruency of music and image. A number of different events follow and the story ends with an abundant fully-grown tree covered in red leaves, growing in the little red-haired girl's bedroom. The congruency of the inspirational final phase of the music, combined with the image of abundance, create the expectation of a brighter future.

In each movement, the pace, tone and structure of the music reflect the ideas and emotions of the images. Images from the book are often interspersed with moving patterns of colours and textures, and this is an example of abstract image bordering on neutral congruency. To ensure abstract images are not in conflict, they need to be part of an integrated whole and this was achieved using colours and textures from the book, resulting in congruency between images. The pace of the moving abstract images was congruent with the tempo of the music. The lyrics were in a number of languages including English and were partially developed through improvisation. Rather than being a typical song where the voice normally dominates the music, the singing was more like an additional instrument to the orchestra. The effect was that rather than words backgrounding the music the voices seemed an integral part of the orchestra.

This music-image combination had the advantage of specifically composed music that perfectly complements the images. This congruency was noted in the reviews: "the rich variety of textures, styles and colours of Tan's illustrations were integral to [the] Yezerski conception of the music"[1] and "the union of music and art [was] effective and seamless"[2]. It is likely that it may be considerably easier to achieve congruency by creating music for image than when creating image for music. This may occur because once music is heard without images, unless it is **program music**, the listener allocates their own personal interpretation. Whereas music created for image could be considered a special type of program music that when first heard is automatically associated with the image it accompanies. As music can take on many meanings, it is unlikely, or less likely, there will be any conflict between the audience's ideas and what is presented at a first hearing. The result is that specifically written music is almost a guarantee of congruency because the music matches the image and the audience has no preconceived ideas about the music before it is first heard. A comment on the performance stated the music is "symbi-

[1] Mathison, L., A Potent Mix, *ACO The Red Tree Concert Reviews* [online] (2008).
[2] Szabo, A., ACO Shines in The Red Tree, *ACO The Red Tree Concert Reviews* [online] (2008).

otically paired with illustrations and text [in a] bold and stunningly rich collaboration [that was] enticingly complex, chaotic and beautiful"[1].

The Red Tree is an example of the successful combining of image and song with music, where neither image nor song detracts from the music but create a congruent combination where attention is maintained on the music-image-song combination without backgrounding the music. This might suggest that *The Red Tree* is multimedia and this is a reasonable proposition. However multimedia presupposes that the mediums will interact and dominance will pass from one media to another and there would normally be some degree of conflict[2]. Therefore it could also be claimed that *The Red Tree* is not multimedia because even though the music is not primary, neither are the images nor the singing. No media dominates the performance, overall nor intermittently, and to a large extent this occurs due to congruency of all media.

Man Machine

For those readers interested only in adding image to traditional classical music, as opposed to contemporary, newstring music or jazz, the following discussion may not be of interest. In Kraftwerk's *Man Machine* (2005) the images were created to accompany the music and the combination is as congruent as is possible with two different media. *Man Machine* does have the advantage of a strong beat, which makes full congruency easier to achieve. The congruency in *Man Machine* (2005) is of a very different nature to that of *The Red Tree.* Kraftwerk, a German group founded in the 1970s, created music that was neither pop nor classical, but a form of minimalist, electronic music, considered avant-garde at the time, and described as electronic chamber music[3]. They developed simple rhythms and repetitive structures, and shared platforms with artists such as Philip Glass[4].

Kraftwerk were strongly influenced by German Expressionism, Dadaism and Futurism and the industrialist aspects of these movements. Typically their concerts present old fashioned images, in marked contrast to their modernist music[5] that could be considered progressive even by today's standards. The Kraftwerk *Minimum-Maximum* DVD, on which the comments in this book are based, is a music video of selected 2004 concert tour performances. The imagery that was projected behind the group in the concert has also been frequently superimposed over the top of the

[1] Botticelli, L., The Red Tree, *ACO The Red Tree Concert Reviews* [online] (2008).
[2] Cook, N., *Analysing musical multimedia* (1998) 106.
[3] Bussy, P., *Kraftwerk: Man, Machine and Music* (2005) 18, 75.
[4] Gray, L., The Classic Kraftwerk, *New Internationalist* 314 (1999).
[5] Bussy, P., *Kraftwerk: Man, Machine and Music* (2005) 81, 95, 120-2, 198.

concert shots in the DVD. The concerts used massive screens that covered the entire back stage except for a horizontal band of colour that ran across the stage from the floor to hip height beneath the screen. Kraftwerk's aim was for the visuals to enlarge their music[1] and they have described their imagery as 'electronic ballets'[2]. Like most of the Kraftwerk imagery, the basis for the *Man Machine* imagery used in the 2004 tour was that used for the original release of the music.

The performance starts with the repeating lyrics 'man machine' sung in darkness as gigantic black silhouettes gradually appear on a red lit background. The lyrics stop and the music begins. The curtains open showing a stage shrouded in red haze with occasional flashes of light and smoke drifting upwards. Kraftwerk stand behind computers, much like staff in a futuristic factory. Synchronised text in a pixelated industrial-like font flashes across the entire back of the stage. The text of the repeating lyric 'machine' is built into architectural-like constructions that form walls that disappear to be immediately rebuilt. The colour palette is black, red and white. Both the industrialised text and construction-like images create congruency with the meaning given to the music by its title *Man Machine*. The dense colours, red and black, are congruent with the feeling of solidity and strength that the words, 'man machine', impart. The colours and words are congruent with the strong mechanical-like repetition of music that includes sounds like tapping, grinding, clanking and the meshing of gears.

There appears to be absolute synchronisation of sound and image creating further congruence. The words give way to dynamic arrangements of lines and geometric shapes that at times fly apart. Later, various architectural-like combinations of red, black and white squares are constructed and deconstructed forming complex patterns reminiscent of changing cityscapes. The shapes, colours and typography are inspired by Russian artist El Lissitzky. Lissitzky's aim was to create an impersonal art, just as machines create impersonal products[3]. Kraftwerk also aim to remove their individual personalities from their music and present themselves as an industrial entity; 'Kraftwerk' means 'power plant' and in concerts the group has been introduced as a man-machine 'die Mensch-Machine – Kraftwerk'[4]. The song achieves congruency in all characteristics as well as the philosophy behind the images and music. The *Man Machine* performance is an example of full congruency where all characteristics of

---

[1] Bussy, P., *Kraftwerk: Man, Machine and Music* (2005) 120-2.

[2] Hütter, R., & Schneider, F., Interview in Alessandrini, P. Kraftwerk, *Rock & Folk* 118 (Nov 1976).

[3] Read, H., in *El Lissitzky: Life.Letters.Texts*, ed Sophie Lissitzky-Küppers, Thames & Hudson (1968) 8.

[4] Bussy, P., *Kraftwerk: Man, Machine and Music* (2005) 28, 121.

music and image are congruent. Kraftwerk's *Man Machine* performance achieves their stated aim of using image to help maintain attention on the music. The same concepts can be applied to classical and contemporary music, to create congruency that focuses attention on the music or the music-image combination.

Neutral congruency

Neutral congruency will not distract from the music but nor will it focus attention on the music.

Neutral congruency refers to a media relationship where all characteristics are neutral and there is neither match nor conflict between the music and image. It would be unusual to achieve neutral congruency over the entire music-image relationship and it is more likely that only some characteristics will be neutral.

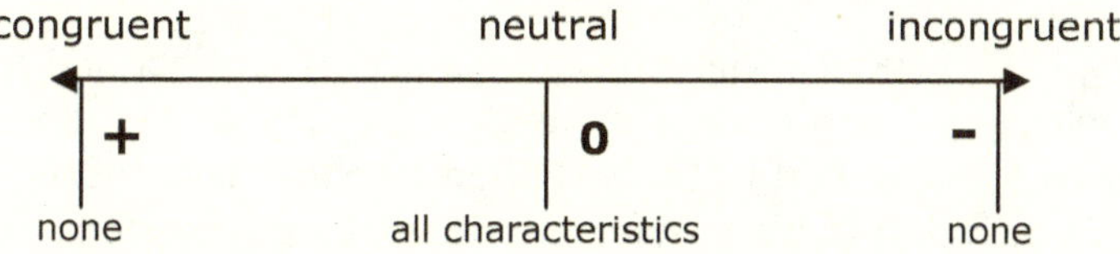

Figure 7 Neutral congruency

Neutral congruency is a **complementary relationship** where each media has its own intrinsic qualities and where each media complements the other but there is no incongruency. A complementary relationship is one which forms a 'balanced whole' where one media adds what is missing in the other media. It also occurs where one media contrasts with the other as occurs with complementary colours but there is no conflict between the contrasting media. In describing neutral congruency, complementary means that the music and images co-exist without one dominating or detracting from the other. While there is not a match, there is no mismatch. Thus a complementary relationship is not incongruent.

One aspect of complementation is that each media allows the other breathing space or 'gaps' so each characteristic maintains its own individual integrity; and this complementation can be understood in terms of media interaction rather than hierarchy[1]. Gaps between the media, used

[1] Cook, N., *Analysing musical multimedia* (1998) 103-107.

in complementation, can be observed in opera when the instrumental music normally becomes quieter and simpler during the actual singing but may return to its original strength and complexity during the periods without singing. Opera could be considered a form of multimedia because dominance alternates between the singing and the music, even though the singing is dominant for majority of the performance. A better term for music in combination with other arts such as singing and the dance is 'multimodal' because it does not have the same connotations as the term 'multimedia'.

Complementation of the music-image relationship in concert involves more than gaps and is not only a simple matter of turning down the volume or simplifying the structure. Complementation between music and image could be likened to polyphonic music, where there are two parts that are independent melodic voices singing at the same time with different melodies and different rhythms but both are clearly identifiable, perfectly complement each other without any conflict, and neither is dominant. Each part maintains its integrity but the whole is greater than the sum of the individual parts.

An example of neutral congruency is the use of abstract and meaningless art where the term abstract is used to identify art that does not directly imitate a real-world object. To have neutral congruency, images should not be recognisable as having a particular genre or era, or as having a particular meaning. For instance, if the image is recognisably from the same period as the music then the genre will normally be congruent. If only some characteristics are neutral and some are congruent, this will be partial congruency. This is a positive relationship but is congruent, not neutral. However if the image is from a recognisably different period that conflicts with the music, such as baroque music being accompanied by abstract expressionist images, this is incongruent, not neutral. Nor should the image be comprised of a dominating colour that could be interpreted as having specific meaning that could be considered incongruent.

Open images such as scenes of ripples on water or leaves blowing in the wind might also be considered neutral, depending on their elements and the overall effect. A relationship where all characteristics are neutral is unlikely. An example of a music-image relationship that could be considered neutral is the first part of *Tour de France 03,* which is described in more detail in the section on non narrative. The images consist of sound levels rising and falling, and these have no relationship to the title and lyrics. They are not actually in sync with the music but nor are they out of sync. As is the case with much in the music-image relationship, the decision as to whether something is neutral or not can be different for different people at different times. These sound levels could be judged as congruent because they appear to be loosely synchronised with the music, or they may be judged as neutral because they have no relationship to the title or lyrics, and because apparent synchronisation is normally supported by congruency of meaning in the music and image. Even so, the music and image are not in conflict.

Neutral congruency may not focus attention on the image, but nor will it focus attention on the music. Therefore neutral characteristics would normally be used in combination with congruent characteristics and the result is the creation of partial congruency.

Partial congruency

Partial congruency is created by a combination of neutral and congruent characteristics. In music concert performance partial congruency may be the relationship that creates the highest level of focus on the music.

Partial congruency is comprised of both neutral and congruent characteristics but there can be no incongruent characteristics. Partial congruency occurs with the music-video where music and image occur in parallel and there is often no precise relation but there are points of synchronisation[1]. Therefore all other characteristics of the music-image relationship can be neutral but if congruency occurs in any one characteristic it should be enough to tie the music and image together creating partial congruency.

The following diagram shows partial congruency created by a combination of congruent and neutral characteristics but no incongruency.

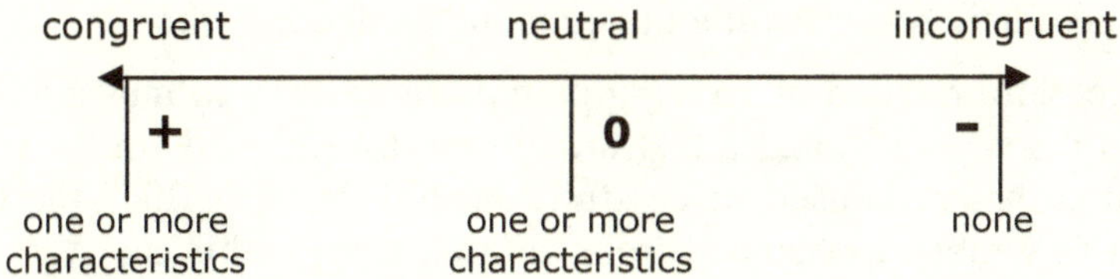

Figure 8 Partial congruency

[1] Chion, M., *Audio-Vision* (1994) 37.

There is a small amount of evidence to suggest that partial congruency may be the most effective method to focus attention on the music. Experiments indicate that a moderate match of audio and visual information results in reduced visual attention[1]. While this result applies to language and image, it is reasonable to apply it to music and image, and if so, these results indicate that during partial congruency of music and image, while focus on image will be reduced, the focus on the music will be retained. This is supported by music-video theory. In the music-video, if only some of the music-image characteristics are congruent, the music-image combination will be workable[2] (workable for the music-video normally includes the music not being backgrounded). Both the theory and experiments referenced above suggest that partial congruency is the most effective way to focus attention on the music.

Given that a moderate match of audio and visual information results in reduced visual attention, it appears that partial congruency is preferable to full congruency. If the congruency is high, the focus will be on the music-image combination. If incongruency occurs, the audience may find it difficult to focus on the music because the attention capacity may be exceeded due to information overload created by incongruency. Achieving the correct balance should create focus on the music. While partial congruency is a mix of congruent and neutral characteristics, and this may be over different music-image characteristics at different times, partial congruency does not include any incongruent characteristics so there will be no conflict at any time in any of the music-image characteristics. Partial congruency also solves the problem of boredom that may be created from too close a match. In cinema it is claimed "what is for the eye must not duplicate what is for the ear"[3] indicating that imagery should not duplicate sound. While the music-image combination needs the stability of similarity and repetition, it also needs variety and contrast[4]. In the music concert this 'contrast' must be complementary where image and music co-exist without detracting from each other.

One successful method of creating partial congruency in music and image is to display still images that are closely associated with the music. This format has been used successfully several times. In 2005 the Brandenburg Ensemble, a chamber group formed from within the Australian Brandenburg Orchestra, performed *Rembrandt's World* and *Cleopatra's Banquet*, using images of artworks to accompany music from the same period. In each case the images were loosely associated with the music

---

[1] Grimes, T., Audio-Video Correspondence and Its Role in Attention and Memory (1990) 15.
[2] Vernallis, C., *Experiencing Music Video: Aesthetics and Cultural Context*, Columbia (2004) 181.
[3] Bresson, R., *Notes on Cinematography* (1977) 27.
[4] Bordwell, D. & Thompson, K., *Film art: an introduction*, McGraw Hill (2004) 62.

but there was no exact match. Neither music nor image was created for the other, although the music was chosen to accompany the images. All other relationships between music and image appeared neutral. Judging by the audience response, both were successful performances. A disadvantage of this formula is that it relies on the audience being interested in the artworks presented, whereas concerts normally rely exclusively on appreciation of a style of music and the skill of the orchestra.

Rembrandt's World

The *Rembrandt's World* (2005) concert performed by the Brandenburg Ensemble comprised paintings from the period of Rembrandt, his peers, and artists who inspired him, such as Titian and Rubens. They were accompanied by music of the same era from composers of the Netherlands, London, Venice, Paris and Germany. Works included Biber's *Partita III from Harmonia Artificioso – Ariosa*, Pachelbel's *Canon and Gigue in D major*, and Albinoni's *Concerto à cinque in G Major. Rembrandt's World* was originally performed at Melbourne's National Gallery surrounded by the *Rembrandt's World* exhibition paintings. In Sydney, photographs of the paintings were projected onto a screen that was slightly above and behind the seated musicians[1].

Before each musical segment, the music, the paintings, and the relationship between the two were briefly discussed. There was no strong relationship between the music and paintings as occurs in program music. Connections were drawn between the meaning of the music and paintings, creating partial congruency. There was no synchronisation with the projected photographs because the changes occurred between pieces or movements. Nothing was out of sync and this created a neutral characteristic. The screen always contained images, even during interval when photographs of performers were interspersed with photographs of paintings. As the projections continued at all times, no incongruency was created by an empty white screen. The musicians formed part of the image by being only slightly below the projections.

In this performance the images enhanced the music and the music enhanced the images. Exquisite images continually filled the screen during the performance. Some characteristics were congruent such as the genre, some were neutral such as the synchronisation, and some, such as meaning and emotions, could have been interpreted either way depending on the individual's response. There were no incongruent characteristics. The overall result was partial congruency that focussed attention on the music. *Rembrandt's World* and *Cleopatra's Banquet* were well received by

[1] *Rembrandt's World*, Verbrugghen Hall, Sydney Conservatorium of Music, 22nd June 2005.

audiences and at least in part this was due to the outstanding nature of the images. It would be difficult to create new images that had the interest level of old masters and there is a limit to how frequently this particular format can be used. It was a simple but elegant concept, and regardless of the risk of overuse, remains an excellent formula when exceptional images are available.

Incongruency

Incongruency between music and image distracts attention from the music and focuses attention on the image. Additionally, incongruency may also result in the inaccurate perception of the music.

Incongruency occurs when there is a conflict between music and image. This may be caused by any type of conflict within any music-image characteristic, and the conflict may occur across one or more characteristics. A complication is that the decision on whether a conflict has been created may vary from one person to another. The diagram below shows some characteristics are congruent, some are neutral and at least one is incongruent. This one incongruent characteristic makes the overall relationship appear incongruent.

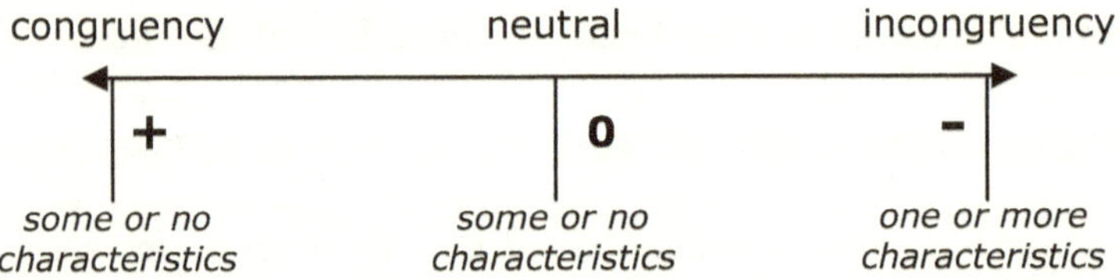

Figure 9 Incongruency

There are a number of issues with incongruency. The first is that it can distract attention from the music and this occurs for multiple reasons. It is widely accepted that vision dominates sound; research shows that visual dominance normally continues even when sound is more intense than image; further, visual dominance becomes overwhelming when there is a conflict between image and sound[1]. This visual dominance that occurs during a conflict with other sensory information often distorts the perception of the other senses and these other senses can become completely

[1] Colavita, F. & Weisberg, D., A further investigation of visual dominance, *Perception & Psychophysics* 25/4 (1979) 345, 347.

excluded during attention-demanding visual tasks[1]. If there is too great a discrepancy between the audio and visual information, the attention capacity can become overloaded and it may become difficult if not impossible to focus on the auditory information[2]. However this is not the only reason to avoid incongruency.

A second issue with incongruency is that it can cause the music to be incorrectly perceived. Research shows that when sound and image diverge, audience judgement falls between the ratings for the visual and the audio, even if the audience are asked to focus on one particular medium. While image and music are processed separately by the brain, this result suggests that the final meaning is additive and the result is a combination of the total associations generated, which is much like a compromise. The result is that when music and image are incongruent neither are perceived accurately.[3]

Incongruency in film

Sound and vision are interdependent. In film, image can affect music and music can affect image, with the result that "when one cannot be 'squared' with the other, credibility itself is threatened"[4]. When this occurs it may no longer be possible to maintain the suspension of disbelief that is necessary for fiction. Art films often create a conflict between music and image to produce an unusual or startling effect. Attempting to create difference and originality in the music-image relationship may create a number of unintentional results. When music and image contain a high degree of contradiction, they risk not being understood; puzzlement is a likely outcome and the effect may be unintentionally comic[5]. The uncertainty created by contradiction may also minimize seriousness and may cause cognitive uneasiness[6]. Another issue is that incongruent music-image combinations, which are often used in film as contrast, can result in a form of satire[7].

Audiovisual harmony is an important part of the music-image relationship and this audio-visual harmony can consist of both dissonance and consonance, with audiovisual dissonance being a 'momentary discord'

---

[1] Posner, M., Nissen, M. & Klein, R., Visual dominance: an information-processing account of its origins and significance, *Psychological Review* 83/2 (1976) 158-9,170.

[2] Grimes, T., Audio-Video Correspondence and Its Role in Attention and Memory (1990) 23-24.

[3] Cohen, A., Film Music: Perspectives from Cognitive Psychology (2000) 362-367.

[4] Kalinak, K., *Settling the score: music and the classical Hollywood film*, Uni. Wisconsin (1992) 29-30.

[5] Gorbman, C., Aesthetics and Rhetoric, *American Music*, 22/1 (2004) 20-2.

[6] Quinto, L., personal conversation, 17 March (2009).

[7] Boltz, M., Schulkind, M., & Kantra, S., Effects of background music on the remembering of filmed events, (1991) 594.

between image and sound[1]. If it is considered that a momentary discord is beneficial, even though it will momentarily focus attention on the image, there are methods that can be used to refocus attention on the music.

Refocusing attention on the music

Attention can move from one sense to another and once attention is turned to a particular sense, it is more difficult to switch attention to a different sense than it is from a neutral state[2]. Therefore if image grabs the attention, it is likely to maintain it unless there is specific action to focus attention back on the music. There are a number of methods for achieving this. One method of returning attention to a particular sense is by consistently following one sense with the other, in which case, the switching of attention becomes easier[3]. However, while switching returns the audience to the music, it is not the aim of the instrumental music concert to regularly focus on another sense.

A better method involves high levels of arousal. While research shows that vision controls attention when competing against other senses, it appears that in a high arousal state visual dominance is reduced and sound may become dominant[4]. Returning focus to the music can be achieved with music that is very emotional and/or exciting. Other musical devices that capture attention include high pitch, discriminating features such as loudness, a change of timbre or texture, or the addition of something new[5]. Synchronisation also has the ability to return attention to the music. Therefore if brief discord is desired, it should be followed with a passage of music that has one or more of the properties previously discussed, so the music has the power to pull the attention back to itself.

The Arrival

The Australian Chamber Orchestra's performance of *The Arrival* (2008) had a number of incongruent characteristics in the music-image combination. A number of issues made this a difficult combination including a narrative that is strong and at times ambiguous. This is discussed further as part of narrative. In this performance, the images from Shaun Tan's picture book, *The Arrival,* were used with the Shostakovich *String Quartet No. 15 opus 144*. The book tells of a man who regretfully leaves his family to find a more prosperous living. He arrives at his destination to

---

[1] Chion, M., *Audio-Vision* (1994) 37.
[2] Posner, M., Nissen, M. & Klein, R., Visual dominance (1976) 167.
[3] Posner, M., Nissen, M. & Klein, R., Visual dominance (1976) 167.
[4] Shapiro, K., Egerman, B. & Klein, R., Effects of arousal on human visual dominance, *Perception & Psychophysics*, 35/6 (1984) 547, 552.
[5] Sloboda, J., *The musical mind: the cognitive psychology of music*, Clarendon (1985) 172-4.

find himself in an alien-like environment. After many hardships he establishes himself, and his family join him for a happier life.

The music is Shostakovich's final string quartet and it is unusual, technically difficult, complex and elusive; it quotes from the Russian Orthodox prayer for the dead; it is an "introspective meditation on mortality ... at times agonisingly slow, but heart-stoppingly beautiful"[1]. Shostakovich was influenced by J.S. Bach and this is reflected in his style, expression and form. Shostakovich's late works, like Bach's, are considered intellectual[2]. There are some congruent aspects of Shostakovich's music and Tan's images. Both have a bleak and haunting beauty[3] and the slow meaningful progression and rhythmic development of the music[4] is reflected in the progression and rhythm of the story. While these similarities between images and music are limited, there are many characteristics that are incongruent.

The narrative of the book, a man seeking and achieving a better life, is incongruent with the music's references to a prayer for the dead and the title of the fifth movement *Funeral March.* Simplicity, clarity, grandeur and serenity are characteristic of Shostakovich's later chamber works[5]. The simplicity and clarity of the music is incongruous with the complexity and strangeness of many of the images, which include weirdly shaped buildings, strange objects and unrecognisable animals. The air of grandeur and serenity of the music is incongruous with the stress and desperation of day-to-day issues such as finding work. The happy ending of the narrative is incongruous with the intention of music that is based around death and a funeral march, which is normally considered a sad event. It is likely many of the audience felt the narrative was inappropriate for the music and this may well have been much more a feeling than an intellectual decision due to the sound of music described as having a simplicity, grandeur and serenity. This may have occurred because the structure of music can dominate the meaning, and influence how the music is perceived. This is discussed in a later section on structure.

In film, music is not capable of modifying visual information that has a clear meaning, even though it can provide a context to ambiguous images[6]. Therefore if an audience feels the music has a specific meaning

---

[1] McBurney, G., Shostakovich String Quartet No.15 [Repertoire Note], Boosey & Hawkes (2008).

[2] Martynov, I., *Dmitri Shostakovich, the man and his work*, Philosophical Library (1947) 98,144,164, 167.

[3] Botticelli, L., The Red Tree (2008).

[4] Martynov, I., *Dmitri Shostakovich, the man and his work,* Philosophical Library (1947) 100.

[5] Martynov, I., *Dmitri Shostakovich, the man and his work,* Philosophical Library (1947) 99, 159.

[6] Bolivar, V., Cohen, A., & Fentress, J., Semantic and Formal Congruency in Music and Motion, *Psychomusicology* 13 (1994) 48.

and the image does not reflect that meaning, the audience will not be influenced by the meaning of the music-image combination. The opposite can also occur and the audience may be alienated by a narrative they feel is inappropriate[1]. As there are more differences than similarities between the images and music in *The Arrival*, this alienation is likely to have occurred in many of the audience. The difficulty of the combination is further born out by several reviews emphasizing this difference, including "abstract images that distracted rather than added to the performance"[2], and also "the marriage ... misfired chiefly because the projected images often seemed to have no reflection in the musical content ... [and only] seemed to fit the aural content fitfully"[3].

Another factor as to why at least some of the audience were less enthusiastic over this performance can be attributed to the audio-visual film theory of 'added value'[4], which states that the addition of sound changes image and vice versa. This widely accepted theory is supported by cognitive psychology experiments where changing facial expressions alter how the music is heard and interpreted[5]. For listeners who had previously heard and enjoyed the music, the addition of image may have changed what they heard and they may have preferred the sound of the music before it was changed by the addition of image.

Ken Healey, who spoke at the pre-concert talk, stated this negative response came from an audience too set in their ways, many of whom were unable to be imaginative and flexible enough to perceive the music differently from the composer's intention[6]. This is somewhat unfair to the audience given that some people would have heard this music previously and others would be influenced by the titles of the movements. When music is heard it is likely that the listener creates associations based on the context and sound of the music. In this case the context is a funeral march and the music itself is "steeped in morbidity". These associations would not be easily altered. Even so, Healey believes we should be free to listen to music without the burden of preconceived ideas, that we should be open to music taking on different concepts, and allow our imagination to form new relationships between music and images.

---

[1] English, H., 'Fantasia' and the Psychology of Music, *Aesthetics and Art Criticism* 2/7 (1942-3) 27; Lindgren, E., *The art of the film*, Macmillan (1963) 139-140.

[2] Szabo, A., ACO Shines in The Red Tree, (2008).

[3] O'Connell, C., Visual feast, young choir in fine voice, *The Age* [newspaper] 17 Jul (2008).

[4] Chion, M., *Audio-Vision* (1994) 21-22.

[5] Thompson, W., Graham, P., & Russo, F., Seeing music performance (2005) 203-4; Thompson, W., Russo, F. & Quinto, L., Audio-visual integration of emotional cues in song, unpublished (2008).

[6] Healey, K., pre-concert talk at the City Recital Hall Angel Place, Sydney, 16 July (2008).

This performance had superb playing, outstanding music and amazing images but the music-image relationship was incongruent. The applause was noticeably less enthusiastic than that for the following item on the program[1] and this supports that claim that congruency is necessary for a performance where the audience expects the music to remain dominant. However not everyone felt the two were incongruent and such a comment was that the Shostakovich music was, with "its bleakness and haunting beauty, the perfect companion to Shaun Tan's book"[2]. Even with this incongruency that for many detracted to some extent from the performance, this was an innovative and exciting concert.

Conclusion

Incongruency between music and image undermines the audience focus on the music. Whereas congruency, particularly partial congruency will help to foreground the music. Congruency should not be difficult to achieve given that music can mean many things depending on the context in which it is performed, and to some extent music will take on the characteristics of any image that accompanies it[3]. However once an association is formed between music and images (even imagined images) it may be difficult to change, and it is likely that the audience will have preconceived images associated with often-heard music. This association may occur from the title of the music even if known only shortly before the music is heard. It may also occur unconsciously if the music references other known works.

A difficulty with a fully congruent relationship is that it may become dull due to music and image being too closely aligned. Another problem is that full congruency may become comical. Incongruency of music and image distracts from the music and can be likened to dissonance in music that distracts attention from the melody. Once the dissonance is resolved the attention returns to the melody but this does not occur with incongruency because once attention focuses on the image it tends to stay on the image. There are however, techniques for returning attention to the music. The relationship between music and image is complex given the number of characteristics involved, and the potential that the music-image relationship, within each characteristic, can change from moment to moment[4]. The complexity of the relationship dictates that time, effort, skill and knowledge of music and image, and how each affects the other, are required to create a successful performance.

[1] The Red Tree concert performance at City Recital Hall Angel Place, Sydney, 16 July (2008).
[2] Botticelli, L., The Red Tree (2008).
[3] Cook, N., *Analysing musical multimedia* (1998) 22-3.
[4] Cook, N., *Analysing musical multimedia* (1998) 113.

3 Narrative characteristic

This chapter discusses various types of narrative and their influence on the music-image combination. The narrative types discussed are **non narrative**, **apparent**, **loose**, **open**, **strong**, **complex**, **ambiguous** and **humorous narrative**, and the narrative created by program music.

Narrative

Narrative distracts audience attention from the music. The degree to which this occurs depends, to a large extent, on the type and complexity of the narrative. Narrative may also impose a story that conflicts with individual meanings allocated to the music by the audience. Therefore if narrative is used to accompany instrumental concert music, it should be a loose, open or apparent narrative, because strong, ambiguous and humorous narrative will background the music.

Definition

Narrative is defined as a story that has a beginning and end, and that communicates specific information about people and/or events that occur over time. Narrative may be created through the spoken word, written down as text, or documented using visual media or any combination of media. In program music the narrative is created by the music title allocated by the composer. The image narrative is created by the content of the images.

Importance of narrative

Narrative engages the intellect and creates interest and continuity. Narrative has been a part of all cultures throughout human history[1] and is an important part of our lives for many reasons. Narrative is at the very basis of human consciousness and our consciousness is created by an understanding of ourselves and our world through narrative[2]. Each person, regardless of time, place and culture, uses narrative to organise the experiences and memories of their day-to-day lives, and this created ongoing narrative gives meaning to each individual's life[3].

---

[1] Barthes, R., *Image Music Text*, Fontana (1977) 79.

[2] Young, K. & Saver, J. The Neurology of Narrative, *SubStance*, 30/1-2/94-95 (2001) 73.

[3] Bruner, J., The Narrative Construction of Reality, *Critical Inquiry*, 18/1 (1991) 4, 20.

The understanding of narrative depends on the ability to interpret it. To understand a narrative from a particular culture we must understand that culture. Narratives must be interpreted because they are concerned with the reason things happen. Great storytellers have the ability to create narrative that may only have a single interpretation, where the narrative is interesting and complex but appears to have only one meaning. However, most narrative is not told by great storytellers and narrative that appears to have only one meaning, is normally created by making the narrative stereotyped. To avoid this banality, narrative normally has multiple meanings that presuppose interpretation and actually challenge us to interpret. Narrative does not provide the actual causes for an event or action but the underlying basis that allows us to interpret the reasons for events. Narrative expresses a meaning and the audience attempts to interpret the meaning. The result is that the same narrative might have different meanings to different people.[1]

Narrative in film

Narrative in film connects the progression of the film as a whole[2], and where images and dialogue tell the story, we focus on those particular events that create the story. Images and dialogue provide constantly accruing meanings that allow us to follow and understand the plot; however this process relegates the music to the sensory background[3]. Most people don't notice music when it accompanies narrative unless it is actually part of the narrative itself, and so film music is not normally heard unless it is part of the plot[4]. This backgrounding of music occurs because the intellectual activities used to understand and interpret narrative in films take attention away from the acoustic properties of the music. This occurs even when it is the intention of the audience to listen to the music, because the music is used to assist in interpretation of the narrative. Therefore film provides a poor model of narrative for the music concert.

Narrative in the music-video

The form and structure of music are backgrounded by narrative so most music-videos do not have a traditional narrative. Rather than creating a story or plot, the music-video follows the form of the song that is normally cyclical and episodic rather than sequential; this is logical for a music-video whose intention is to draw attention to the music because if

[1] Bruner, J., The Narrative Construction of Reality (1991) 7-13.
[2] Eisenstein, S., *The Film Sense*, Harcourt, Brace & World (1947) 3.
[3] Gorbman, C., *Unheard Melodies: Narrative Film Music*, British Film Institute (1987) 12.
[4] Marks, M., Music, Drama, Warner Brothers: The Cases of Casablanca and The Maltese Falcon, *Michigan quarterly review*, XXXV/1 (1996) 112.

the focus was on the narrative, the song would be backgrounded[1]. If the music-video does have a narrative it is often a superficial narrative that is brief and closer to a daydream[2]. This can be referred to as apparent or loose narrative because it often strings together non-contiguous moments and is more a spinning out of ideas rather than actual narrative[3]. This results in music-videos providing a better narrative model for the music concert than cinema.

Backgrounding of music by narrative

The claim that narrative backgrounds the music is supported by observations of eye fixation density (viewing time and intensity). Eye fixation occurs when the eye is in sharp focus and at rest on an area. These observations show that narrative in art is given priority over other information processing. When perceiving an art image, the eyes spend more time looking at narrative aspects than non narrative aspects[4]. The narrative elements are those that help us understand the meaning of the image. They add information to, and help explain the story we construct from the picture. Given that narrative is basic to society and self understanding, as well as facilitating memory, it is not surprising that it so easily engages the intellect and distracts attention from other activities, including listening to music. The main factors within the narrative that determine the level of backgrounding of music by narrative are: the congruency of the narrative with the music; the intellectual processing load of the music-image combination; and the type of narrative.

Congruency of narrative

The first factor in determining whether the music will be backgrounded is congruency. Congruency of narrative and music is essential for the instrumental music concert. The issue of dramatic appropriateness was important when adding music to silent film, and it is equally important that added image be appropriate to music. However appropriateness, and therefore congruency, may be different for different people. Inappropriate image can destroy the listening experience and the music for the listener. This occurred for many people with Walt Disney's use of Beethoven's *Pastoral Symphony* in the film *Fantasia*, "which was so destructive ... I feared I should never be able to efface Disney's images from my mind, and my enjoyment of it [the *Pastoral Symphony*] would

[1] Vernallis, C., *Experiencing Music Video* (2004) 3-4, 13.
[2] Hennion, A., The Production of Success: An Anti-Musicology of the Pop Song, *Popular Music*, 3 (1983) 163.
[3] Vernallis, C., *Experiencing Music Video* (2004) 4.
[4] Marschalek, D., What Eye Movement Research Tells Us about Perceptual Behavior of Children and Adults: Implications for the Visual Arts, *Studies in Art Education*, 27/3 (1986) 123-7.

be permanently marred"[1]. I sympathize with this view. I was too young when I saw *Fantasia* to permanently associate the music with the image but find it distressing to hear classical music from the repertoire accompanying television shows and advertisements and go out of my way to avoid hearing the music and purchasing the products.

To achieve congruency of narrative, given that different people have different interpretations of music, the story and the images that create the narrative must be flexible enough to allow various interpretations. The image must remain a multiple-meaning symbol as could occur with a graphic sequence of a grey-haired old woman, a white horse and a snow-covered roof, which could indicate either old age or whiteness, and would eventually be clarified as the sequence continued[2]. An exception is program music where congruency can be achieved based on the narrative identified by the title(s) allocated by the composer. However, achieving congruency of narrative is much more than adding images that follow the story created by the titles of program music. The narrative must follow the structure of the music because structure defines the narrative of all music. When music is especially written to accompany image, the music structure will follow the narrative structure.

Information overload

The second factor that backgrounds music is that too large an amount of intellectually demanding information will overload the brain's processing power. If the brain's ability to process is slower than the pace the information is presented, it may cause loss of information. Vision supplements information missed when listening, but vision itself can cause loss of information if the brain's pace of processing the information is lower than the pace the information is presented; this loss may not occur with people who are very knowledgeable of, or familiar with the particular music and image being used because they can process the information at a much faster rate than people who are unfamiliar with the material[3]. As unusual and surprising stimuli attract more attention and require more mental effort,[4] strange and unfamiliar images will add to the information burden. Because people who are knowledgeable in an area can process information faster than those who have little knowledge, the problems associated with exceeding mental processing capacity during a concert may not be apparent to those involved in creating the image. This may apply to the artistic director and image creator, who due to their

[1] Lindgren, E., *The art of the film* (1963) 138-140.
[2] Eisenstein, S., *Film Form: Essays in Film Theory*, Harcourt, Brace and World (1949) 65.
[3] Kozma, R., Learning with Media (1991) 194-5.
[4] Kahneman, D., *Attention and effort*, Prentice-Hall Kahneman, (1973) 4.

knowledge, expertise and familiarity with the material, may not experience this information overload.

Types of narrative

The third factor in the backgrounding of music is the type of the narrative. Narrative comes in many strengths and flavours resulting in many different types of narrative. The types of narrative discussed here are non narrative, apparent, loose, open, strong, complex, ambiguous and humorous narrative as well as the narrative of program music.

Narrative can range from having almost no story line through to a strong storyline. Most dramas and thrillers have strong storylines and mysteries will have complex and often ambiguous storylines. Action films and comedies often have weak storylines. Art films often have ambiguous storylines. Most music-videos fall into the loose, apparent or no storyline category. Music concerts traditionally have no storyline but this has been changing since the sixties and today many pop concerts are more like stage musicals and are often filmed for release as music-videos.

The type of narrative determines how much the music will be backgrounded, to what extent the acoustic properties of the music will be lost, and which members of the audience will be most affected. Backgrounding of music is more pronounced with certain types of storyline. A strong story line will background the music because the narrative elements receive more attention than non-narrative elements[1]. An ambiguous narrative will also background the music because the music is used for interpretation of the narrative and this may result in the acoustic properties being lost[2].

The different types of narrative discussed are: non narrative, a series of disconnected images that do not tell a story; apparent narrative, a brief, superficial story that skims over the details; loose narrative, comprised of loosely linked image themes but with no traditional storyline; open narrative, the narrative is open to accept many different overlays allowing the viewer to construct their own meaning; strong and/or complex narrative, a strong traditional style story that dominates all else and demands attention to be understood; ambiguous narrative, where the narrative is unclear and demands the viewer decipher the information to find the correct interpretation; program music narrative, where the story has already

---

[1] Marschalek, D., What Eye Movement Research Tells Us about Perceptual Behavior of Children and Adults (1986) 123-7.

[2] Cohen, A., Associationsim and musical soundtrack phenomena (1993) 173; Film Music: Perspectives from Cognitive Psychology (2000) 363, 366-8, 373-4.

been suggested by the title allocated by the composer; and, humorous narrative. The following table expands on these descriptions.

Figure 10 Table of narrative types

Non narrative	A series of disconnected images that can be comprised of two types of images. The first type of image is where individual images have meaning but even if these images are all on the same subject, there is no storyline relating them to each other. The second is where the images themselves have no intended meaning, such as patterns and colours.
Apparent narrative	A brief, superficial story that skims over the details but has a beginning and end; often used in music-videos.
Loose narrative	Loosely linked image themes as often occur in music-videos but with no traditional storyline.
Open narrative	The narrative is open to accept many different overlays allowing the viewer to construct their own meaning but (importantly) the narrative does not demand to be deciphered.
Strong / complex narrative	A strong story that dominates all else; a complex narrative that demands attention to be understood such as mysteries. A strong complex narrative normally occurs in dramas, thrillers and mysteries.
Ambiguous narrative	The narrative is unclear and demands the viewer decipher the information to find the correct interpretation, as often occurs in mysteries and art films.
Program music narrative	Narrative that has already been suggested by the title allocated by the composer; alternatively, music written specifically to accompany another art form.
Humorous narrative	A narrative created for cartoons and comedy.

A single story may include different types of narratives. It is common for thrillers to have a strong story line, while often including ambiguous scenes where we don't know what is happening, as well as humorous scenes. To discuss all at one time, or to discuss the various permutations, would be both impractical and confusing. It may be somewhat artificial to define narratives as only being a single category, but is necessary for clarity. For instance, a thriller movie would normally be a combination of strong storyline with a level of ambiguity and often added humour but each narrative type is discussed separately as shown below.

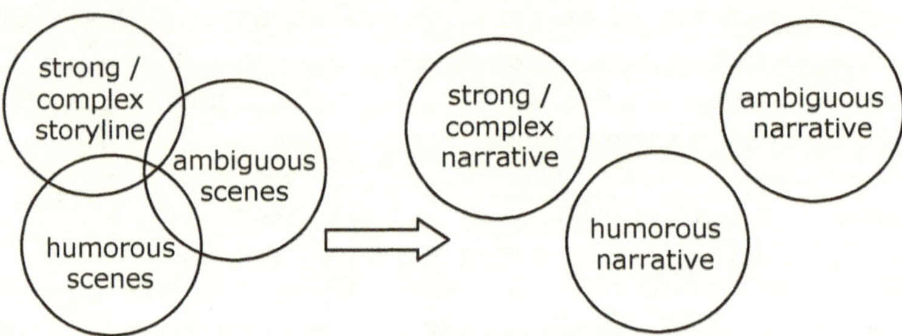

Figure 11 Breakdown of combined narratives

Differences between non narrative, apparent and loose

Non narrative, apparent and loose narratives are similar and could be created from similar artwork. Images might also be a combination of these forms of narrative. Non narrative could be a series of photographs of the environment. An apparent narrative could be a series of photographs of the landscape as it changes over time. A loose narrative could use themes such as weather patterns. Regardless of whether there is one type of narrative or a combination, there must not be a plot that creates drama and requires deciphering and where resolution is critical because these will background the music.

Differences between open and ambiguous narrative

An image within a narrative may have multiple interpretations and this is a double edged sword. Image that is open allows the audience to overlay their own meaning on the music and this results in a positive outcome for the music-image relationship helping to create congruency. Ambiguous image is very different. Ambiguity that is obscure requires deciphering and distracts attention from the music. This difference between open narrative and ambiguous narrative is subtle but important and is discussed further.

Narrative and its effect on backgrounding music

The different types of narrative have different influences on music and differently affect the focus on the music. Any type of narrative created by images will normally reduce the focus on the music to some extent. Non narrative will theoretically allow the highest focus on the music. Apparent or loose narrative will allow focus to be primarily on the music. Open narrative will create focus on the music-image combination. Strong, complex and/or humorous narrative will background the music. Ambiguous narrative will result in backgrounding of the music to the extent it may not be heard. The following diagram shows an approximate hierarchy for the type of narrative that will create most focus on the music through to the type of narrative that causes focus on the image, thus

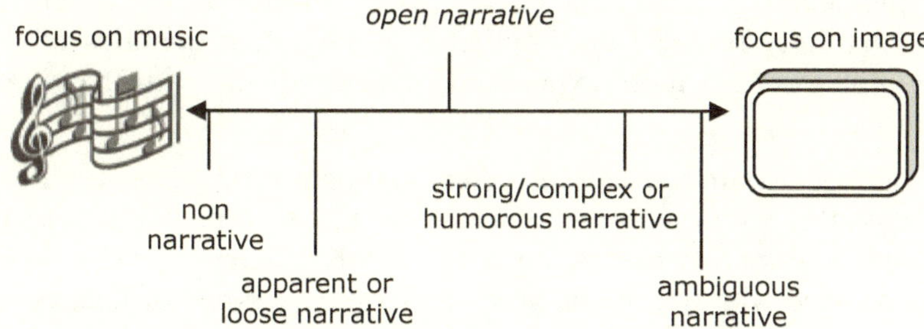

backgrounding the music.

Figure 12 Types of narrative and their influence

Non narrative

Non narrative images can provide a satisfying visual accompaniment for music, provided the images are congruent with the music across multiple characteristics.

Non narrative occurs where a series of images do not tell a story even if the images are about the same topic. While narrative might be necessary in film to provide continuity[1] a storyline is not necessary for music concert images because music itself provides continuity[2]. However there does need to be a level of congruency between music and non narrative images. A non narrative series of images might consist of images that have no meaning, or images that individually have meaning but collec-

[1] Eisenstein, S., *The Film Sense* (1947) 3.
[2] Vernallis, C., *Experiencing Music Video* (2004) 21.

tively do not form a narrative. If images have no meaning whatsoever, and it is clear that no meaning is intended, there can be no ambiguity. For instance a video jockey (VJ) or video performance artist might use computer generated patterns based on the structure of the music and these images will have no previous meaning that can associated by the audience. Meaningless non narrative might also be comprised of colours and patterns.

Meaningful images that are non narrative could be a series of photographs where the individual photographs themselves may have a meaning but together do not create a storyline. The music will be more dominant when the images are relatively abstract, whereas more representational images tend to create tension between music and narrative[1]. It might seem that the use of a sequence of unconnected images could result in fragmentation but this need not occur. Music has the ability to enforce continuity because the implied and suggestive qualities of the music complement the more explicit and specific qualities of the words and pictures[2].

Themes without a narrative can be used to maintain interest, as they do in the music-video, with multiple themes or strands, such as colours, seeping through multiple scenes as the music-video progresses[3]. This same idea can be used with non narrative images where a series of images relates to a single concept but does not create a story. A single concept series is often used by the Australian Broadcasting Corporation's television program Sunday Arts to accompany the end titles. A concept may be a series of paintings or photographs by one artist, or a series of works by several artists in a single exhibition that has a specific theme. This is invariably an example of a skilful selection of both music and image to create an interesting music-image combination.

Music creates its own meaning by stealth without drawing attention to its role[4]. Creating a series using non narrative images is an effective visual component in the music-image relationship that allows the music to suggest a story and meaning and allows the audience to interpret this as their own. While this concept of non narrative seems simple enough the other music-image characteristics must be considered as each one can background the music.

---

[1] Cook, N., *Analysing musical multimedia* (1998) 179.
[2] Cook, N., *Analysing musical multimedia* (1998) 22.
[3] Vernallis, C., *Experiencing Music Video* (2004) 21-23.
[4] Cook, N., *Analysing musical multimedia* (1998) 20.

Pink Floyd's early performances

Pink Floyd was one of the first pop groups to use images during performance. In the second half of the 1960s they were at the "creative heart of the drug-fuelled social and artistic movement that became known as the counterculture"; from the time they played at an Essex University Rag Ball in March 1966, "a key Floyd component fell into place" when a film taken by a paraplegic while travelling around London, was projected during the performance[1]. Shortly after this concert they were using three projectors to flood the group, the walls and sometimes even the audience in vivid but static colours; later that year they used strange images projected onto the band members in time with the music; from then on, each concert featured bigger and better effects[2]. A lighting rig was created that consisted of a row of spotlights each covered in a different colour and each with its own on-off switch; even though these were low powered, they threw a huge shadow behind each member of the band, and this was very effective[3]. These effects progressed to hypnotic and frenzied patterns of liquid-coloured lights creating honeycombs, galaxies and throbbing cells that whirled around the group, accelerating as the music developed[4].

Various light treatments were developed. A vibrating mirror set at an angle of 45 degrees in front of a long lens created Lissajou patterns[5]. The addition of chopper and colour wheels, along with varying the speed of the wheels, created 'worms of colour'. Another creation used a film light pushed beyond its recommended limits, with motorized coloured glass wheels that spun at extremely high speeds mounted in front, and these created rainbows of spectacular silvery purple metallic colours on the back projection screen. Due to their unstable nature from lack of temperature control combined with their shaking and banging, they often shattered, resulting in shards of glass flying at the group, so these whirling monsters were called 'the Daleks'[6] in tribute to their robot-like nature and their hostility to humanoids.[7]

In May 1967, Floyd played an event billed as "space-age relaxation for the climax of spring – electronic composition, colour and image projection, girls and The Pink Floyd"[8]. By 1973, with the release of *Dark Side*

---

[1] Manning, T., *The Rough Guide to Pink Floyd*, Rough Guides (2006) 23-24.

[2] Miles, B., *Pink Floyd: The Early Years*, Omnibus (2006) 67.

[3] Miles, B., *Pink Floyd: The Early Years* (2006) 67.

[4] Mason, N., *Inside Out: A Personal History of Pink Floyd* (2004) 50.

[5] Lissajou patterns are patterns of sound frequencies as created by an oscilloscope.

[6] Daleks are an evil extraterrestrial mutant race from the BBC's Doctor Who science fiction television series.

[7] Mason, N., *Inside Out: A Personal History of Pink Floyd* (2004) 70-3.

[8] Manning, T., *The Rough Guide to Pink Floyd* (2006) 37.

of the Moon, Pink Floyd stage shows included light projections, film backdrops and pyrotechnics, and the group itself was dwarfed by these theatrical spectacles[1]. These images had no narrative but were integrated into the performance by being projected onto and/or directly behind the group. Pink Floyd created effective non narrative images that were leading edge at the time. In photographs[2] of performances in the second half of the sixties, these effects, which were described as both grotesque and beautiful, look unusual and exciting even today.

Tour de France 03

Kraftwerk have created around eleven versions of *Tour de France* and there are two versions on the *Minimum-Maximum* DVD (2005). The two different versions on the DVD show three different types of narrative as well as different types of synchronisation, which are discussed later. The imagery in the first half of *Tour de France* 03 on track 4 (referred to as the 03 version) is non narrative, the second half is loose narrative, and *Tour de France* track 6 (referred to as the original version) is apparent narrative.

The 'Tour de France' is a bicycle race of the same name, which is an invitation only event, first staged in 1903, which covers over 3,500 kilometres mainly through France. The race is broken into around twenty stages, normally over twenty three days and winning is based on cumulative times.

The first half of the 03 version starts with a short series of sustained chords that are repeated then followed by the words 'Tour de France' spoken slowly by a computer voice. The melody starts, followed by the sound of gears in the background. Only after the music is established is the somewhat minimalist imagery displayed. The screen is filled with changing volume levels, moving up and down, as they would appear on a sound panel. These changing volume levels are royal blue and the broad horizontal band of coloured lighting at the base of the screen is a medium blue.

The images of sound-levels stop temporarily leaving a blank, black screen that focuses attention on the group standing in front of it. The sound-level images restart with a different colour combination, white sound-levels with a red horizontal band below. The colours change again, this time to red sound-levels with a royal blue horizontal band. The sound-level images are at times shown in front of the group. This

[1] Miles, B., *Pink Floyd: The Early Years* (2006) 148, 150.

[2] Photographs of Pink Floyd at UFO in Mason, N. *Inside Out: A Personal History of Pink Floyd* (2004) 41-51.

sound-level imagery becomes monotonous and could have been varied by such things as changing the perspective and angles of the imagery. Even though this is non narrative, the music has been designated as a narrative by its title and lyrics and this is supported by the sound of bicycle gears. The images of a sound level panel do not represent cycling, but to some extent match the melody and beat. This is an example of non narrative imagery that is dull and unimaginative. This need not be the case as is shown with Kraftwerk's *Numbers,* discussed in the section on structure. *Numbers* uses patterns and repetition to create an exciting combination of music and image. Given the quality of most of the imagery on the Minimum-Maximum DVD, it is difficult to understand the rationale behind this choice of imagery for the first half of *Tour de France 03*.

Apparent Narrative

Narrative distracts attention from the music, however an apparent narrative can be created that appears to have the structure of narrative but is a series of loosely connected images that create only a feeling or outline of a story.

Apparent narrative strings together non-contiguous moments and is more a spinning out of ideas rather than actual narrative[1]. This form of narrative is like a novel that fast-forwards over the details; a superficial narrative that is brief and closer to a fairytale merging of daydream and reality[2]. It is likely that this form of narrative, which is used with pop music in the music-video, can be adapted to and will be acceptable for classical and contemporary music provided the narrative is simple and slowly paced. However, in reducing the level of narrative in the music-image combination, inconsistency or a lack of satisfying resolution may be unintentionally introduced and these problems can occur due to ambiguity of truth and temporality[3]. In other words, the aim is to create a story that has a sense of validity and legitimacy of meaning over time, and with a beginning and an ending which comes to some type of resolution. Music structure has the ability to provide meaning, continuity and resolution[4] so these should not be difficult to achieve, provided the images or video follow the structure of the music.

---

[1] Vernallis, C., *Experiencing Music Video*, (2004) 4.
[2] Hennion, A., The Production of Success (1983) 163.
[3] Vernallis, C., *Experiencing Music Video* (2004) 10.
[4] Vernallis, C., *Experiencing Music Video* (2004) 21; Gorbman, *Unheard Melodies* (1987) 2.

Book of Longing

An apparent narrative was created by the music-image combination in the *Book of Longing* (2008) collaboration by Philip Glass and Leonard Cohen. This multimedia performance consisted of a series of songs composed by Philip Glass to accompany the poetry of Leonard Cohen. The ensemble included electronic keyboards (one played by Glass), flute and base clarinet, hand percussion, violin, cello, double bass, oboe and English horn, with four vocalists. Voice recordings by Cohen were included, as were many of his drawings. The drawings included sketches of people and faces, doodles, scribbling and words written in Cohen's handwriting. Lyrics were clearly enunciated so Cohen's words could be easily understood with the poetry dominating the music. The poetry was specifically selected by Glass to create a continuous and meaningful journey that had a beginning and an end[1]. This musical and poetic journey with related images created the effect of an apparent narrative.

Tour de France

Tour de France, track 6 on the *Minimum-Maximum* DVD, is an example of apparent narrative. The performance starts with an image of the three colours of the French flag stretched across the entire back of the stage with blue at the top, white in the middle forming a cycling track, and red below. On the white 'track' is a drawn image of four cyclists. This could be considered as creating a beginning to the narrative as they prepare for the race to begin. The song starts with heavy panting in time to the music, followed by the repeating words 'Tour de France'. The imagery changes to black and white film footage of a cycling race from the first half of the 20th century. The cyclists are moving slowly as if the race has just started. The streets are lined with spectators and we see a cyclist organising a bag across his shoulder as he rides.

The scene moves to the leading cyclist on a lonely mountain road. Shots alternate between the leader and the cycling pack as they travel through crowded towns, misty mountains and sunny seaside villages. Along the sides of the road, spectators wave, clap and smile. We see the faces of individual cyclists, their expressions and actions such as using sponges to drink and cool down. At other times the leader rolls down a mountain track or cyclists drink and splash water over themselves as they ride. The song finishes with a winner being congratulated. Even though this is the end of a stage rather than the full race, it gives a sense of completion.

The images that accompany this version of *Tour de France* when analysed are not as contiguous as they at first appear. The coherence of the

[1] Glass, P., pre-concert talk, Sydney Opera House, 12 October (2008).

story is due to there being a story beginning and ending, long takes (long-held shots), long (distance) shots, slow motion, limited cuts and the continuity created by the music. All give the feeling of beginning, coherence, genuineness, time passing and finalisation. Close-ups of competitor and spectator faces create a story about people and their activities leading to a personal involvement of the audience and this is typical of traditional narrative. The result is an apparent narrative of a cycling race. The narrative does not distract from the music, as it would if the plot were more detailed. This apparent narrative provides the barest essentials to create a feeling of a story and this minimalist congruent story supports focus on the music.

Loose narrative

Narrative that is loosely based and created on themes rather than plot creates a low level of distraction from the music which will not normally background the music.

Loose narrative occurs where themes provide loose connections throughout the story. This is not the same as a weak storyline because in loose narrative there is no intention to create a traditional plot. The themes give continuity, and form an association between various image segments but they must follow the structure of the music. These themes have been referred to as 'strands' in the music video and 'lines' in film.

The music-video often has a loose storyline and it is sometimes said that the music-video is anti-narrative, a type of 'post-modern pastiche' that defies the conventions of narrative. As the purpose of the music-video is to showcase the star and the song, it is logical that it doesn't use story or plot as film does. If there was a regular narrative, the audience could become so focused on the actions, characters and plot that the song would be backgrounded, as occurs with film music. The music-video holds back plot information, and any loose narrative is created by the music-image relationship unfolding over time. Instead of using characters and plot, the music-video's richness and complexity are created by multiple strands. These strands are comprised of various elements and these elements may be such things as colour, a part of an image, or a particular type of motion. The connection between strands is based on the principle of 'contagion' where an element, such as a colour within one strand, seeps into the next strand. Loose narrative can maintain cohesion and interest by the use of these multiple strands, with their elements seeping into subsequent strands, as the music-video progresses.[1]

A similar concept is that of 'lines' in film. Lines run through a film, and these lines are continuous themes that create continuity over time. A line could be a building of emotion and intensity, or it could be a direct relationship between sound and visuals such as voices and faces of singers. Each scene or series of scenes need contain only some of these lines and occasionally all the lines. Each scene or series of scenes has a responsibility to add to the complete film as well as continuing at least some of the individual themes that run through the film. There is also the difficultly in fusing the individual pieces to achieve the "composite sensation of all the pieces as a whole". The lines running through the film provide the continuity to achieve this composite sensation.[2]

In the music concert, themes create a similar effect to 'strands' and 'lines'. Themes consist of multiple elements, which can include colour, mood, shapes, patterns, people, objects and types of movements. While it might seem that the use of a sequence of loosely connected images could result in fragmentation, even if they are linked by themes, this is not normally the case. Music has the ability to enforce continuity because the implied and suggestive qualities of the music complement the more explicit and specific qualities of the images; the attributes of music are normally transferred to any image it is associated with because music creates coherence and makes connections that are not in the original images, and can even engender its own meaning; all this is done by stealth, without the awareness of the audience[3].

The type of artworks used to accompany the end titles of the Australian Broadcasting Corporation's television program, Sunday Arts, varies, and can be non narrative or loose narrative, and at times apparent narrative. A non narrative could occur with a series of photographs that have a single subject, such as the landscape. If a series of photographs showed a particular type of landscape in a particular area this could be a loose narrative. If a similar series of photographs showed a single landscape changing over a period of time, this could be an apparent narrative. Such a series could show the land altering over a number of years as it changes from drought conditions to flood and back to drought. Loose and apparent narrative may be very close or may be combined.

[1] Vernallis, C., *Experiencing Music Video* (2004) xi, 4, 16-17, 21-23.
[2] Eisenstein, S., *The Film Sense* (1947) 75-7.
[3] Cook, N., *Analysing musical multimedia* (1998) 20, 22.

Tour de France 03

The second half of Kraftwerk's *Tour de France 03* track 4 is an example of loose narrative. Even though it is likely the scenes used in this 03 version are from the same race as those used for *Tour de France* track 6 (apparent narrative), they create a different effect.

The imagery in the second half starts with the bottom of a gigantic wheel that covers almost the entire back of the stage. This is a creative start to the film but does not start a narrative. The scene changes to the back view of the cycling pack on a mountain road disappearing into a tunnel with the race well underway. Slow motion shots of feet and wheels are followed by a yellow map of France on a red, white and blue background with a rapidly drawn cycling route. It is immediately replaced with a long (distance) shot of cyclists. Red streaks flash along the route. White animated contour lines spread out across the landscape. A triangular blue block of solid colour follows these contour lines up the mountain. Blocks of red and blue with lyrics in white, or vice versa, are overlaid on the film footage emphasising the route and the cyclists. A flash of yellow indicates a winning cyclist. Moving pictures change momentarily into moving drawings, with one cyclist drawn as yellow, another as red and another as blue. A helicopter hovers over the pack, is motionless, and becomes a drawing in the colours of the French flag. Scenes of riders become motionless and are surrounded by blocks of colour. All images are related to the race but none create a story.

The 03 version ends with an image of the Eiffel Tower emitting radio transmissions from its peak. While this forms an ending to the song it is not an ending to a narrative. There is no intimacy in the graphic images or shots of spectators and riders who are seen mostly from a distance with frequent views of backs and feet cycling. Scenes are predominately long (distance) shots showing the landscape. Closer shots are not clear enough to see individual facial expressions. Blocks of colours and patterns, diagrams of gears, still shots and drawn images add impact but not a story. None provide personal information about the competitors, spectators or the race results. The scenes would be disjointed without the unifying effect of the music. The imagery is of scenes in a race, rather than a story of a race, but the music weaves these disconnected scenes into a loose narrative.

Differences between loose and apparent narrative

The two versions of *Tour de France* previously discussed show the difference between loose and apparent narrative. Both versions are created from black and white archival film footage that is edited and has added coloured graphics. Both versions use the same colour palette. The original version has a beginning and an ending to the narrative, while the 03 version has neither. The original version shows faces of cyclists and spectators clearly enough to see their expressions, while the 03 version focuses on feet, pedals and wheels. The 03 version has more added graphics such as flashes and blocks of colour as well as drawings of gears, bikes and helicopters. These added graphics disrupt any apparent narrative that might start to form. In the 03 version the various techniques that reduce the narrative effect are: added graphics, long (distance) shots, and the many shots that focus on feet, wheels and peddling. All reduce the impact of the narrative and create a different feeling between the two versions of the song.

Open narrative

Narrative that is open to the overlaying of different meanings does not impose a plot that conflicts with individual interpretations of the music. The result is that open narrative should not background the music.

Open narrative is a less common form of narrative. It occurs where the story is open to the overlaying of a personal meaning by each member of the audience. This occurs when the meaning of the images is open to interpretation but the images are not abstract or ambiguous. The open narrative must not be ambiguous because ambiguity needs to be deciphered and this takes attention from the music. An example of open narrative is a scene of a woman walking slowly along a beach looking out at the ocean with no indication as to why she is there or what she is doing. However there is no ambiguity, the scene is very clearly a woman walking on a beach in an unhurried manner. This narrative doesn't demand deciphering and allows different individuals to allocate their own personal meaning to the woman, her thoughts and her reason for being there.

Music-videos often have an openness to interpretation that gives the audience the space to determine the meaning of the music and images to suit their own emotional and intellectual requirements[1], and to construct their own personal meaning[2]. Open narrative in the music-video has also been called digital narrative; this is defined as narrative where the visuals are non-linear, are only loosely related to the music, and may either reinforce or juxtapose the meaning; open narrative is more suggestive of

[1] Björnberg, A., Structural Relationships of Music and Images in Music Video (1994) 51.

[2] Jones, S., Cohesive But Not Coherent: Music Videos (1988) 25.

meaning rather than explicit, and allows the audience to allocate their own individual meaning[1].

Music-video viewers often state that while watching videos they are entranced by the images and their mind wanders; the result of this openness, that allows the imagination to create an individual meaning, is what makes the music-video popular[2]. This drifting is a form of trance that can also occur listening to music without image. The listener becomes lost in their own internal world, which may or may not include internal images. A strong narrative normally inhibits this internalized trance state. A person may become 'entranced' with a film but the focus is externalised not internalised.

Open versus ambiguous narrative

The difference between open narrative and ambiguous narrative is subtle but important. Open narrative is not ambiguous. Ambiguity creates a need to answer questions so as to be able to understand the narrative. In open narrative there should be no requirement to decipher the image. Openness refers to the ability of the image to accept multiple meanings, the personal meaning allocated by each individual member of the audience. This openness of a narrative that allows overlaying of different meanings and emotions is important because this is normally what music offers. Music offers each person the flexibility for an interpretation that meets their own needs[3]. Therefore this flexibility should be maintained when image is added to music, and it can be achieved with open narrative. In summary, when the narrative is ambiguous then the audience is deciphering the ambiguity rather than thinking about the music. When the narrative is open the audience is thinking about the music-image combination.

Surrealist images

In the music-video it is not reasonable to expect a clearly defined plot[4] and the same applies to the music concert. Open narrative does not need to be logical, and surrealist images can provide visuals that allow the audience to overlay their own meaning. A loose or open narrative series of images can be illogical provided the plot and individual images are not ambiguous. An image is ambiguous if it demands to be deciphered but images can be illogical without needing to be deciphered. For instance, much surrealist artwork is illogical, such as Dali's melting clocks. There

[1] Jones, S., Cohesive But Not Coherent: Music Videos (1988) 16-21.
[2] Jones, S., Cohesive But Not Coherent: Music Videos (1988) 26.
[3] Meyer, L., *Emotion and Meaning in Music* (1956) 265.
[4] Cook, N., *Analysing musical multimedia* (1998) 170.

is no difficulty in interpreting these images. Dali's melting clocks are instantly recognisable as clocks that are melting. Nor is there any requirement to determine why they are melting. We don't ask ourselves if these melting clocks indicate global warming, they are just accepted for what they are, illogical. Much surrealist art is open to overlaying of a personal meaning rather than being ambiguous, and surrealist images are often compared to dreams.

Dream-like image sequences

Loose narrative can be likened to a dream sequence. Dreams weave loose narratives from disconnected images and this same approach, a series of unrelated images that emphasise dislocation of time and place, is used in the music-video[1]. There may be concern that dream-like sequences may not be acceptable to an audience and may just appear silly, but there is evidence to the contrary. The music-image combination grants validity to dream-like image sequences that image alone may not otherwise have.

Cognitive psychology experiments show that when image and music are combined, depending on the congruence of the match, our perception of reality is a construct that may or may not match reality. Further, this music-image combination provides for the ability to suspend disbelief and heighten our sense of reality. Therefore we may accept as real, situations that are not real and these music-image combinations may seem more real than reality itself.[2]

In summary, dreams are commonly disconnected or illogically sequenced, without continuity of action or narrative, but do not demand deciphering. At the same time, dreams are open to overlaying various meanings. Therefore dream-like image sequences and surrealist art that has a dream-like quality are likely to be a successful accompaniment for music. *The Red Tree* is an example of open narrative that uses dream-like imagery.

The Red Tree

The Australian Chamber Orchestra's performance of *The Red Tree* (2008), previously described, is an example of the successful pairing of image and music where the music is not backgrounded by the narrative within the images. This is because the narrative is open to the overlaying of multiple interpretations. The illustrations in 'The Red Tree' picture book form an open narrative that allows the audience to create a personal

[1] Kinder, M., Music Video and the Spectator: Television, Ideology and Dream, *Film Quarterly* 38/1 (1984) 5.

[2] Cohen, A., Film Music: Perspectives from Cognitive Psychology (2000) 369, 265, 366.

meaning. It is also an example of loose narrative with its many themes, and apparent narrative because it has a beginning and ending with a sense of time passing and resolution.

The Red Tree narrative could be considered contemporary mythology. It is about a little red haired girl and the feelings and reactions she experiences. The story could be more accurately described as a set of loosely connected images, with the words forming titles for the images, as opposed to creating an actual plot. The images have a dream-like quality. The narrative starts in the girl's bedroom. She stands waist-deep in dried leaves. The music's first movement, *Black Leaves*, reflects an uncertain emotion but even though it is odd that the room is half-flooded with leaves, there is nothing menacing in this image. The child is not restrained by the leaves and has no difficultly leaving the room. The mood is open to interpretation, which could be distress or just resignation to one-of-those-days.

While the image is open to interpretation, it is not ambiguous. There is no difficulty in recognising the bedroom and the leaves, even though it is obvious there is some level of problem. The image allows the viewer to overlay their own mood, which could range from a somewhat light-hearted inevitability through to despair. The artistic director, Richard Tognetti describes this image as being a little girl waking in a bad mood, with the narrative being about child depression, and describes the narrative as depressing at times.[1] To me, the narrative was about resignation to life and whatever it presents, about the ability to keep going and move on. I found it inspiring, especially as the music is accompanied by the beauty and freshness of children's voices, which can be interpreted as creating a feeling of promise for the future.

The words from the book are used as introductions to each movement of the music and are interspersed between many of the dream-like illustrations. The words 'Darkness overcomes you' are displayed before a movement that shows an image of the little girl walking along a street under the shadow of a huge open-mouthed fish. Others in the street seem unaware there is anything strange. The image is open and dream-like and could be seen as nightmarish or menacing but it could also be seen as a feeling of resignation or even a disregarding of problems. The next image is of a lonely beach with the little girl in a diving bell helmet. She sits quietly inside a partially water-filled bottle that has been washed up on the pebbles. There are no obvious repercussions from sitting in this bottle, but that is for the viewer to decide.

---

[1] Tognetti discussed *The Red Tree* project on a video at the ACO web site at: www.aco.com.au

The image and setting change completely with the next illustration and the title states 'the world is a deaf machine'. This scene, of a massive building with a huge doorway showing steps leading upwards, is reminiscent of the film *Metropolis* (1927) by director Fritz Lang. On top of this huge open doorway is a form of the Egyptian winged solar disk symbol. The little red-haired girl is walking away and a glowing light bulb shows inside her chest. This could be interpreted in a number of ways and at a number of levels, from a simple child-like interpretation of the light in her heart representing that she is alive and well, through to the winged solar disk symbol indicating psychic powers of perception.

The pictures are often interspersed with moving patterns based on colours and textures from the book, which add to the dream-like qualities of the imagery. The images continue in a surreal, dreamlike, disconnected way with continuity created by the music. Resolution comes after various trials, with the girl returning to her now leaf-free bedroom. There is a shaft of light coming through the open door, illuminating a small red plant growing out of the floor. The narrative ends with a tree, fully grown, covered in red leaves and a contented expression on the face of the little red-haired girl.

This narrative is loosely connected by various image themes. As well as *The Red Tree* narrative being open and apparent, it is also a loose narrative with a major theme with several sub-themes. The main theme is the day-to-day mood and/or problems of the little red-haired girl. The sub-themes include the patterns and colours of the images as well as various opposing concepts. These opposing concepts are: decay and growth in a natural environment such as dead leaves and growing trees; strange occurrences in a normal environment; and, benign and overwhelming environments such as a calm beach and a turbulent ocean. An important factor of this open narrative is that while the images are part of themes and sub-themes, each image is complete in itself, and does not draw on the following images for explanation. With these dream-like qualities, loose themes and openness to interpretation, it is easy to understand why the book has been used by the medical profession as part of treatment for mental illness[1].

To summarise, the series of images that accompany *The Red Tree* music form a loose, apparent and open narrative that is not ambiguous but is open to the audience to engage in flights-of-fancy and to turn their thoughts inwards to create a personal meaning. Even though the music closely follows the image, this does not inhibit many different interpreta-

[1] *The Red Tree* Concert Tour Program Notes available from the ACO web site at www.aco.com.au

tions. This is an achievement by the illustrator, who has created images that can express a narrative, while at the same time both images and narrative are open to an interpretation that allows each person to overlay their own meaning.

Strong and complex narrative

Strong and/or complex narrative grabs the attention at the expense of other senses and distracts audience focus from the music. Neither should be used in the instrumental music concert.

Strong and/or complex narratives background the music and this occurs for a number of reasons. The first is that narrative elements receive more attention than non-narrative elements[1]. The second is that our attention capacity is limited and while this capacity can be increased according to our state of arousal, normally one of the stimuli is given preference over the others and may even exclude the others[2]. This preference is normally given to vision. The third issue occurs if the narrative is in conflict with the meaning of the music as interpreted by the audience. Even though music can provide context to image, music is unable to modify visual information that has a clear meaning[3]. The result is that if the audience feels the music has a clear and specific meaning and the image reflects a different meaning, they will consider that the music and image are incongruent.

A strong storyline, unless it clearly reflects the intention of the music, as occurs with program music or specifically composed music, risks alienating the music lover. This alienation occurred in response to Walt Disney's *Fantasia.* Music critics and many musically sensitive listeners at the time groaned with distaste at the use of much loved and well known classical music to complement cartoon narratives[4]. Listeners may feel that inappropriate narrative is so destructive that their enjoyment of a particular composition is permanently marred[5]. Therefore, if the audience feels the image is symbolically out of step with the music, they will be forced into a situation where they must try to ignore the images, otherwise those images will dominate the music creating a conflict of meaning. Ignoring the visual aspect of a performance is difficult to do

[1] Marschalek, D., What Eye Movement Research Tells Us about Perceptual Behavior of Children and Adults (1986) 123-7.

[2] Kahneman, D., *Attention and effort,* (1973) 3, 8-11.

[3] Bolivar, V., Cohen, A. & Fentress, J., Semantic and Formal Congruency in Music and Motion, (1994) 48.

[4] English, H., "Fantasia" and the Psychology of Music (1942-3) 27.

[5] Lindgren, E., *The art of the film* (1963) 139-140.

when a conflict occurs, normally the image will prevail at the expense of the music.

A narrative may appear to be weak and therefore appear less inclined to distract attention from music, however many narratives that have weak storylines often have other strong elements that dominate attention. Action films often have weak stories but the action itself creates a strong effect and the music is backgrounded due to the attention grabbing nature of the action. Readers may prefer stories that have a high degree of surprise and suspense[1], but it is likely these will background the music. Action and surprise should be left to the music, with the image creator following the composer's lead.

Ambiguous narrative

Ambiguous narrative distracts audience focus from the music because it requires deciphering. Where the music should remain dominant, ambiguous narrative should not be used.

Narrative is ambiguous when the narrative needs to be deciphered to be understood. Narrative normally has some level of ambiguity. This level of ambiguity may range from being easily and quickly interpreted and understood, through to being difficult and needing to be deciphered. Strong narrative is often also ambiguous. This idea may at first seem contradictory, but this combination frequently occurs in dramas, thrillers and mysteries, where the plot unfolds over time. Once the plot is fully revealed it is no longer ambiguous, but this normally does not occur until the end of the narrative. For example, an Agatha Christie mystery will have considerable intentional ambiguity at the beginning and requires the audience to be totally focused on the unfolding events. While a narrative might initially be ambiguous, once understood it becomes clear. This does not change the fact that while the audience is deciphering the ambiguity, the music is being backgrounded because it is used for the deciphering process. A second viewing of a narrative may result in less or no backgrounding of the music because the narrative is then understood. This is why the artistic director and image creator, who have an ongoing involvement, are unlikely to find the narrative ambiguous, and it will not be apparent to them that ambiguity and its negative effects will be experienced by the audience.

[1] Boltz, M., Schulkind, M. & Kantra, S., Effects of background music on the remembering of filmed events (1991) 601.

There are situations where images may be ambiguous but the ambiguity may not be apparent. One of the most common types of image in film is where the image is ambiguous when out of context, but when in context is not ambiguous. Context is determined by additional information such as music and sound effects and these determine the meaning. For instance, a scene where a woman is asleep in bed late at night, which is accompanied by soft, gentle music, elicits a very different interpretation to when the same scene is accompanied by irregular, discordant music. The scene is actually ambiguous but the accompanying elements, in this case the music and its perceived meaning, clarify the context. This often occurs with narrative because narrative frequently depends upon multiple senses. Each sense is limited and the senses overlap, resulting in different senses assisting each other to understand the objects and events[1]. In this situation, where it is not apparent that music is being used to provide the context of the image, it may not be apparent that the music is being backgrounded.

Ambiguous narrative backgrounds music because when additional information is needed to make sense of the visual narrative, the attention will focus on the interpretation of the image, and any information that is available, including the music, will be unconsciously drawn upon to interpret and understand the narrative. This was shown in cognitive psychology experiments using two video excerpts. In one a woman is chased by a man, while the other shows two men fighting. Music that contrasted with the image was used with both scenes. In the male-female chase, the music strongly influenced the interpretation. Where the music had previously been judged as representing conflict, the male-female chase was interpreted as violent. Where the music had previously been judged as representing love, the male-female chase was judged as non-violent. However, when the contrasting music was used with the fight between the two males, it had little effect on the interpretation. Therefore, as previously stated, whether the music is used to interpret the image and if so how much, depends to a large degree on the level of ambiguity in the image. When the music is unconsciously drawn upon to interpret and understand the narrative, the music becomes transparent and the acoustical information is ignored. Thus ambiguous narrative can lead to backgrounding the music.[2]

---

[1] Marks, L., *The unity of the senses : interrelations among the modalities*, Academic (1978) ix,185.

[2] Cohen, A., Associationsim and musical soundtrack phenomena (1993) 173; Film Music: Perspectives from Cognitive Psychology (2000) 363, 366-8, 373-4; Bolivar, V., Cohen, A. & Fentress, J., Semantic and Formal Congruency in Music and Motion, (1994) 48.

Ambiguity also occurs with the music-video. The music-video is improved by holding back information and this creates ambiguity[1]. Two situations may result from ambiguous music-video narrative: the audience may find this ambiguous narrative style to be liberating because they can construct their own meaning; or, the lack of information may be confusing because the audiences is unable to make sense of the images[2]. The first situation, where the narrative is liberating, allows the audience to construct their own meaning, and this occurs with open narrative. The second, where the lack of information causes confusion or where it demands deciphering to be understood, occurs with ambiguous narrative.

Regardless of beliefs and evidence of visual dominance[3], image is much more ambiguous than it may at first appear. Interpretation is strongly influenced by sound and this can be seen in the film *Good Bye Lenin* (2003). This film, which is set in 1990, is about a young man trying to protect his fragile mother, who has come out of a long coma. He is concerned that if she learns that her beloved nation of Communist East Germany no longer exists, the shock might be fatal. To protect her he recreates history, changing the speeches on film footage from the time of the fall of the Berlin wall, to a context that would please his mother. This change of wording, which is very different to the original, is added to original archival newsreel footage and totally reverses the meaning of the images, while at the same time appearing to be completely natural. For anyone not familiar with the history there would be no reason to doubt the authenticity and the naturalness of the newsreels. The film's director Wolfgang Becker states:

> What's interesting here is that we didn't shoot one single new shot for this. All we had to do was take the existing archival footage and put it in a different context. You can see how quickly you can fake things with picture and with a slightly altered commentary; which makes you doubt whether the pictures were already completely truthful in their original context. And how much truth is to be found in pictures to begin with.[4]

Based on research and examples such as *Good Bye Lenin*, it is clear that much image we take for granted as being definitive is actually ambiguous, and it is the accompanying sound that makes it unambiguous. Further support for the influence of sound on image, and that sound determines how image is perceived, comes from experiments where people

---

[1] Vernallis, C., *Experiencing Music Video*, (2004) 4.

[2] Jones, S., Cohesive But Not Coherent: Music Videos (1988) 25.

[3] Colavita, F. & Weisberg, D., A further investigation of visual dominance (1979) 345, 347.

[4] Becker, W., *Good Bye Lenin* DVD (2003).

were asked to evaluate the qualities of paintings after listening to different types of music while watching the paintings. The type of music had a strong affect on the evaluation, and the same paintings were evaluated by different groups as having very different qualities when each group listened to different music[1].

There are two different types of ambiguity. The first type, which has already been discussed, is where image can be ambiguous because the meaning of the image is unclear even though we can clearly discriminate the image itself. Alternatively, the image may be ambiguous because we cannot clearly identify all or parts of the image. This second type of ambiguous image is where all or part of the image is strange and difficult to recognise. When we look around us it is impossible to take in everything at once so we select key parts of a scene; we scan constantly looking for these key parts and then fill in other details from memory and experience; therefore, when we see an image, it is a combined construction of the real world and our memory[2]. At the same time, unusual and surprising stimuli attract more attention and require more effort to understand[3]. The result is that if the image contains a great deal of unfamiliar information, we are not able to easily fill in this information from memory as we normally do when looking at a scene, and therefore the information may be interpreted incorrectly or it may take much longer, and more attention, to interpret it. This type of ambiguity often occurs with science fiction and fantasy images.

The Arrival

The Australian Chamber Orchestra's 2008 performance of *The Arrival* has already been discussed as part of incongruency. The images are also an example of narrative detracting from the music. The images used in the performance, which are from the picture book 'The Arrival' by Shaun Tan, create a strong narrative that is at times also ambiguous. These images are accompanied by the Shostakovich *String Quartet No. 15 opus 144*.

The narrative tells of a man who is unhappy to leave his family who are living in poverty, but he does so to find a more prosperous life. After he arrives at his destination, the natural environment, animals, the city buildings, vehicles and equipment are all strange, and could be from science fiction or the supernatural. The program notes state the images are a wordless story that takes time and focus and must be 'read' as one would

[1] Lindner, D. & Hynaan, M., (1987) Perceived structure of abstract paintings as a function of structure of music listened to on initial viewing, *Bulletin of the Psychonomic Society*, 25/1 (1987) 45.

[2] Greenfield, S., The Mind's Eye, *Brain Story*, BBC Television (2000).

[3] Kahneman, D., *Attention and effort* (1973) 4.

text[1]. The attention required to 'read' this story in pictures occurs at the expense of the music.

The performance starts with an image of a face, and progressively more faces are added until a large number are displayed simultaneously. These are faces from different ethnic backgrounds and many have troubled expressions. Recognising faces is such a demanding and complex task that the brain has a dedicated subsystem specialized for facial recognition[2]. Even one face demands substantial attention so it is likely that many faces will overload the brain's processing power. Vision supplements information missed when listening, however vision itself can cause loss of information if the brain's pace of processing the information is lower than the pace the information is presented[3]. When looking at images in a book, we choose our own pace to move from one to another, however in concert, the images are presented at a pace chosen by someone familiar with the images, having worked with them. This continuous addition of new faces, before the previous face can be fully comprehended, is likely to create information overload with loss of information, including loss of musical information. As the narrative progresses, information overload is also created by images of weirdly shaped buildings, unrecognisable objects and otherworldly animals. These have a vast amount of detail and strangeness, which needs to be deciphered.

This overload is further aggravated by the music. The style, expression and form of Shostakovich's late works, like J. S. Bach's, were considered intellectual and demanding[4]. As *The Arrival* images are also intellectually demanding, the combination is extremely challenging. This is supported by the comment that "the emotional landscape produced by the combination of the music and the images was quite a lot to take in and kept me haunted"[5]. Even so, the more knowledgeable a person is of the material being presented, the faster the information can be processed, so the less demanding the combination will appear[6]. Thus there will be variation of overload for different people of different experience and knowledge and those people working with the material such as the image creator may not suffer this overload and may not find the images distracting. The complexity of each art form and the difficulty of the combination are further born out by a reviewer who was unhappy about

[1] Cuncannon, B., *The Red Tree* Concert Tour Program Notes (2008).

[2] Greenfield, S., The Mind's Eye, *Brain Story* (2000).

[3] Kozma, R., Learning with Media (1991) 194-5.

[4] Martynov, I., *Dmitri Shostakovich, the man and his work,* Philosophical Library (1947) 98,144,164,167.

[5] Botticelli, L., The Red Tree (2008).

[6] Kozma, R., Learning with Media (1991) 195.

the 'abstract' images, which presumably referred to the science fiction-like elements of the drawings. The review stated "abstract images ... distracted, rather than added to the performance"[1].

Issues that detract from music

Overall there were five main issues that interfered with the focus on the music. The first was the strong and often ambiguous storyline. Music in a film may call unwanted attention to itself where it has a strong and clearly defined melodic line[2]. Similarly, a strong narrative calls unwanted attention to itself in the music concert. Narrative elements receive more attention than non-narrative elements[3], and a strong narrative focuses undue attention on the story, backgrounding the music[4]. This occurred with *The Arrival.*

The second issue was the large number of faces presented reasonably quickly, one after the other. As faces require a large amount of processing power[5], loss of information can occur when the brain's pace of processing the information is lower than the pace the information is presented[6]. Much of the audience attention would have been used for interpreting the sequence of faces presented at the beginning of the performance, with little attention left for the music. Once the attention is taken away from the music, it is more difficult to return it than from a neutral starting point[7], so these faces started the performance with attention taken away from the music. For many people, it is likely it stayed that way for a substantial part of the performance.

The third issue that interfered with the focus on the music was the incongruence of the narrative with the meaning of the music. Music is unable to modify visual information even though music can provide context to ambiguous image[8]. Therefore if listeners feel the music has a specific meaning and the image does not reflect this meaning, they will not be influenced to accept the image as representing the music. They may actually be alienated by a narrative they feel is inappropriate[9]. As there are more differences than similarities between *The Arrival* images and the

---

1 Szabo, A., ACO Shines in The Red Tree, (2008).
2 Lindgren, E., *The art of the film* (1963) 139.
3 Marschalek, D., What Eye Movement Research Tells Us about Perceptual Behavior of Children and Adults (1986) 123-7.
4 Marks, M., Music, Drama, Warner Brothers, (1996) 112.
5 Greenfield, S., The Mind's Eye, *Brain Story* (2000).
6 Kozma, R., Learning with Media (1991) 194-5.
7 Posner, M., Nissen, M. & Klein, R., Visual dominance (1976) 167.
8 Bolivar, V., Cohen, A. & Fentress, J., Semantic and Formal Congruency in Music and Motion (1994) 48.
9 English, H., 'Fantasia' and the Psychology of Music (1942-3) 27; Lindgren, E. *The art of the film* (1963) 139-140.

Shostakovich music, this alienation, at least to some extent, is likely to have occurred in many people.

The fourth issue was the intellectually demanding nature of images that had many unusual features and at the same time contained high levels of detail. This occurred with the science fiction-like buildings, animals, plants and appliances. When we look at a scene it is not possible to take in everything at once so we select key parts and construct an image calling on memory and experience to fill in the missing details[1]. We construct our own internal view of strange and unfamiliar images and this requires more attention and effort[2]. It is likely that the attention and effort required to construct a mental view of these unusual images distracted attention from the music.

The fifth issue that interfered with the focus on the music was the ambiguity. There were two levels of ambiguity, the ambiguity of the narrative and the ambiguity within many of the individual images. *The Arrival* program notes direct us to the problem of the ambiguity of the narrative, stating the story created by the images works by "inspiring memory and urging us to fill in the silent gaps, animating them with the addition of our own storyline". This is not the overlaying of meaning and emotion previously discussed in *The Red Tree* (2008), but the deciphering of narrative that was ambiguous and difficult to understand. The second level of ambiguity was from the science fiction-like images with strange details that took considerable deciphering to understand, if they could be understood at all. When ambiguous narrative and images need to be deciphered, the music is called upon to assist in the deciphering process[3]. When deciphering of image is required, the music becomes transparent and the acoustical information is ignored. The result is the music is backgrounded.

Conclusion

It is easy for strong, dramatic and at times ambiguous narrative to distract attention from the music. Once that distraction occurs, it is much more difficult to return attention to the music than it is to have the audience focus on the music from a neutral starting point[4]. There are characteristics within the music that will bring attention back to the music, as previously discussed. The Shostakovich music, although strong and dramatic, does not contain enough of these characteristics to continually pull the attention back to itself. Therefore this performance was a situation

[1] Greenfield, S., The Mind's Eye, *Brain Story* (2000).
[2] Kahneman, D., *Attention and effort*, (1973) 4.
[3] Cohen, A., Associationism and musical soundtrack phenomena (1993) 173.
[4] Posner, M., Nissen, M., & Klein, R., Visual dominance, (1976) 167.

where the ambiguous and intellectually demanding nature of the image kept pulling attention away from the music, and the dramatic nature of the music frequently tried to pull it back, but this was often not successful.

Audience pleasure appeared to be reduced by this conflict between music and image. This claim is supported by several reviews and by the audience applause, which was noticeably less enthusiastic for *The Arrival* than for second item of the concert *The Red Tree*[1]. Even so, many people found *The Arrival* a pleasurable and worthwhile experience. Comments included that it had a "haunting beauty"[2], and "the connection between this man's journey and Shostakovich's meditation on death was intriguingly ambiguous; nevertheless, the overall impression was compelling"[3]. For part of the audience it may not have mattered that the images distracted from the music.

The Arrival was a fascinating concept and unique concert. The audience response was positive, although not to the same extent as the following item, *The Red Tree*, which has already been discussed. The Shostakovich music and *The Arrival* images are both outstanding works of art and it is their very nature that makes this combination so difficult. This performance was leading edge experimentation in the use of image with classical music. Even with the issues discussed, it was to a large extent successful due to the calibre of the Australian Chamber Orchestra and its artistic director and lead violin, Richard Tognetti.

More on ambiguous versus open narrative

Ambiguous narrative and open narrative are very different. Ambiguity revolves around the need to answer questions, to enable us to understand the image and/or narrative. This need to interpret the image draws on the music to help resolve the ambiguity, and in doing so, the acoustic properties of the music are lost to the listener[4]. Ambiguity causes the audience to use the music for interpretation and background it, whereas open narrative and images do not ask questions that need to be resolved. Openness allows the audience to overlay their own emotions, and these emotions that the audience experience while listening to the music will normally be initially aroused by the music itself.

The Arrival and *The Red Tree* picture books are excellent examples of the differences between ambiguity and openness. *The Arrival* (2008)

[1] *The Red Tree* concert performance at City Recital Hall Angel Place, Sydney, 16 July (2008).
[2] Botticelli, L., The Red Tree (2008).
[3] Mathison, L., A Potent Mix (2008).
[4] Cohen, A., Film Music: Perspectives from Cognitive Psychology (2000) 363, 366-8, 373-4.

starts with a man being forced to leave his family due to circumstances beyond his control. We don't know where he's going or when he'll be back and this begs one of the most important questions that can arise for a human being 'Will he see his family again?' For the vast majority of people, this would create a very strong desire to stay focused on the narrative to learn the outcome. There is no overlaying of individual variations of emotion here. This is a very clear narrative about pain of loss of home and family with the possibility it may be permanent.

It might be said that the images in *The Red Tree* can have a negative association and we might ask 'What does a room half full of leaves represent?' However this is unnecessary because the image can be accepted on multiple levels. *The Red Tree* does not demand deciphering. The book is used by psychiatrists and psychologists in analysis confirming its openness to the overlaying of personal meanings and emotions. Determining which narrative and images are ambiguous and which are open, is not necessarily easy but it is important if the music is to remain the focus of the music concert.

Program music narrative

Program music does not suffer from many of the negative effects of narrative because the music has been written specifically to be congruent with a concept and the title conveys that concept before the music is heard.

Definition

Program music is specifically composed to represent or accompany a concept or narrative. It was popular in the Romantic period. While opera and song could in theory be considered program music, the term is normally used only for instrumental music.

Program music

Program music starts life accompanied by a specific concept or narrative and is created for that purpose, which may exclude it from many of the negative effects created by narrative.

There are two reasons that program music can support narrative and these are the high levels of congruency, and the audience expectation. The first, a high level of congruency, occurs because the music is specifically composed for the particular narrative, with this congruency encouraging focus on the music. The second reason that program music can support narrative is because the narrative of program music is normally clearly identified before the music is initially heard. This occurs through the titles of the piece and its movements, and any program notes that accompany the music. Any internal images and emotions generated by program music will normally be based around the narrative specified by the composer. The amelioration of the negative effects of narrative is due to top down processing. Top down processing occurs where we know something from previous knowledge and experience. When we experience this music we fill in the gaps (in this case the narrative) according to our previous associations. If accompanying images are based on the program music title allocated by the composer then it can be claimed that "no violence is done to the composer's intent"[1].

An example of expectation determining the understanding of the music, and the extent to which this occurs, can be seen with a situation that occurred with one of the great romantic composers. Schumann was told he was listening to Mendelssohn's Italian Symphony, when it was actually the Scottish Symphony, with the result that he stated he could clearly see the Italian landscapes represented in the music[2]. If a master of music such as Schumann can so easily allocate the 'wrong' meaning to music, it shows how easily unknown music can take on suggested characteristics. More importantly for the addition of image to program music, it also shows how easily an audience will accept the proposed narrative provided they have not previously allocated their own meaning. This suggests that the most successful combinations of image and music may be when music is specifically written to accompany the image.

From the moment it is first heard, program music is automatically associated with the image it is written to accompany such as *The Red Tree* (2008) and *Sinfonia Antartica* (2007) performances. Even so, techniques such as slowly paced images help maintain the music as the focus of attention. Slowly paced images were used with both *The Red Tree* and *Sinfonia Antartica.*

Sinfonia Antartica

Vaughan Williams' Symphony No.7, *Sinfonia Antartica,* presented by the Sydney Symphony Orchestra in 2007 is an example of the use of images with program music. This music-image concept, combining the *Sinfonia Antartica* Symphony with photographs from the Scott Antarctic expedition, was an in-house production[3]. Vaughan Williams initially

[1] English, H., "Fantasia" and the Psychology of Music (1942-3) 28.
[2] Davies, S., Representation in Music, *Aesthetic Education* 27/1 (1993) 16, 20.
[3] Wilson, R., The concept for the *Sinfonia Antartica* (2007) music-image combination was created by the Sydney Symphony's Artistic Administration Manager, Raff Wilson.

wrote *Sinfonia Antartica* in 1947-48 to accompany the film *Scott of the Antarctic*.

The images were the actual photographs taken during the Scott expedition and the content was amazing. That they were taken at all, given the size and primitive level of photographic equipment in the early 1900s, was an outstanding achievement. Such powerful images might normally dominate the music-image relationship but the congruency of music specifically created to accompany images of the Antarctic, ensured the music held its own. Perhaps the only note of incongruency was the sepia tint of the photos. While this was genuine, it gave warmth to the scenes that would not have been in the landscape itself. Changing it to a blue tint would have created a more authentic feeling of location. However, the sepia tint did give an authentic feeling of the historical aspect of the event.

Vaughan Williams' grand and majestic music reflects the immensity of the alien landscape of the Antarctic with its powerful timeless majesty. The music creates a "sense of desolation and hostility, man pitted against pitiless nature ... the triumph of Nature over adventure". The first movement evokes the foreign landscape with a "constant tonal shimmering [which is] heightened by the addition of a wind machine, female chorus and solo soprano". In the second movement we hear the sound of whales in the low brass, and the sound of comical penguins in woodwinds. The denseness of the third movement equates with the immensity of the ice. In the last movement the music tells of the struggle to survive before Scott and his men are overwhelmed. The music accurately reflects the struggle and loss of Scott's journey in this harsh environment.[1]

The congruency between music and image was enhanced by the skilful selection of particular photographs to present at specific times in the performance, creating a seamless and inspiring music-image combination. Even though these photographs were dramatic, they did not detract from the music due to the congruency and audience awareness of the narrative. While this music-image combination was simple in concept, the music and images were a stunning combination and the audience response was extremely enthusiastic.

[1] *Antarctic Symphony* program notes, (2007).

Humorous narrative

Humour is inherently demanding and attracts attention to the detriment of all else, including music. Humorous narrative should not be used in the instrumental music concert because it will distract audience focus from music.

Humour is frequently used as an attention getting device and it is common practice to start lectures and speeches with jokes. Humour is a powerful force that assists development of the sense of self and it can be used as a coping mechanism and assists in the solving of problems[1]. Humour is so forceful that it substantially reduces the importance of and need for narrative in film[2]. It appears that not only will humour background music but it will also background narrative.

The power of humour is such that congruency of music and image during a humorous narrative is not normally powerful enough to maintain focus on the music, not even program music. The humorous narrative that occurs in cartoons and comedies focuses attention on the image at the expense of the music. In cartoons the music is frequently used to explain characters and plot. The fast action of the cartoon does not provide time to develop the plot, character and emotions so the music provides an instant assessment that tells the audience how to react. If the cartoon character is attacked and beaten, the music informs us whether the character is dejected or angry. The music is used to provide an instant interpretation of the action in much the same way that music can be used to interpret ambiguity in image. The result is that the music is often not heard in comedy.

Much the same thing happens in concert, where the humour can so distract the audience from the music that the acoustic properties are lost. This was apparent in the Sydney Symphony Orchestra's performance of *Gold Rush,* even though the score was created by Chaplin specifically for the film. The following description shows the extent to which the music can be backgrounded by humour. In this performance of *Gold Rush,* the score was performed live while the film was projected on a screen above the orchestra.

---

[1] Woods, P., Coping at School through Humour, *British Journal of Sociology of Education* 4/2 (1983) 122.

[2] McKee, R., Interview, *Sunday Arts,* ABC1 [television] 21 June (2009). Robert McKee is a screenwriting lecturer.

Gold Rush

In 2007 the Sydney Symphony Orchestra performed the score for Charlie Chaplin's *Gold Rush* to accompany the film of the same name (1925), which is a comedy about a tramp that joins the Klondike gold rush. The accompanying music was created by Chaplin for the film's 1942 revival, and is a combination of popular, classical and original music. This performance is an example of close synchronisation where a close match between music and image adds to the humour. While the congruency in *Gold Rush* might help to focus attention on the music, the humorous narrative focuses attention on the image and this can be seen from the following description of the performance and the description of the audience reaction.

> My experience watching Chaplin's *Gold Rush* with the Sydney Symphony playing the score live was a very enjoyable one, much more enjoyable than if I had watched the film or listened to the concert separately. I knew that the performance was a unique occasion and that made it very special. There was something clearly spontaneous about music that was being conducted to fit the screen at that moment.
>
> The experience was a little disconcerting as well. I didn't know what to watch: the orchestra's performance or the film on the screen. I had not seen *Gold Rush* before, and I wanted to know what the film was about, and how the music was related to the film. On the other hand, I wanted to see the players' performance and particularly the conductor's mediation between the film and the orchestra. I wished I could see both simultaneously. Anyway, even when I was focusing my sight on the screen or the orchestra, the way I perceived one was influenced by the presence of the other.
>
> At the beginning I was focusing more on the orchestra than on the film, but as the film evolved, I started to focus more on the film. This was more evident for the rest of the public. At some point all the audience was focusing on the film and paying little attention to the orchestra. The fact that the film was being played totally changed the feel of the concert hall. People would start overtly laughing at certain scenes in a fashion that I had never experienced when attending a concert without film. They would also laugh more than if they were watching the film in a cinema. I felt a lot more amused by watching the film with a live orchestra than I would have done if watching the film alone. The orchestra seemed to reinforce the drama and the

> comedy of the film, and the film seemed to reinforce the power of the music played by the orchestra. I really wish I could watch all films like this!
>
> I was under the impression that the conductor and the orchestra were responding to the audience reaction. For instance, there was a scene towards the end of the film in which a cabin is pushed near a precipice by a snow storm. Then, as Chaplin and his friend move to one part of the cabin, the cabin starts swinging while balancing on the side of the cliff. I don't know how it happened, but everything felt so intense at this moment – so much more than when normally watching a film in the living room or the cinema. The moment became very comic. The music was mimicking the film. For instance, if the house was hanging down, the orchestra would play a falling scale. Everyone started laughing. A lady was laughing incredibly loud, and many people actually starting laughing at her laugh. Then the orchestra seemed to grasp the audience excitement, and I think the musicians started exaggerating the music just for that scene.
>
> Even though at that point almost everyone was focusing on the screen, we could all see the players' movements as they related to the film. It was great fun.[1]

Based on the audience response, *Gold Rush* was a very enjoyable experience and a successful performance for the Sydney Symphony Orchestra's *Kaleidoscope* concert series. *Kaleidoscope* is an ongoing series that aims to attract an audience that would not normally attend a classical music concert. This concert had none of the 'straight-jacket' stiffness of the usual classical concert where the audience is expected to remain still and absolutely silent. It would have been a refreshing and exciting experience for those who felt they could not be part of the 'elite' classical music set.

The format of the *Gold Rush* performance successfully achieved its objective of introducing new audiences to an enjoyable orchestral performance. This type of event is ideal for attracting a new audience and this is the intention of Sydney Symphony Orchestra in providing these more unusual events. The downside is that serious classical music listeners may not be happy to attend a rowdy performance where the music frequently becomes relegated to the background.

[1] Neve, E., Sydney Symphony Orchestra's performance of Gold Rush at the Sydney Opera House, 30 August 2007. Eduardo Neve is a PHD candidate at Durham University, UK.

Conclusion

Narrative normally demands attention and this normally occurs at the expense of the music. It is difficult to add any form of narrative that will not detract from the music, and often the best that can be achieved will be to limit the distraction created by the narrative. When narrative is used, it should be apparent, loose or open to multiple meanings. There may be only small differences between non narrative, apparent, loose and open narrative and several may be combined in a single performance.

Adding a strong, complex, ambiguous or humorous narrative to music should be avoided if the music is to remain the primary focus. If it is considered desirable to background the music as might be advantageous in an amateur performance, or if the aim is to attract an audience that does not normally attend instrumental music concerts, then a strong, complex, ambiguous and/or humorous narrative can be used to achieve these objectives.

Each image within a series, where the image has a meaning, should be complete in itself and satisfying as a story within itself. Abstract images, patterns and shapes can be used and will not be ambiguous provided they do not have strong or dominating elements that create their own meaning.

Where a composer has added narrative through the title, or where music has been composed to accompany narrative, then narrative is appropriate. Even so, the implementation of the narrative needs to be subtle so the music remains the primary art form because this is concert rather than film, theatre, or multimedia.

Narrative may be entertaining and pleasurable, but where the aim is to present a concert where the music remains dominant, or at least is not backgrounded, then narrative must be used with care.

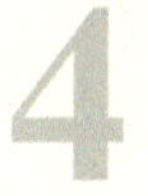

Synchronisation and tempo-pace characteristics

This chapter discusses different types of synchronisation and how each type can be used in the music-image combination to create congruency between music and image. The types of synchronisation discussed are: neutral, perceived, apparent and continuous synchronisation; synchresis[1]; and, mickey-mousing; as well as the synchronisation created by sync points, film editing, patterns and repetition. Also discussed is the relationship between the tempo of the music and the pace of the image.

Synchronisation

Synchronisation can be used as the glue that holds the music-image combination together, creating coherence that may not otherwise be present. Synchronisation of music and image is often essential to maintain audience focus on the music. However the synchronisation may need to be subtle in the case of classical and contemporary music.

Definitions

Synchronisation refers to a regular process of recurring accents of music and image that appear to occur at the same time. An accent in music can be made using tone, loudness or beat. An accent in images can occur through movement or change.

Rhythm in music is the grouping of separate sounds into structured patterns. While strictly speaking, beat and metre are separate to rhythm, here the term 'rhythm' is used loosely and includes all three temporal modes: rhythm, beat and metre.

Beat or pulse is a regular rhythmic pattern of music; it is a basic time unit of a piece of music. A metronome can be used to sounds out the basic beat of music.

Metre in music, like the beat, has a consistent rhythmic pattern. Unlike the beat, metre is characterized by alternating strong and weak beats.

Images are like music in that they have a rhythm created by the beat, tempo and accent of movements within the images, but rhythm in film is also created by editing[2]. Rhythm in films can also be created by alternat-

[1] The term synchresis was coined by Chion, M., *Audio-Vision* (1994) 63.
[2] Bordwell, D. & Thompson, K., *Film art: an introduction* (2004) 360.

ing different shots[1]. Therefore in images, rhythm is created by movement, the type of shots and editing.

Synchronisation of music without a beat

Much classical and some types of contemporary music normally do not have a steady beat due to expression markings such as rubato, presto, largo and fermata that temporarily change the rhythm and tempo. The impact of these expression markings is that many of the following synchronisation concepts will be more difficult to achieve than with music that has a regular beat. The exception to this is continuous synchronisation, which can be used with all types of music. If you are creating image for only traditional classical rather than contemporary music, you may prefer not read the reviews of the Kraftwerk concerts. While these reviews will be helpful in understanding the concepts involved in synchronisation, it will require imagination to see how different aspects might on occasion be applied to the classical concert.

Rhythm

Rhythm is part of our daily lives with all spoken language and all normal movements having rhythm[2]. There are two very different types of rhythm that are sometimes confused: natural rhythm as occurs in normal speech and body movements, and stylised rhythm as occurs in metered poetry, music and dancing[3]. The following diagram shows the two types of rhythm, natural and stylised with the rhythmic patterns of stylised rhythm comprised of rhythmic motives.

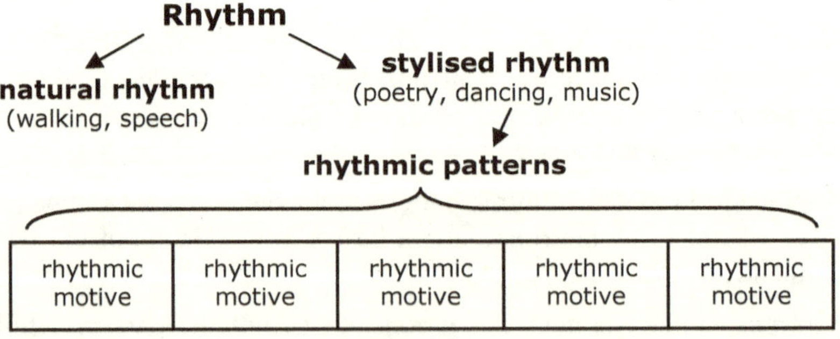

Figure 13 Different types of rhythm

---

[1] van Leeuwen, T., Rhythmic Structure of the Film Text, (1985) 216-9, 222.

[2] Allen, G., Speech Rhythm: its relation to performance universals and articulartory timing, *Journal of phonetics* 3 (1975) 75-9

[3] van Leeuwen, T., Rhythmic Structure of the Film Text, in *Discourse and communication: new approaches to the analysis of mass media discourse and communication* (1985) 216-9, 222.

This stylised rhythm of music with its structured rhythm patterns is formed by the interaction of pitch, intensity, timbre, texture, harmony and duration. These patterns of rhythms are comprised of multiple levels of small rhythmic motives that each have their own shape and structure. These small rhythmic motives together create extended rhythmic patterns that form the larger rhythmic organisation.[1]

Rhythm is extremely important in music; so important in fact that a change in the rhythmic structure, changes the perceived tonality of the music[2]. The tendency of rhythm to dominate perception is shown by experiments where melodies, even though they were different, were judged as being similar when their rhythms were identical[3]. Additionally, music through rhythm has the ability to unify image that is not chronologically coherent[4]. A strong rhythmic beat will continually bring attention back to the music, but as music normally lacks a strong beat, maintaining focus on classical and some contemporary music is more challenging than it is for pop music.

The concept of rhythm in classical and some contemporary music is more complex than popular music. It could be argued that the rhythm of much of this type of music exists between natural rhythm and stylised rhythm. While each bar has a time signature, the tempo can be changed by musical notation terms and symbols such as 'accelerando', which indicates that the tempo should be gradually increased. While this term refers to the tempo, its gradual implementation means that it disrupts, at least temporarily, the regular beat. The term 'rubato' indicates that the strict tempo is to be temporarily abandoned to create a more emotional tone, which gives the musician freedom to alter the tempo many times. Other terms such as 'presto' (very fast) and 'largo' (very slow) may change the tempo from one bar to the next. There is also the 'fermata' (pause) symbol indicating the particular note should be sustained, which temporarily halts the tempo. While all these terms and symbols refer to tempo, if used within a movement they also change the rhythm by changing the regularity of the pulse. This is an important consideration when adding synchronised images to music.

Rhythm is also an important part of image. Film and video have rhythm even if there is no music. Movements and cuts in video image may create one rhythm while the musician's gestures, facial expressions and body

---

[1] Cooper, G. & Meyer, L., *The Rhythmic Structure of Music*, University of Chicago (1963) 1-2.

[2] Hershman, D., Rhythmic Factors in Tonality, *Psychomusicology* 14 (1995) 4.

[3] Kidd, G., Boltz, M. & Jones, M., Some Effects of Rhythmic Context on Melody Recognition, *American Journal of Psychology*, 97/2 (Summer 1984) 170-2.

[4] Kalinak, K., *Settling the score*, (1992) 47.

movements may create different rhythms[1]. Rhythm in films can be created by techniques such as alternating between accented shots and non-accented shots and this difference, which creates rhythm, occurs because accented shots such as close-ups are more conspicuous and have greater psychological impact; even before editing and cuts impose a rhythm, and before music is added, a film may have its own rhythm through image and sound[2].

The music-image combination always has multiple rhythms because individually music and image always have some type of rhythm, and within each there may be multiple rhythms; these multiple rhythms and their interaction form the rhythm structure[3]. Even though both music and image have rhythm, visual rhythm and sound rhythm are very different because it is not easy to tap your feet or dance to image unless it is something like a flash or strobe light[4]. As music and image each have their own individual rhythm, each can undermine the qualities of the other, however the opposite may also occur; by creating connections between music and image through elements such as synchronisation and rhythm, the music can be accentuated[5], and this is the aim in the instrumental music concert.

Synchronisation

Synchronisation is one of several elements that can create congruency in the music-image relationship and congruency unifies the music-image combination. This synchronisation that unifies also creates impact, and when a visually accented image is synchronised on a music beat, the combination will have more emphasis than the separate elements[6]. When music and image are out of sync the similarities are weakened but when music and image are synchronised the similarities are strengthened; this strengthening occurs because synchronisation draws attention to the music-image relationship[7]. As the music-image relationship is weakened when music and image are out of sync, this should not be allowed to occur in the music concert because it creates a conflict that will distract from the music. However, there is a difference between being out of sync and a neutral situation of not being in sync.

---

[1] Martinec, R., Rhythm in Multimodal Texts (2000) 289.

[2] van Leeuwen, T., Rhythmic Structure of the Film Text, (1985) 216-9, 222.

[3] Martinec, R., Rhythm in Multimodal Texts (2000) 289.

[4] van Leeuwen, T., Rhythmic Structure of the Film Text (1985) 221.

[5] Vernallis, C., *Experiencing Music Video*, (2004) 14, 190.

[6] van Leeuwen, T., Rhythmic Structure of the Film Text, (1985) 222.

[7] Johnson, W., Sound and Image: A Further Hearing, *Film Quarterly* 43/1 (Autumn, 1989) 6, 7, 25.

An example of synchronisation strengthening the relationship and creating emphasis can be seen in Kraftwerk's *Trans Europe Express* (2005). Old film footage of Trans Europe Express trains, which have long been decommissioned, show colliding buffers that appear to be cleverly cut and paced to coincide with a crashing sound in the music. On initial viewing, if the synchronisation is not carefully observed, these repeating collisions seem to be exactly timed with the music but on subsequent viewings, when observing the synchronisation, many of the collisions are not in sync with the crashing sound. At times these collisions occur when there is no crashing sound at all. This is an example of where we notice the synchronisation because it strengthens the music-image combination but we don't notice similar situations where it doesn't occur because these images and sounds are weakened when not in sync. To create this impression, that everything is in sync, requires a certain number of the synchronisations to actually occur.

Something similar occurs in Kraftwerk's *Numbers* (2005), discussed in detail in the section on structure. In any music-image combination, audience attention will be focused on those parts where congruent image is rhythmically synchronised to the music and the result is that those parts are emphasised, appear more congruent and are better remembered[1]. This occurs in the instrumental sections of the song *Numbers* where hundreds of numbers flash on the screen, but where the eye focuses on those numbers that are flashing in time to the music. The result is the entire image appears synchronised with the music. In this instance the quantity of numbers not in sync is probably more than the quantity of numbers in sync, but the effect is strong enough to result in apparent synchronisation. An important point is that due to the volume of displayed numbers involved, and the quantity of sounds occurring in a short space of time, nothing appears out of sync. It is likely that determining whether the desired synchronisation result will be achieved is a matter of actually testing the music-image combination and observing the results.

Types of synchronisation

The different types of synchronisation are: **neutral**, **apparent** and **continuous synchronisation**; **mickey-mousing**; and, **synchresis**. While each type of synchronisation is different, a single piece of music may contain multiple types, however this may not be readily apparent.

[1] Marshall, S. & Cohen, A., Effects of Musical Soundtracks on Attitudes toward Animated Geometric Figures, *Music Perception* 6/1 (1988) 108.

Neutral synchronisation	There is no synchronisation but nothing is out of sync.
Apparent synchronisation	There appears to be synchronisation. There are two types: sound creates apparent visual movement where there is an expectation of movement but none actually occurs; or, the synchronisation occurs within a window of time that appears synchronised but if measured precisely would not be.
Continuous synchronisation	The synchronisation of the music and image occurs in parallel over a period of time with nothing out of sync. The music and image may wax and wane in unison, or may start and end on a sync point.
Mickey-mousing	Close synchronisation of music and image as is often seen in cartoons.
Synchresis	Unlikely combinations of sound and image that become associated because of synchronisation.

Figure 14 Types of synchronisation

The following diagram shows the different types of synchronisation that range from mickey-mousing, which is close synchronisation, through to being completely out of sync.

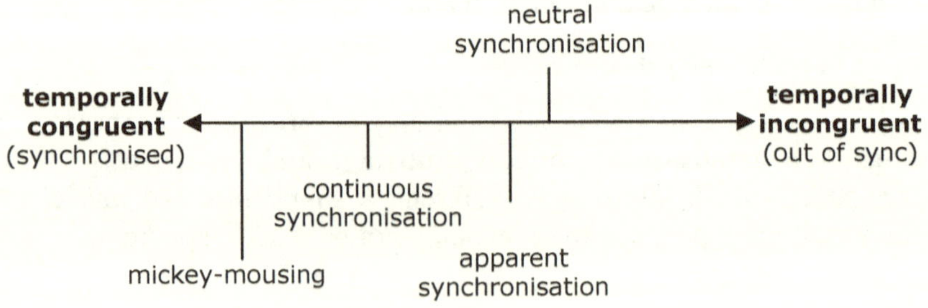

Figure 15 Synchronisation range

Neutral synchronisation

Neutral synchronisation is like neutral congruency in that it doesn't create emphasis but neither does it detract from the music-image combination. In neutral synchronisation there is no apparent synchronisation but at the same time the music and image do not appear out of sync. Neutral synchronisation was used in the performance of *Rembrandt's World* (2005) previously discussed, where the images were changed between pieces and movements. There was no rhythmic synchronisation between the still images and the music but neither were they rhythmically out of sync.

Apparent synchronisation

There are two types of apparent synchronisation. The first is where a sound creates an apparent visual movement. The movement is perceived as coinciding with the sound, but in fact there is no movement. The second type is synchronisation that occurs within a window of time where sound and image appear synchronised but if measured precisely by equipment, it would be obvious that they were not in sync.

Sound and apparent movement

Sound can create a sleight-of-hand effect by creating the impression of a rapid movement that in fact is not there. This occurred in the George Lucas *Star Wars* film, *The Empire Strikes Back* (1980), where the automatic opening and closing doors were an illusion created by the sound. They are seen closed and then seen open, and it is the imagination, prompted by sound, that creates the impression they are seen actually in the process of opening and closing.[1]

Something similar occurs in the song *Pocket Calculator* where we see a hand above a calculator and when we hear the sound of the button being pressed, we 'see' the finger move. This is an example of apparent movement creating synchronisation by 'sleight-of-hand'.

Pocket Calculator

Kraftwerk's *Pocket Calculator* (2005) is an example of apparent movement. It is a playful song that includes sounds from calculators, and in early performances of the song, the group performed with calculators[2]. Keeping an audience entertained while pressing calculator buttons must

---

[1] Chion, M., *Audio-Vision* (1994) 11-12, 15.
[2] Bussy, P., *Kraftwerk: Man, Machine and Music* (2005) 115, 179-180.

be considered quite an achievement given that some artists perform actions as radical as smashing guitars to impress their fans. This is an example of the transference of the qualities of the music to the image where the image is made more interesting by the music.

The performance starts with a stark white screen behind four suited figures standing at their computers with pink lights shining down creating pink heads. The effect is much like looking at four accountants at work in a futuristic finance office. A calculator emerges from the back right of the screen, increasing in size as it moves to centre screen. This is followed by two columns of Japanese text moving inwards from both sides to form columns either side of the 'accountants'. A massive hand moves across the calculator image with the extended index finger pressing buttons, apparently in sync with the music. On subsequent viewings with closer analysis, it can be observed that the hand often moves to the button slightly before the beat rather than synchronised with the beat. The hand and fingers move as one and the fingers do not move individually. It may be that we unconsciously link the hand hovering above the button as getting ready to press the button and we 'see' the button being pressed when the appropriate sound occurs. However this perception is an illusion because the hand (or finger) doesn't move once it is above the button. We expect the button to be pressed in sync with the sound and the button actually does appear to be pressed at that time. This is an example of sound animating the image. This indicates that synchronisation of image with the music in live performance may be less of a problem than would be initially expected and it is a matter of testing and literally seeing if an effect works.

Synchronisation, rhythm and time perception

Many factors influence how we perceive rhythm and whether we hear it accurately. Some of these factors are obvious, such as musical training, musical sensitivity and actual changes in rhythm and tempo. However other influences on how we perceive rhythm are surprising. Changes in music pitch may create one rhythm, while changes in volume may create another rhythm[1]. Monotony is another factor, and can reduce attention to rhythm and affect the accuracy of how we perceive rhythmic regularity[2].

[1] Martinec, R., Rhythm in Multimodal Texts, *Leonardo* 33/4 (2000) 289.

[2] Sink, P., Effects of Rhythmic and Melodic Alterations on Rhythmic Perception, *Research in Music Education* 31/2 (Summer 1983) 111-2; Effects of Rhythmic and Melodic Alterations and Selected Musical Experiences on Rhythmic Processing, *Research in Music Education*, 32/3 (Autumn, 1984) 177.

Therefore, music "is not necessarily heard as it is played"[1] and research supports the idea that our perception of sound is often inaccurate and the hearing of rhythm is perceived rather than being objective, as equipment would measure it. This is shown in experiments where the last unit within a rhythm cycle is perceived differently, and is unconsciously expected to be longer; when the last unit is not longer, it is perceived as shorter[2]. This has a natural logic considering that a singer may momentarily pause for a breath at the end of a phrase even if the music theoretically does not allow additional time, but this is not perceived by the listener as a fault. Additionally, we talk about timing that allows the music 'to breathe' and something similar occurs in conversation where it is natural to pause at the end of phrases and sentences.

As well as perceiving the end of musical phrases inaccurately, we may perceive entire phrases as rhythmic when they are not. Perceived rhythm is also affected by differences in pitch and loudness. Time intervals that are approximate, but not exactly equal, will normally be heard as exactly equal. Any sequence of pulses that is not overly slow or overly fast, will appear to have a rhythm even if there is none. Rhythm dominates humans to the extent that it is impossible to move without a degree of rhythm.[3]

This inaccurate perception of rhythm continues with the music-image combination and if there is enough similarity between image and music it allows the pictures to absorb the rhythmic qualities of the music resulting in the image taking on those rhythmic qualities, much like ventriloquism[4]. However, the ability for image to take on specific rhythmic qualities of the music appears to depend on whether the events occur within a window of time, which allows the audience to compensate for audio and visual characteristics that are slightly out of sync[5]. At times natural rhythm, such as body movements, can be perceived as stylised rhythm if it occurs within this window because perception of rhythm is fluid rather than hard wired.

Inaccurate perception of rhythm in the music-image combination can be observed looking out a window on a windy day while listening to music. Most times, the leaves and branches of the trees will appear to be moving to the beat of the music. While there may be some movements that are in

---

[1] Miller, B., Time Perception in Musical Meter Perception, *Psychomusicology*, 12, (1993) 151.

[2] Lehiste, I., Rhythmic units and syntactic units in production and perception, *Acoustical Society of America* 54/5 (1973) 1233-4.

[3] Allen, G., Speech Rhythm: its relation to performance universals and articulartory timing, (1975) 75-9.

[4] Cook, N., *Analysing musical multimedia* (1998) 78.

[5] Bolivar, V., Cohen, A. & Fentress, J., Semantic and Formal Congruency in Music and Motion (1994) 49.

synchronisation to the music, the bulk of the movement will not be. Our eyes look for and focus on those movements that occur within an acceptable window of time and we see these as synchronised. The image designer can use this trick where precise synchronisation is not possible. Whether it works is an artistic decision that can only be made by observing the music-image combination. The entire rhythmic structure should be taken into account when creating synchronisation because the music-image combination can at times create unexpected results due to the complexity of this structure, along with the fact that synchronisation is perceived rather than hard wired. Timing, rhythm and emphasis can change the meaning of spoken words. In the same way, the addition of image to music can change the apparent timing and emphasis of the music, thereby changing its perceived structure[1].

Semantic congruency and apparent synchronisation

The perception of synchronisation between music and image is influenced by the semantic congruency of the music-image combination. When the mood and meaning of music and image are congruent, the temporal aspects of the media are more likely to appear congruent[2]. Therefore, even if music and image are synchronised, if their mood and meaning do not match, they may appear out of sync. Semantic congruency is normally necessary to achieve apparent synchronisation. Congruency of meaning and synchronisation go hand in hand in the role of gluing music and image together to create a coherent combination that focuses attention on the music.

Tour de France

Tour de France (2005) track 6 on the *Minimum-Maximum* DVD, has already been described in apparent narrative, but it is also an example of apparent synchronisation that is created by events coinciding within an acceptable window of time, and, by the congruency of the meaning and mood of music and image. It also shows natural rhythms that appear to be stylised rhythms. The music starts with a continuous melody with no beat. The opening image is formed by the three colours of the French flag, blue at the top, red at the bottom and white in the middle forming a cycling track containing a drawn image of four cyclists.

The lyrics start with the repeated word 'budup' followed by a beat with heavy panting in sync with the rhythm. The image changes to black and white film of cyclists racing along streets lined with spectators. Various

---

[1] van Leeuwen, T., *Speech, Music, Sound,* MacMillan (1999) 137-141.

[2] Bolivar, V., Cohen, A. & Fentress, J., Semantic and Formal Congruency in Music and Motion (1994) 44, 49.

shots including close-ups and distant shots show the group of cyclists peddling in what appears to be synchronisation to the music. This is an illusion because the movements are natural. Movements, such as drinking while cycling and waving of the spectators, create natural rhythms, but these natural rhythms appear synchronised to the stylised rhythm of the music. This apparent synchronisation occurs because these natural and stylised rhythm movements coincide within an acceptable window of time. Apparent synchronisation is reinforced by semantic congruency created by the sounds of cycling such as bicycle gears with the image of the race. An instrumental 'solo' section in the middle is accompanied by scenes of slow motion cycling with huge feet on pedals, followed by massive shadows of cyclists filling the entire back of the stage. Part of the instrumentation for this solo section is the sound of heavy breathing, which cyclists would make in a race, and this breathing creates a beat without melody.

Kraftwerk fans believe the group has captured the mood of cycling in the sounds and music. This can be seen in a comment on amazon.com from the user *nicjaytee* which suggests using the entire eleven released versions of *Tour de France* in shuffle mode to accompany serious cycling[1]. *Tour de France* has congruency of mood and meaning in music and image, and this along with movements and beat occurring within an acceptable window of time, creates apparent synchronisation.

Synchresis

Synchronisation glues together unlikely combinations of sound and image. A sound can be associated with an image on a sync point and seem correct even though that sound was not originally and is not normally associated with that image. Our logic should tell us that that the combination is illogical but instead we accept the new combination. This is 'synchresis', a word created from a combination of the words synchronism and synthesis. Additionally, synchresis allows a wide variety of very different sounds to be accepted by the audience as appropriate to a particular image, such as a single face may have many voices that sound appropriate. Random combinations of music and image can result in synchresis but it may not always be obvious why this has occurred. Synchresis does not always occur and a variety of factors determine whether synchresis of a particular sound and image is achieved.[2]

---

[1] *nicjaytee*, London, http://www.amazon.com/Tour-France-03-Kraftwerk/dp/B0000A2ZUF/ref=sr_1_1? ie= UTF8&s=music&qid=1231218447&sr=1-1 (2005) accessed 15 February 2008.

[2] Chion, M., *Audio-Vision* (1994) 54, 63, 115.

In the music concert synchresis allows music to be associated with image that is clearly illogical. For example, a series of loud, dramatic chords might be played in sync with images of crashing waves. Logic says that waves do not create music tones but we readily accept these chords as the sound of waves and this association continues. This special meaning created by sound and image would not have occurred without the synchronisation. Synchresis cannot be determined by an intellectual decision and whether synchresis is created by the combination of an unrelated sound and image will be determined by how the effect is perceived. Synchresis can be dramatic or not. Synchresis that creates a dramatic effect should only be used when the music is already dramatic, because synchresis should not be used to create effects that were not part of the original music. The song *Radioactivity* contains an example of synchresis.

Radioactivity

Kraftwerk's *Radioactivity* (2005) has been described as electronic chamber music. This song was admired and used by the great German art film director Rainer Werner Fassbinder. The title *Radioactivity* is a play on words, and some of the images are a visual pun, such as radio broadcasting, at odds with the nuclear power message. This message was too subtle for some non-European audiences who seemed confused by the song, which at times was interpreted as pro nuclear power. Hopefully the meaning of the song has been clarified since it now starts with an anti-nuclear statement. Kraftwerk's use of noise in music, such as *Radioactivity,* was avant-garde at the time.[1]

Congruent, repeating images such as the radio active symbol, the atom, and explosions caused by colliding atoms, are synchronised with the music. The performance also includes voice and displayed text. The use of voice and text, rather than detracting from the music, highlights and reinforces the music, and this is achieved through minimalism, rhythm and congruency.

Radioactivity includes an example of synchresis with animated radio waves emanating from a tower synchronised to beeping sounds. The combination of the two events, the images of radio waves and the beeping sounds, are immediately associated. This association occurs even though we know that radio waves can not be directly seen nor heard. When we hear the beeping sound again, even if we don't see the images of radio waves, the beeping will be accepted as the sound of radio waves being broadcast. Such is the power of synchresis.

---

[1] Bussy, P., *Kraftwerk: Man, Machine and Music* (2005) 73-6, 95.

Continuous synchronisation

Continuous synchronisation is a form of synchronisation that does not require a beat. It can be used to create congruency in the music-image relationship when the music and image occur in parallel, and where the music flows or waxes and wanes but does not have a steady beat.

Sync points in the music-image relationship are not necessarily essential to create synchronisation. Instead, the music and image can be more like two musical instruments playing together where the movements of both the music and the image are complementary[1]. When this occurs, particularly where the music waxes and wanes, synchronisation can exist as a continuum rather than as explicit synchronisation on the beat; this is more correctly referred to as a 'smear' than a sync point, with a gradual unfolding of music and image over time[2]. Continuous synchronisation occurs when a beginning and ending point within the music coincides with a beginning and ending point within the image. Note that the starting and ending points may or may not be sync points. There are no actual synchronisation points between the start and the end but at the same time nothing should appear out of sync. This is discussed further in the section 'Creating and using sync points' with the example of the song *The Model* using both sync points and parallel continuous synchronisation.

The following diagram shows continuous synchronisation from a start point through to an end point with no sync points between and nothing out of sync. In this case the start and end points would normally be sync points.

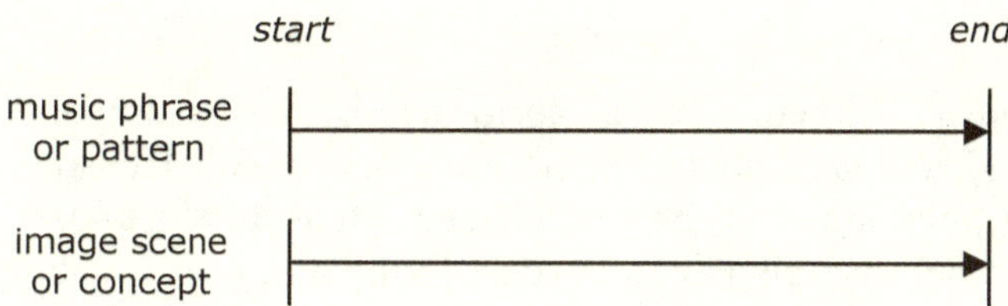

Figure 16 Continuous synchronisation between points

[1] Chion, M., *Audio-Vision* (1994) 11, 13-14.
[2] Vernallis, C., *Experiencing Music Video* (2004) 181-2.

The following diagram shows music and image waxing and waning in parallel. The start and end may or may not be sync points.

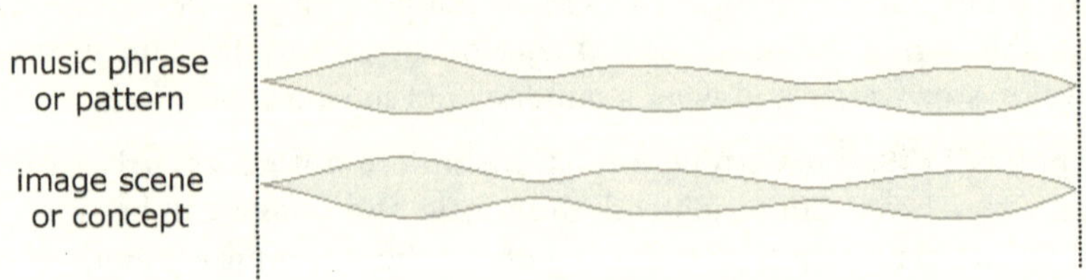

Figure 17 Continuous synchronisation waxing and waning

This type of continuous synchronisation can be just as important for creating congruency as the sync point because much classical and contemporary music does not have a steady beat, but often waxes and wanes. An example of music where continuous synchronisation would be essential is the flowing music by Debussy. Debussy's music is normally considered impressionist even though Debussy himself indignantly claimed it was symbolist. Normal synchronisation would be difficult with this flowing music, and continuous synchronisation provides an alternative. In the Kraftwerk *Tour de France* song previously discussed, the gigantic bicycle wheel apparently in sync with the music is an example of a smear creating continuous synchronisation, This can be also be seen in Kraftwerk's *Planet of Visions* and *Neon Lights*. While all have a steady beat, it is often less dominant than the melody, which is probably the reason the melody was chosen for continuous synchronisation in these works.

Luminous

The *Luminous* (2005) concert was performed by the Australian Chamber Orchestra and included photographic artworks by Bill Henson[1] and has already been mentioned in the first chapter. Henson was chosen for this collaboration because his works have a "lilting and lyrical quality"[2]. The performance comprised a wide variety of songs and instrumental music that ranged from classical through to pop classics as well as specifically created soundscapes. Composers included Alfred Schnittke, Benjamin Britten, Gabriel Yared, Astor Piazzolla, REM, George Crumb, Peteris Vasks, Leoš Janáček and soundscapes by Paul Healey. The works are listed in the section on genre-style. The soundscapes were specifically created to add coherence to this unusual combination of music. The *Lu-*

[1] *Luminous* performance at City Recital Hall, Sydney, 13 April 2005.
[2] Richard Tognetti in *Luminous* [documentary], *Sunday Arts*, ABC1 [television], 1 June (2008).

minous sound sculptor, Paul Healey, described the collaboration as part concert, part cinema and part cabaret, creating a cinematic experience that immerses the viewer in an aesthetic of photography and music, which has a dark, romantic beauty[1].

Henson wanted to create an interesting conversation between music and image and did this by the intermittent use of videos of the selected artworks. He stated that when music and image are used together it is often the case that each medium is an illustration of the other and each becomes compromised by the other. He wanted each media to have the space to become everything it could be. Henson believed a dynamic visual presence could be achieved by filming his still artworks so they could unfold in a more physically demonstrative manner.[2]

While Henson believed that motion was essential, this is not necessarily the case because "the [still] photographic message is a continuous message"[3] so we don't necessarily need to accompany continuous music with moving images as was shown with the still images of *The Red Tree* (2008). However, Henson did create a 'conversation' between music and image, but at times this 'conversation' halted unexpectedly with no image while the music continued. Being unexpected it seemed somewhat unnatural so this halting of the image was a form of incongruency and the music and image became out of sync. The blank screen also created the problem that the screen needed to be regularly checked by the audience who were looking up at it suspended high above the orchestra. This may not have been as much of a problem for those seated in the upper levels as it was for those seated at the front of the concert hall, where viewing the screen involved a conscious effort and unnatural head position.

The film Henson created consisted of slowly changing shots that often started as close-ups, and then slowly zoomed out to reveal more and more of the artwork. This created continuous synchronisation between the music and image and worked especially well between the landscapes and soundscapes, which were specifically composed for the music-image combination. The combination of the landscape and soundscape, which introduced the second part of the performance, was a particularly elegant merging of music and image to create continuous synchronisation.

The extreme close-up shots that Henson often started with were the reverse of typical film shots. Film normally uses an establishing long shot

---

[1] Healy, P. in *Luminous* [documentary], *Sunday Arts*, ABC1 [television], 1 June (2008).

[2] Henson, B. in *Luminous* [documentary], *Sunday Arts*, ABC1 [television], 1 June (2008).

[3] Barthes, R., *The Responsibility of Forms: Critical Essays on Music, Art and Representation*, Oxford: Basil Blackwell (1986) 5.

(long distance shot) to set the scene[1] and this long shot at the beginning ensures that the audience is oriented before the zoom focuses in to introduce a character or concept. Henson's extreme close-ups, without the preliminary orienting long shot, were often ambiguous until enough of the image was revealed to allow the viewer to become oriented. As discussed in the narrative chapter, ambiguity normally distracts attention from the music. Tognetti described these zooms in and out as a telescopic type of rapport; even though the music didn't change when the camera was close up, it felt like the music was closer; when the camera pulled away, it felt like the music was also further away; he thought this was an interesting effect not normally experienced with music alone[2]. However, this effect was not obvious to me sitting in the audience near the front of the stage. A short introduction by Tognetti mentioning his ideas on the music-image combination would have ensured these were observed and would have enhanced the audience pleasure.

These shots that started as extreme close-ups and slowly zoomed out were normally long-takes. Long takes are shots held for an extended period. In film, long takes are used for a number of reasons including allowing time for complex and densely saturated visual information to be absorbed[3]. As these shots were often extreme close-ups, the lack of details sometimes gave the feeling of excessive slowness. They also created ambiguity from the uncertainty of what the image actually was, and this uncertainty, when the image could not be deciphered, interrupted the focus on the music. Humans recognise a face from the slightest hint of a facial configuration, which is why we see the man in the moon and faces in clouds[4], so there was no ambiguity when the close-ups were of faces where the eyes were apparent. However sometimes in images where the eyes were closed it was difficult to recognise an extreme close-up as a face.

These issues of ambiguity and excessively slow long-takes were not apparent in the documentary of the performance[5] because it included techniques commonly used in film, such as overlaying images where a semi transparent image sits on top of another. This overlaying of image-on-image or artist-on-image created interest and relieved the feeling of excessive slowness during close-ups that contained little detail. Another technique that the documentary used, which could have been included in

---

[1] Orpen, V., *Film Editing: the Art of the Expressive,* Wallflower (2003) 127.

[2] Tognetti, R in *Luminous* [documentary], *Sunday Arts*, ABC1 [television], 1 June (2008).

[3] Orpen, V., *Film Editing* (2003) 127.

[4] Farah, M., Director, Center for Cognitive Neuroscience, University of Pennsylvania in Greenfield, The Mind's Eye, *Brain Story* (2000).

[5] *Luminous* [documentary], *Sunday Arts*, ABC1 [television], 1 June (2008).

the performance, was the use of overlaying the same image but at different focal lengths. This would have resulted in a type of still zoom, an interesting and effective alternative to the continual use of the standard zooming in and out. These more innovative techniques were not included in the live performance, which may have benefited from the involvement of an experienced filmmaker. The apparent aim of keeping the artwork discrete from the performers reduced the impact of the continuous synchronisation and lessened the ability of each media to become part of an integrated whole.

Artistic Director, Richard Tognetti, stated that the choice of repertoire was a slow, arduous process and the aim was to combine unlikely music to 'en-trance' the audience, with the widely different styles of music chosen to reflect the extremes of light and day that appear in Henson's artworks[1]. However, each artwork has a combination of light and dark within it, but the music alternated between light and dark compositions, so this relationship was not readily apparent to the audience. While this widely different music created an interesting concert, it was disjointed and seemed, at least to some extent, less satisfying than it might have been had there been greater congruency between the music works. The soundscapes did create a bridge between specific pieces, but they were used only intermittently.

The sometimes mournful music, such as the Schnittke *Trio Sonata* (1985), described by Tognetti as dark, depressing, morbid, thick and dense, created continuous synchronisation with the long-takes, but the music-image combination seemed excessively slow and laboured. This slow laboured result seemed to reflect Tognetti's statement that the choice of repertoire was a slow arduous process. In contrast to the Schnittke, the music by Vasks, Violin Concerto *Distant Light* (1996-97), had "great lightness" and Tognetti stated the aim was to put unlikely things together to en-trance[2]. Tognetti's aim of creating entrancement through extremes in the music was unlikely to succeed because extremes do not usually create trance-like states. Trance states are normally created by either constant repetition or by music that allows the listener to 'drift'. While this drifting might have been created by the Vasks music, the Schnittke would not have induced trance-like drifting.

The combination of the Vasks music with landscape in continuous synchronisation highlighted both the lightness of the music and the light aspects within the artwork. The long takes were more appropriate with landscapes than images of people because these landscapes held more

[1] Tognetti, R., in *Luminous* [documentary], *Sunday Arts*, ABC1 [television], 1 June (2008).

[2] Tognetti, R., in *Luminous* [documentary], *Sunday Arts*, ABC1 [television], 1 June (2008).

detail to keep the eyes satisfied. This is necessary because the human visual system continually roams for information, with the eyes initially gazing at the centre of the image then moving in a series of cycles looking for areas of interest, which are viewed intensively; when perceiving an art image, the eye movements are so rapid that the viewer is not aware of this process[1]. The Henson landscape provided a wealth of visual information with even the close-ups filled with detail.

The documentary solved the problem of excessively long takes by overlaying semi-transparent images of the performers over the top of the Henson images, and then overlaying image over image to create a double image, as well as moving back and forth between image and performers. Another issue that seemed less of a problem in the documentary was the lighting, which appeared darker than in the live performance, making the blank screen less obvious. The documentary used a wider range of more interesting film techniques and was physically more comfortable to view. Had a filmmaker been assisting Henson to achieve his aims of a conversation between music and image, a number of the issues discussed here would have been resolved.

Many of the issues highlighted here may have been corrected in subsequent performances and others who attended the concert may consider this review harsh, which it may well be. This review was written from the perspective of achieving the best possible music-image combination. Even with the problems discussed here, *Luminous* was outstanding and achieved its aims of creating a performance that was new and exciting.

Neon Lights

Kraftwerk's romantic *Neon Lights* (2005) is an example of a more traditional style of song using continuous synchronisation. The song starts with light aqua-blue neon signs moving across the screen to the sound of the melodic words 'Neon lights, shimmering neon lights'. This is much more a normal style of song but even so the voice does not dominate the music. The overlaying of many neon signs forms patterns with a wide variety of colours, however the signs are well chosen to harmonize and match the soft, romantic feel of the music. As occurs with much iconography used by Kraftwerk, these images of neon lights have "an air of retro futurism" with many of the images dating back to a 1978 promotional video[2].

[1] Marschalek, D., What Eye Movement Research Tells Us about Perceptual Behavior of Children and Adults (1986) 123-7.

[2] Hagström, A., Neon lights - Signs of Düsseldorf (2004-5).

Neon Lights has a strong melody as well as a steady beat but there is little use of sync points in music and image. Occasionally there is a loose synchronisation when the appearance of a neon sign synchronises with the first phrase of the melody, and a flash of light at times synchronises on the first of an eight beat sequence, but there is no precise or regular synchronisation of image to the beat. While the beat is steady, it is not dominant. Due to the continuous synchronisation, the melody is emphasized. This is an example of continuous synchronisation creating a music-image relationship where there at first appears to be no synchronisation. This continuous synchronisation is dependant on congruency of mood and emotion between music and image and this is an example of congruent mood and emotion emphasising continuous synchronisation.

Planet of Visions

Kraftwerk's *Planet of Visions* (2005) starts with a melody but no beat. Continuous synchronisation is created with a parallel relationship between the melody and the green flowing patterns that move on a black background. After a few moments these patterns are reflected on the faces of the group creating an intriguing effect. A portion of the pattern becomes massive covering the entire back of the stage except for a green horizontal band of colour that stretches around a metre high across the stage below the screen.

A beat starts but the image continues to flow in parallel with the melody. The intermittent lyrics are 'Man, Nature, Technology, Planet of Visions, The Twenty-first Century'. The electronic voice with its deep resonating and distinctly un-human sound is used more like an instrument than as a singing voice, so it does not dominate the music. A building complex of a futuristic city drifts in space, its constant rotation creating the effect of the viewer flying in a spacecraft around and over it. The construction's open white framework shows four robots at its centre, working at their computers with a screen above each of the robot's heads. At times these four screens show the four group members.

In the second half of the song the voice and melody stop but the flowing imagery continues synchronising, but the synchronisation is now with the beat not the melody. This is an interesting situation, with a flowing image but an instrumental beat without melody. This is a smear to a beat rather than to a continuous melody. Such innovation by Kraftwerk is not unexpected because as in most of their creations, Kraftwerk concepts are original. The melody restarts and our tour continues around and above these futuristic buildings, which seem to be drifting in space. The images become green and blurred and it looks and feels as if our speed is increasing, as if we are travelling very fast through corridors, perhaps flying through a constructed time warp where images stretch and morph. This flowing imagery continues the smear effect with the music.

The song finishes with a return to the original green flowing pattern, again reflected on the group's faces. The pattern then reduces in size and moves upwards to the left until it disappears. *Planet of Visions* is an example of continuous synchronisation, which is just as successful as using sync points, to glue the music-image relationship and keep the focus on the music.

Conclusion

Expression markings such as rubato, presto, largo and fermata temporarily change the tempo of music, thus interfering with the regularity of the beat. When this occurs, any synchronisation based on this regularity, such as sync points, will become out of sync. Continuous synchronisation of music and image offers an alternative to maintain synchronisation while allowing freedom of expression of the musician.

Mickey-mousing

Synchronisation of music and image that is overly close will normally focus attention on the music-image combination but may lack interest and may also create unintentional results including humour. Very close synchronisation should be used with care.

Mickey-mousing refers to a very close synchronisation of music and image, which can easily and unintentionally slip into cartoon mode[1]. It can also refer to the duplication of action by music or dialogue, which may in film be considered a weakness.

Mickey-mousing is an important and valid method that is commonly used in the music-video and most music-videos co-ordinate movements or the pace of editing, at least some extent, with the rhythmic elements of the music [2]. Therefore mickey-mousing may also be appropriate for the music concert to focus attention on the music and it should not be considered a weakness in the music-image relationship provided it is handled with care. The following diagram shows synchronisation of emphasised points that creates mickey-mousing.

[1] Chion, M., *Audio-Vision* (1994) 54.
[2] Björnberg, A., Video.2. Structure, *Gove Music Online* ed L. Macy (2008).

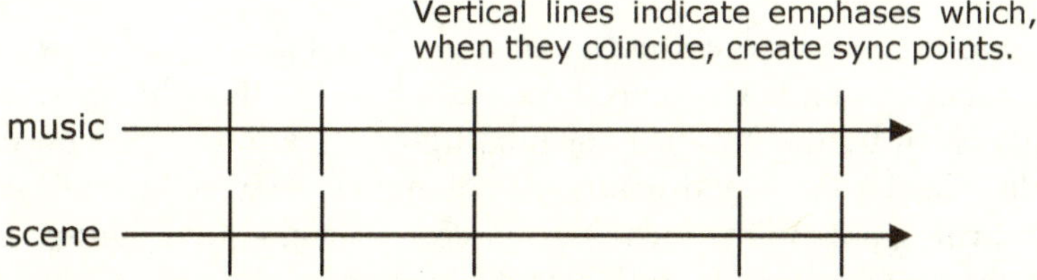

Figure 18 Emphasised points creating mickey-mousing

Close synchronisation is often used to create and support humour in films. *Much Ado About Nothing,* based on the Shakespeare play and directed by Kenneth Branagh, successfully uses synchronisation to create a humorous effect. This is especially noticeable in the opening scenes where the image is obviously slowed to synchronise with the music. The slightly comic result is described as "particularly inspired, with the male characters riding into the film in heroic slow-motion, like refugees from *The Magnificent Seven*"[1]. This humorous slow motion effect of men on horses galloping in time to the music is certainly intentional, and while being light hearted, is an exhilarating opening to this comedy-drama.

Comedy focuses attention on the image and the action and while this is appropriate in films it should not be part of the instrumental music concert unless its negatives are understood. The Sydney Symphony Orchestra have used humorous performances, such as Charlie Chaplin's *Gold Rush* (2007) previously discussed, because their aim in that series was to attract a new audience, such as younger people, and those who had not previously attended a classical concert. However if the aim is to maintain the focus on the music, close synchronisation should not become comical otherwise the humour will distract attention from the music.

Elektro Kardiogramm

The song *Elektro Kardiogramm* (2005) from the Kraftwerk *Minimum–Maximum* DVD shows synchronisation that could be classified as mickey-mousing due to both the constant synchronisation of music and image, as well as the duplication of the music and words by image and displayed text. However this is an example of mickey-mousing that is interesting and not comical. The song starts with the green point of a cardiogram wave moving across the screen, which occupies the entire back of the stage. Heavy breathing is heard that coincides with the cardiogram

[1] Sutton, M., Much Ado About Nothing, *DVD Times*, (2008).

heart rate waves, and a heart beats almost imperceptibly in the background.

Out of the dimness emerge sections of a luminous green grid on a dark, royal blue background. It slowly becomes apparent that this grid is on body suits worn by the group. Four blue lights streaming down on them create blue heads, faces and hands. A column of hazy light, led by the moving cardiogram point, moves from left to right highlighting each member the group. This is followed by a cardiogram wave bouncing across the back of the stage, which is now a luminous green grid on a dark, royal blue background, duplicating the pattern on the body suits. As the electronic singing starts, the text 'Electro Kardiogramm' is displayed in white electronic-style lettering. Music, image and words appear perfectly synchronised but the image doesn't try to match the speed or complexity of the **music rhythm**. A closer analysis reveals that the cardiogram imaging, the breathing and the music are only very loosely synchronised.

At times the hazy light reappears, moving across the stage and highlighting each member of the group in turn. Multiple cardiograms bounce across the background to a more complex rhythm created by multiple forms of heavy breathing, which sound much like snare drums. This is an instance of voice being used as a percussion instrument. The lyrics are extremely simple and do not detract from the music. A 'solo' percussion section mid-song uses various electronic sounds. The cardiogram image is frequently shown in front of the performers and this is a visually effective device added to the DVD. While the synchronisation in *Electro Kardiogramm* could be classified as mickey-mousing there is no weakness in these multiple levels of synchronisation created by sync points, and at no stage does the performance slip into cartoon mode. Part of the reason it does not appear comic is the complexity of the rhythm created by a combination of breathing sounds and the music. Man, music, voice, image and text form into a synchronised, integrated whole.

Music Non Stop

Kraftwerk's *Music Non Stop* (2005) is an example of mickey-mousing that is intended to be humorous. The comic strip depictions of the lyrics 'Boing, Boing, Bumm, Tschak, Peng and Zong' are displayed in comic strip style lettering. The words appear and disappear, sometimes in exploding stars, sometimes in smoky rings, sometimes expanding then disappearing, all in an outlandish colour pallet of red, yellow, blue, purple and aqua. This mickey-mousing of the lyrics to music, using comic strip depictions creates a cartoon-like effect.

The song enters a different style with words ‘Music non stop’, which are displayed in white lettering. Robot faces appear and disappear. A robot face is constructed on screen to the music with a very serious expression and at times surreptitiously moves its eyes synchronised to the music. The group is displayed on the screen drawn as hollow grid men as if these are blueprints for a future man. The grid men’s movements appear synchronised to the music, grid feet tap the beat and grid hands move to the music. The seriousness of the robot, along with the mickey-mousing of the robots and the grid men’s movements, all in strict synchronisation, add to the humorous effect.

As the music changes to a flowing style and the image changes to music notes and symbols flowing across the screen, the synchronisation becomes continuous and the imagery loses its comic nature. Massive control panel buttons emerge like growing cities and we tour along a landscape created by an image of a sound control panel that fills the entire back of the stage. The song finishes with each member of the (live) group setting the controls on their computer, then bowing and leaving the stage in turn. The music continues and as the curtains close, the imagery of the eyes and nose of the robot covers the curtains. This song was the last in the live performances with the apparent intention of providing a light-hearted finish to the concert.

Shots, editing and cuts

There are a number of different filming and editing techniques that can be used to achieve different types of synchronisation between music and image, with the most important form of editing for the music-image combination being the cut.

Rapid cuts and intensified continuity

Editing and cuts can be used to synchronise the image with the music but there are dangers involved in using excessive or fast cuts and this can be observed from their use in films. Films are rhythmic even before they are edited; these rhythms that have already been created from the sound and image determine how the editing will be carried out, even so the cut is an important part of the rhythm of image[1]. The type of shot and the editing have a dramatic effect on the feel of the image. A series of short shots

[1] van Leeuwen, T., Rhythmic Structure of the Film Text, (1985) 217.

helps to create a rapid tempo, whereas longer shots will tend to slow the rhythm down[1].

Creating scenes from rapid cuts does not normally create good films and is a technique used by some B-grade filmmakers. Rapid cuts combined with close-ups create **intensified continuity**, which is intended to create shock and suspense with moment-to-moment anticipation. Rapid cuts glue the viewer to the screen in case something is missed in these rapidly changing images, and even normal scenes are heightened. Today, editing is more rapid in the average film than ever before with the result that fast cuts can lead to a breakdown of spatial continuity and coherence making it difficult to understand what is happening. The fast cut and its associated elements, such as the close-up, which also creates intensified continuity, favour the small screen (television). Therefore this trend towards the intensified continuity of the fast cut and close-up has been influenced by the use of video-based production and editing tools as well as the release of films in video form for television.[2]

This gluing of the viewer to the screen occurs because we cannot ignore movement. Normally objects that interest us, hold our attention for periods of time; sudden events attract our attention whether we are interested in them or not, even though they may not continue to hold our attention[3]. The image cut, which creates a sudden impact, grabs our attention from the music, even if we would prefer to maintain our attention on the music. Fast cuts also create other problems. The James Bond film *Quantum of Solace* (2008) was almost forty minutes shorter than the previous Bond movie and this resulted in a degraded plot, dialogue and atmosphere; this fast pace created confusion because it wasn't possible to understand what was happening; these problems were due to over-editing and over-cutting[4].

Film shots

The long take long-shot (a single extended time shot taken from a long distance) may be more appropriate for the music concert than frequent cuts. The intensified continuity created from frequent cuts and close-ups may well be one of the major factors in backgrounding film music. Continual cuts demand constant attention to visual cues and may cause confusion so they are not appropriate for image that accompanies music.

---

[1] Bordwell, D. & Thompson, K., *Film art: an introduction* (2004) 360.

[2] Bordwell, D., Intensified Continuity: Visual Style in Contemporary American Film, *Film Quarterly* 55/3 (Spring, 2002) 14, 16-17, 22, 24.

[3] LaBerge, D., Attentional Processing in Music Listening: A Cognitive Neuroscience Approach, Psychomusicology 14 (1995) 21.

[4] Stratton, D. & Pomeranz, M., *At the Movies,* ABC1 [television], 19 November 2008.

Even the number of cuts used to create rhythm and synchronisation should be limited. While cuts are frequently used to synchronise music and image, it is not always necessary even in cinema, and in the past cinema did not necessarily do so; an example is the shot of Fred Astaire and Ginger Rogers dancing to the music *Swing Time* in the film *Waltz in Swing Time* (1936); this is a single long take long-shot[1]. It allows the scene to unfold and create its own rhythm without the need for cuts.

In the music-video, tracking shots (shots taken from a camera mounted on a moving support) can create rhythm that will go in and out of synchronisation with other rhythmic elements of the song[2]. This moving in and out of synchronisation, that can provide partial congruency, is an effective method of focusing attention on the music.

Responsive cuts

The combination of certain elements of image and sound, such as movement and beat, create rhythm in the music-image combination. Cuts and editing of image will be somewhat restricted by the music and its beat because the rhythm of the image must coincide with the acoustic rhythmic accents[3]. Further, changes to music are much less flexible than changes and cuts to film; for instance cutting and splicing music is likely to disrupt and detract from the music while cuts to film are a normal part of the process[4]. While a fast cutting rate can create fragmentation that helps to build a climax[5], a climax created by image is not appropriate unless it matches a climax in the music.

Cuts and the way they are used for image in the music concert will be very different to those of film, and will be closer to the music video. The editing of the music-video is different to film editing in that it is responsive to the music and also aims to ensure that no particular element, whether it be the narrative, the setting, the performance, the star, the lyrics, or the song, becomes dominant; music-video editing has a rhythmic basis that closely follows the song highlighting certain aspects[6]. Anyone editing video for concert would benefit from reading the Vernallis chapter on music-video editing[7].

[1] Bordwell, D. & Thompson, K., *Film art: an introduction* (2004) 360.
[2] Vernallis, C., *Experiencing Music Video* (2004) 35.
[3] van Leeuwen, T., Rhythmic Structure of the Film Text (1985) 218-9.
[4] Eisenstein, S., *The Film Sense* (1947) 77.
[5] Cook, N., *Analysing musical multimedia* (1998) 191.
[6] Vernallis, C., *Experiencing Music Video* (2004) 27.
[7] Vernallis, C., *Experiencing Music Video* (2004) chapter 2 Editing.

A cut can create a sync point between music and image[1]. A sync point is formed by emphasis, and cuts normally create some type of emphasis. Cutting scenes in time with the music beat is a form of synchronisation that strongly emphasizes the temporal similarity of the music-image combination[2]. In film, it is the dramatic appropriateness of the music combined with the synchronisation between music rhythm and visual rhythm that is important, rather than the intrinsic quality of the music[3]. In much the same way, in the music concert it is important that the image is dramatically appropriate and that it supports the synchronisation. For instance quiet, melodic music with a violent image will emphasise the violence due to the strangeness of the combination and will detract from the synchronisation effect. The result will be focus on the image rather than the music. Synchronisation glues the music-image combination together and creates focus on the music, but synchronisation can be undermined if the dramatic appropriateness of the music does not match the image. Other aspects of the image such as its quality and originality are of less importance.

Creating and using sync points

In the music-image relationship synchronisation can be achieved using sync points. In music, sync points can be created using beat or changes in loudness, tone or melody. In image, sync points can be created using added graphics, actions, changes, or cuts as previously described. Sync points create phrasing in the audio visual flow and these sync points can also be used to create synchronisation where music and image occur in parallel and there is no precise relation other than the sync points[4]. Therefore all other characteristics of the music-image relationship can be neutral and if sync points are used they will be enough to tie the music and image together.

There are many different connections that can be made when combining music and image. These can occur across a wide range of elements including beat, contour, dynamics, setting, colour and type of shot, and it is these connections and the patterns they form that accentuate the music in the music-video[5]. These connections can also be used in concert. Syncopation is another important part of synchronisation in the music-image relationship because syncopated combinations of movement provide va-

[1] van Leeuwen, T., Rhythmic Structure of the Film Text (1985) 216.

[2] Johnson, W., The Liberation of Echo: A New Hearing for Film Sound, *Film Quarterly* 38/4 (1985) 7.

[3] Lindgren, E., *The art of the film* (1963) 139.

[4] Chion, M., *Audio-Vision* (1994) 37, 59.

[5] Vernallis, C., *Experiencing Music Video* (2004) 190.

riety[1]. Using syncopation of music and image to create a sync point on the musically accented offbeat can create an interesting music-image combination without undermining the rhythm[2]. Sync points may or may not be used with other forms of synchronisation.

Tour de France 03

Kraftwerk's *Tour de France 03* has three different types of images. The first half of the song is accompanied by images of sound-levels. The next part is an extended period of continuous synchronisation between black and white archival film footage and music. The last part makes extensive use of graphics superimposed over the archival film footage to create sync points and these include the use of coloured shapes and lines. Flashes of colour highlight the route. White animated contour lines of the mountain, which are parallel to the winding road of the cycle route, spread out across the landscape. A triangular blue block of solid colour follows the contour lines up the mountain. Blocks of red and blue with lyrics in white, or vice versa, form geometric shapes around the route and the cyclists. Moving pictures change into moving drawings, with one cyclist drawn in yellow, another in red and another in blue. A helicopter hovers over the pack, is motionless, and becomes a drawing in the colours of the French flag. Scenes of riders become motionless and are surrounded by blocks of colour.

All graphics are overlaid on film footage to create points of visual emphasis that coincide with the beat in the music and this synchronisation of music and image creates sync points. Different beat patterns created by different electronic instruments also add to the complexity of the arrangement with multiple beat patterns offering more opportunities for sync points to be created by the combination of music and image. Sync points are also created by cuts. The beat is fast and the shots would not be comprehensible or even visible if they synchronised with each beat, so cuts are used to synchronise with various beats within the music. Sync points, created by cuts and graphics dominate the synchronisation of the last part of *Tour de France 03*.

The Model

Kraftwerk's *The Model* is an example of continuous synchronisation created by starting and ending sync points. *The Model* was a prototype for high quality electro-pop music; it was also one of the Kraftwerk songs arranged for string quartet, which indicates the classical aspect and the subtlety of some of their arrangements; the film footage was originally

[1] Eisenstein, S., *The Film Sense* (1947) 83.
[2] Vernallis, C., *Experiencing Music Video* (2004) 171.

used with the initial release of the song and was created from old French and German news clips of Pierre Balmain and Yves Saint-Laurent models from the fifties and sixties[1]. *The Model* (2005) has music and image occurring in parallel where there is no precise relationship other than intermittent sync points created by cuts. This creates continuous synchronisation that starts and ends on these intermittent sync points.

The Model starts with a count of four followed by the melody accompanied by a strong beat. Nostalgic black and white film footage shows a model's dark provocative eyes peering at us, her face seductively half covered by raised arms that are draped with long elegant sleeves. She slowly drops her arms, fully revealing her face. A cut moves to models on a catwalk and on the third cut, the lyrics start in this traditional style of song where the words tell a story and are possibly more important than the melody. Some shots show the press taking photographs but most are of models on the catwalk. One shot shows the models sipping drinks as the song refers to champagne.

The shot time varies from around four seconds with some shots held for as long as eighteen seconds, and many around eight to twelve seconds. These shot times might not be considered long with more activity occurring but there is very little happening in these scenes so they give the impression of long takes. The intermittent cuts occur on the first beat of a phrase that is comprised of at least two bars, but often more. As there is very little action other than slow walking and the camera circling the body, these scenes create a slow deliberate atmosphere. At times the film appears to be slowed but this is not always easy to discriminate given the models are already walking slowly and deliberately. It is this slow, deliberate and somewhat artificial movement that was the reason for *The Model* being included in the *Man Machine* suite of music[2]. The longer held shots are an example where cuts are not needed to create synchronisation as was shown with Fred Astaire and Ginger Rogers dancing to the music *Swing Time* in the film *Waltz in Swing Time*.

One particularly evocative shot where time seems to stand still is of a motionless model apparently in a boat, which glides under weeping willow branches moving in the breeze. This movement appears in sync with the music and even though the beat continues, the continuous synchronisation with the melody is highlighted. This highlighting of the melody occurs throughout the song because of the slow pace of the movements of the models, along with the parallel relationship of music and image, and the irregular sync points. All combine to create a slow, languid feel

[1] Bussy, P., *Kraftwerk: Man, Machine and Music* (2005) 105-6, 118, 187.

[2] Bussy, P., *Kraftwerk: Man, Machine and Music* (2005) 106.

to the song that backgrounds the beat and highlights the melody. This is further reinforced by the stillness created by many models looking fixedly at the camera. *The Model* uses cuts to create intermittent sync points. The medium and long shots often feel like long takes due to the limited activity. These create the feeling of synchronisation in this parallel relationship.

Kraftwerk songs may give the impression that it is easy to maintain focus on the music using continuous synchronisation but Kraftwerk have the advantage of a beat that keeps bringing the focus back to the music regardless of synchronisation. A beat is not normally available in classical and some contemporary music. Even so, *The Model,* with its use of intermittent sync points, waxing and waning, and parallel relationship of music and image, is an example of continuous synchronisation that could be used with music that may not have a steady beat.

Patterns and repetition

Patterns and repetitions of images can be used to create synchronisation that focuses attention on the music.

Patterns and repetitions can create sync points within the image sequence and these sync points accentuate the music; this can occur where a particular object within the image reappears, perhaps from a different perspective or distance[1]. Much of Kraftwerk's imagery, such as *Man Machine*, creates sync points through patterns and repetition using repeating visual text and images. Images that are limited and repetitive can focus attention on the music and this is shown in an analysis of the bicycling scene from *Jules et Jun* where the limited and repetitive structure of cycling images focuses attention on the accompanying music[2]. Something similar occurs in both versions of *Tour de France*, already discussed; both use the natural movement patterns and repetitions created by cycling, to achieve continuous synchronisation.

Even where patterns are not intended, almost any combination of images may, at least to some degree, create perceptible and apparently intentional patterns, and this occurs with a kaleidoscope[3]. The imagery in Kraftwerk's *Numbers*, discussed in detail in the section on structure, consists almost entirely of patterns and repetition, which appear to be synchronised to the music. Given the quantity of numbers displayed this

[1] Vernallis, C., *Experiencing Music Video* (2004) 182, 190.
[2] Kassabian, A., *Hearing Film* (2001) 53.
[3] Cook, N., *Analysing musical multimedia* (1998) 186.

synchronisation is more likely to be random than actually created. Another method of forming patterns can be with visual micro-rhythms such as curls of smoke, rain, or a flickering candle[1]. These visual micro-rhythms can reflect the structure and patterns of music and are often used in the music-video[2]. Many films created to accompany live pop music overuse patterns and repetition resulting in dull imagery. This might not be noticeable to those dancing but it does become boring to watch. While the music-image combination needs the stability of similarity and repetition it also needs variety and contrast[3] to remain interesting.

Creating synchronisation in live performance

Synchronisation between image and live performance may be challenging but is achievable. While Kraftwerk have pre-programmed music sequences on their computers, the performances can and do vary noticeably from one concert to another and many sequences are initiated live[4]. Therefore much of the synchronisation is achieved using windows of time perception that allow for small variations between music and image while still appearing to be synchronised. Even so, some music will be easier to synchronise than other music due to its structure and this is the case with much of Kraftwerk's music.

Differences in synchronisation created by cuts and graphics

A comparison of the two versions of *Tour de France* on the *Minimum-Maximum* DVD shows how differences in music and image can affect perception of synchronisation and create different forms of synchronisation. These differences between the last part of the 03 version (track 4) and the original version (track 6) include differences in cuts, editing, and the use of graphics.

Both versions have natural rhythms created by the cyclists' movements and both have stylised rhythm created by the lyrics, music, image, edits and added graphics. Both versions use the same colour palette. Both versions have riders on bikes that create continuous synchronisation. Both contain many movements that appear synchronised due to the window of time, which allows for the compensation of audio and visual events that are close but not actually synchronised. In both, the vision focuses on those movements that appear synchronised with the music, and tricks the mind into believing that the overall image is synchronised with the music. Even so, the last part of the 03 version is quite different to the

---

[1] Chion, M., *Audio-Vision* (1994) 16.
[2] Vernallis, C., *Experiencing Music Video* (2004) 179.
[3] Bordwell, D. & Thompson, K., *Film art: an introduction* (2004) 62.
[4] Bussy, P., *Kraftwerk: Man, Machine and Music* (2005) 178-9.

original version. The original version has a constant, steady sound created by the melody, except for the instrumental section in the middle, which includes the heavy breathing of cyclists and the buzzing of cycle gears. This original version feels slower at times even though the beat is stronger and more dominant. This slower feeling is probably because there are less cuts and less added graphics.

In the last part of the 03 version, the music and image are more intense and more complex. Once this part begins, there are more added synchronisation devices such as flashes of colour along the route, blocks of colour, and words of the song that are displayed as text. These added graphics increase the opportunity for sync points with all graphics appearing to be synchronised to the beat. The music has a different sound created by multiple forms of beats that result in complex patterns, even though these beat patterns are less dominant and often backgrounded by the continuous music. The faster and more complex beat, with more added graphics and more cuts, provide more opportunities for perceived and actual synchronisation. This increased synchronisation reduces the narrative feeling. When compared to the original version, the 03 version with its more complex arrangement of the music, multiple beat patterns, and more added graphics, appears more synchronised more often.

Out of sync

The focus on the music can be maintained with many different types of synchronisation but if the music and image are out of sync it will distract from the music. Just as synchronisation can glue music and image together, an out of sync combination can degrade the relationship.

The Necks

The Necks are an Australian avant-garde group who create long, improvised, minimalist soundscapes often described as hypnotic and intoxicating. The group comprises pianist Chris Abrahams, drummer Tony Buck, and bass player Lloyd Swanton with video art created by Buck. This performance[1] was a minimalist style of music that gradually unfolded and increased in intensity over time. The concert used three large screens, situated behind and at a level considerably higher than the group. This arrangement mandated that much of the audience make a conscious decision between looking up at the screens or at the group on the stage.

[1] The Necks, Sydney Opera House Studio, 31 May (2008).

Before the performance started, all three screens displayed photographs of an old staircase from different angles. This was interesting and created anticipation while waiting for the concert to begin. The performance started with music that was slow and quiet with little light on the musicians, however the photographs were of a brightly lit staircase and this brightness was incongruent with the feel of the music and the sombre level of lighting on the musicians. The start could have been improved by gradually dimming the staircase images as the musicians walked onto the stage so the level of brightness matched that of the musicians. This would have better matched the mood of the music.

As the music progressed, a still image of a blurred naked female figure walking up the stairs appeared on the right of the three screens. This image was interesting with the soft, blurred style matching the mood of the music. As the music became more intense, the image of the woman changed from blurred to being clearly defined. Every so often the image changed so that the woman was positioned higher up the staircase. However there was no beat to synchronise the change of image, so these abrupt image changes seemed clumsy because they were out of sync with the continuous, flowing music. This abrupt change unnecessarily emphasised that these images were two-dimensional. "The connections between shots are as important as the shots themselves"[1] and a slow fade-out/fade-in would have created continuous synchronisation, which would have resolved the issue.

Buck stated that his visuals do not contain a narrative; that they are very slowly moving and unwinding, and they match the morphing of the music. He also stated that they are not really a visual accompaniment to the music; they don't direct or dictate how the audience should think about the music, and they are like slowly changing paintings[2]. The problem is the images didn't change slowing, they didn't morph. After the initial blurred image of the woman, subsequent images cut from one movement to another. Even though the images were of the same woman on the same staircase, without a beat to synchronise on, each image change was distractingly obvious. At the same time visuals do direct our thoughts. If a naked women is presented at different places on a staircase, that's the concept that our thoughts are directed to. While the images are to some extent open, the openness is limited. In this image of a naked woman there was little of the composition that differentiates art photography

[1] Katz, S., *Film directing shot by shot: visualizing from concept to screen*, Michael Wiese (1991) 321.

[2] Buck, T. Who's Necksed?, interview in *Timeout, 4 June, Sydney* (2008).

from the photo snap. This image seemed more as a nude to titillate the male audience, than an image to enhance the music.

Buck stated "films are existing in their place and the music exists in its own and it's not like one is accompanying the other"[1]. This is not so. Audio-visual film theory and multimedia theory both state that music influences our perception of image and vice versa. The theory of *Added Value* states that one sensory perception influences another and transforms it, resulting in us not seeing the same thing when we are listening, and not hearing the same thing when we are seeing[2]. Multimedia theory states that when mediums interact and dominance passes from one media to another and where there is some degree of conflict between the mediums then the result is the emergence of something new[3]. Both theories support the claim that when music and image are experienced together each affects the other, and each is perceived differently than when experienced alone. The Necks' combination of obvious image cuts with flowing music, along with an image that didn't seem connected to the music, was incongruent and abrasive, and negatively affected the music.

The second piece in the concert was accompanied by images that flashed on and off, much like a home slide show. I found this flashing difficult to watch and so distracting from the music that I closed my eyes for much of the time and do not feel able to discuss the performance. Overall this was a disappointing concert due to the incongruency over multiple characteristics between music and image, poor image editing, poor integration of music and image especially during image changes, the location of the images high above the musicians, and the home-slide flashing effect. Buck might have achieved a better result working with a professional image creator such as a graphic designer or filmmaker. My opinion and that of the friends who accompanied me, was that the images detracted from the music and we would have enjoyed the concert more without them.

Conclusion

Synchronising image with music may be less of a problem than it initially appears. It might initially seem that synchronisation, especially with live improvised works, would be almost impossible. In the early days of silent film there was much criticism of the music, including synchronisation of the music performance with the film[4]. It would seem

[1] Buck, T. in The Necks, *Sydney Morning Herald,* 24 May (2008).

[2] Chion, M., *Audio-Vision: Sound on Screen,* Columbia (1994) 5.

[3] Nicholas Cook developed these multimedia models which are described in his book, Cook, N., *Analysing musical multimedia* (1998) viii, 82-86,98-106,113.

[4] Lindgren, E., *The art of the film* (1963) 138-139.

logical that these could apply equally to the use of recorded image with concert. Kraftwerk have successfully overcome these problems by the use of: congruency of music and image; complex multiple beat patterns that offer more opportunities for music-image synchronisation; and, the skilful use of apparent synchronisation with the flexibility it grants.

Tempo-pace

The tempo of music and the pace of image cannot normally be matched due to the differing abilities of the senses when processing incoming information. However, the tempo of the music should feel the same as the pace of the image and this is often achieved when the image is paced considerably slower than the music.

Definitions

Tempo is the rate of speed that the music is performed. It is traditionally indicated by the Italian markings such as 'largo', 'andante', and 'presto'. Since the nineteenth century tempo has also been indicated by a metronome marking.

Pace refers to the speed of change of the image, and this is created by movement. In film, the cut often dominates the pace but movement within a scene, depending on how obvious it is, is also a factor. With still image the pace is determined by the rate the images are changed.

Tempo and rhythm

Tempo and rhythm are not the same and it is the tempo of the music that will to a large extent create the mood[1]. Due to the psychological nature of tempo, changes in tempo can change the impression of the rhythm and alter the character of the music[2]. This is supported by experiments, which indicate that during a performance, changes to the tempo of the music will result in the rhythmic structure of the music being modified[3].

Congruency, tempo and pace

Tempo is subjective as well as objective; while different pieces of music may be the same actual speed, one may sound faster, due to how the time is filled, and the patterns that fill it[4]. This subjective evaluation of tempo

---

[1] van Leeuwen, T., Rhythmic Structure of the Film Text, (1985) 221.

[2] Cooper, G. & Meyer, L., *The Rhythmic Structure of Music*, (1963) 3.

[3] Clark, E., Structure and Expression in Rhythmic Performance, in *Musical Structure and Cognition* eds Howell, Cross & West, Academic (1985) 217.

[4] Cooper, G. & Meyer, L., *The Rhythmic Structure of Music*, (1963) 3.

is further complicated by the addition of image. Research shows that image can drive the perception of tempo in music. In studies using amateur musicians and non musicians as subjects, the tempo of a scene was judged from memory using a metronome; while music students were more accurate, the overall results clearly indicated that visual tempo significantly influenced the perceived music tempo with both music and non-music students[1]. Tempo and pace must appear congruent but this is a subjective evaluation that must be made based on the type, the content and the perceived meaning of the music and image.

Pace and perception

If a film is compared to a painting, the painting invites the viewer to investigate its many aspects, allowing the viewer's imagination to interpret the image into whatever it fancies and at its own pace. This cannot be done with a film. No sooner is an image shown than it changes, interrupting any imaginative associations. These constant sudden changes of fast moving images in film create a shock effect, which creates a state of heightened awareness that is far from the leisurely pace of an art museum.[2]

This shock created by a too much, too fast in the image, should be avoided. If detailed or meaningful images are shown during the concert, either as still or moving images, this needs to be done slowly so they can be absorbed without creating a shock effect because in the music concert the aim is for the music to create the effect. Additionally, fast-paced images can cause loss of information if the brain's pace of processing the information is lower than the pace the information is presented[3]. By maintaining a slow pace, the senses are not overloaded as so often occurs in film. Still images are an alternative to film because, as stated previously, "the [still] photographic message is a continuous message"[4]. As the unmoving image is less distracting than the film, the proposal that a still image is ongoing is a useful concept when creating images for music. We don't necessarily need to accompany continuous music with moving images.

The *Sinfonia Antartica* performance (2007) is an example of photographs creating a continuous message as is *The Red Tree* (2008) with its use of drawings. Both performances use still images to create an ongoing scenario that didn't feel two-dimensional. At the same time these still

---

[1] Vitouch, O., Sovdat, S. & Holler, N., Audio-vision: Visual input drives perceived music tempo, *9th International Conference on Music Perception and Cognition*, Bologna, August 22-26 (2006) 88,

[2] Benjamin, W., *Illuminations*, London: Pimlico (1999) 231-2.

[3] Kozma, R., Learning with Media (1991) 194-5.

[4] Barthes, R., *The Responsibility of Forms* (1986) 5.

images were less distracting than moving images. This continuous effect, of both the *Sinfonia Antartica* and *The Red Tree* images, was greatly assisted by the congruence of music and image. Another advantage of still images is that pace can more easily be controlled in a live situation than can be done with film.

Image and eye movements

When perceiving an art image, eye movements are so rapid that the viewer is not aware of what is actually happening. While our visual field is wide, only a small area, approximately two degrees, is available for sharp detailed viewing. Therefore fast eye movement is essential for information gathering. Initially the eyes gaze at the centre of the image then move to areas of interest and these are viewed intensively. Animate objects such as humans attract greater density (time and intensity) of viewing fixations than inanimate objects. Eyes, nose and mouth receive the greatest viewing time, and narrative elements receive longer viewing time than non-narrative elements. The eye doesn't move smoothly around the image, but perception in adults is usually comprised of a series of cycles, which may connect and compare different areas of the image. When scanning, the eyes look for strong structural characteristics, fix on angles rather than lines, and look for areas of interest rather than outlines.[1]

If the image or part of the image being viewed lacks detail, and a close-up shot forces the viewer to look at a particular part of the image for an extended period, this can restrict the eyes' natural information gathering activity. However faces are an exception, given the human brain is adapted to seeking out and analysing any form that resembles a face[2].

Image needs to allow this unconscious scanning by the eyes. Using an extreme close-up of part of an image for an extended period, unless it is highly detailed, inhibits this natural information gathering and may create frustration or boredom without the viewer understanding the reason. Frustration and boredom are unlikely to occur with close-ups that are maintained for only a short period or in an outdoor setting where the natural environment itself provides rich diverse imagery. In a concert hall, where the environment is limited and may lack richness of detail, it might be prudent to create imagery that allows the viewer's focus to find and select its own areas for concentrated attention.

---

[1] Marschalek, D., What Eye Movement Research Tells Us about Perceptual Behavior of Children and Adults (1986) 123-7.

[2] Greenfield, S., The Mind's Eye, *Brain Story* (2000).

A lack of detail to allow natural eye scanning occurred at times with the Australian Chamber Orchestra's *Luminous* (2005) concert, which used extreme close-ups for extended periods. This was not apparent in the documentary of the concert[1], which faded images in and out with views of the musicians. If the live performance had been able to achieve some of the concepts used in the documentary, the problem would not have occurred. This problem, the lack of detail for the eyes to scan in extreme close-ups, could have been solved by the integration of image and musicians, such as the screen behind the musicians.

Matching tempo and pace

There is disagreement as to whether the eye or ear is faster in comprehending its medium. Regardless of the various arguments, for the music-image concert there is evidence that the ear processes information faster than the eye. We can discriminate several different tones in a second but if different images were presented as quickly, they would become blurred and impossible to interpret. This was observed with the Rimington colour organ, which associated colours with keys; when the music was played at a fast tempo, the effect was 'blinding'[2].

Image cannot match the tempo of sound, and sound will determine what is seen if the image is too fast to be clearly comprehended. Sound may lead us to see movements that don't exist or to miss movements that do exist. As discussed in apparent synchronisation, this occurred in the George Lucas *Star Wars* film, *The Empire Strikes Back* (1980), where the automatic opening and closing doors were an illusion created by the sound. They are seen closed and then seen open, and it is the imagination, promoted by sound, that creates the impression they are seen actually in the process of opening and closing.[3]

The difference in the processing speed of music and image is a basic problem when combining the two media. The tempo, even in slow music, is normally faster than the pace of change of the images. Normally the pace of the images should be slower than the tempo of the music otherwise the apparently fast images will distract from the music and focus attention on the image. This occurred in Fantasia's *Rite of Spring* sequences, where the camera, and therefore the image, was in constant motion with the result that the image dominated over the music[4].

---

[1] *Sunday Arts*, ABC Television, 1 June (2008).

[2] Scholes, P., Colour and Music, *Oxford Companion to Music*, Oxford (1970) 207.

[3] Chion, M., *Audio-Vision* (1994) 11-12, 15.

[4] Cook, N., *Analysing musical multimedia* (1998) 208.

Negative effects of slowed image

The pace of the image and the tempo of the music cannot normally match, however the necessity for different speeds between the two media may create problems. While slow and slow-motion images can allow time for contemplation, they can also create unwanted effects. The combination of fast music with a slow moving image can create a languorous, mysterious effect; alternatively it can startle or be comical[1]. This amusing effect intentionally occurs in Kenneth Branagh's comedy-drama film version of Shakespeare's *Much Ado About Nothing* (1993) where, in the opening scene, the pace of horses and riders are slowed to match the music. Slow motion should be used with care so that unintentional effects are not created.

Sinfonia Antartica

The *Sinfonia Antartica* concert[2] (2007) is an example of perfect pacing of photographs of the original Scott expedition accompanying Vaughan Williams' Symphony No.7, *Sinfonia Antartica.* Whereas films, with fast moving frame after frame, scene after scene images, don't allow time for contemplation[3], the images of the Antarctic expedition progressed slowly, compared to the tempo of the music, not distracting from the music and allowing time for contemplation of both image and music. By maintaining a slow pace, the senses were not overloaded and there was no loss of information. Each image presented a scene that allowed the eyes to gather information at their own pace and move to the area of the image that the individual viewer perceived as interesting. These images were powerful and stunning, as is the Antarctic itself. However their rate of presentation allowed time to fully absorb and contemplate both the sound of the music and the projections of the landscape.

Conclusion

In summary, fast images that are used to match fast music are more likely to distract because they cannot be fully comprehended. Images should be synchronised with fast music rather than match the tempo. Image elements should agree or be neutral with the music tempo but not disagree as this will focus attention on the image. Slow images or slow components of an image can be linked with fast music. Provided the music and image are synchronised and the other characteristics are congruent or partially congruent, the image will appear to temporally match the music, regardless of differences in tempo and pace.

---

[1] Bordwell, D. & Thompson, K., *Film art: an introduction* (2004) 364.

[2] Performed by the Sydney Symphony Orchestra in March 2007 at the Sydney Opera House.

[3] Benjamin, W., *Illuminations* (1999) 231.

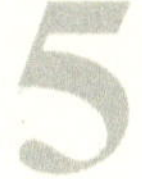

Meaning, emotion and structure characteristics

This chapter discusses whether or not music and image have an actual meaning, the emotion generated by music and image, the structure of music and image, and how the structure of one influences the other.

Meaning and emotion

The music-image combination should allow each individual within the audience to create their own meaning, a meaning that represents their own emotional or internal experience, which for each person is generated by that particular music at that particular time and place.

Congruency of meaning and emotion

Congruency of meaning and emotion between music and image is essential for maintaining audience focus on the music. The problem with attempting to create congruency is that the same music can mean different things and generate different emotions for different people. This can complicate or simplify the process, depending on whether the factors involved are understood.

Meaning and emotion in music

There has been much written about the meaning of music, and the debate on whether music has meaning, divides composers, filmmakers, musicologists and listeners. There are many arguments with widely differing views. So discussed is the area that we are at risk that these "continuous explosions of meaning eventually result in the total loss of meaning"[1]. Even so, when creating image to accompany music, it is useful to understand how diverse the views are on whether music has meaning and/or emotion. This section only scratches the surface of this controversial topic. The aim of discussing music and emotion here is to show the flexibility of music to accept different images, provided the music does not previously have a meaning or emotion associated with it.

Many people including composers, performers, theorists, aestheticians and critics from all cultures and persuasions, believe that music has meaning and that this meaning is communicated to the listener; there is

[1] Koopman, C., Essay Review of Gender & Aesthetics, *Action, Criticism & Theory for Music Educ* 5 (2006) 7.

also evidence based on reports from listeners, composers, performers and critics that music can create an emotional response[1]. Even if it is agreed that music has meaning there is not necessarily agreement as to what particular music means. Each piece of music can have multiple meanings, depending on the time, place, the person, their background and experience. Where the listener believes that a piece of music does have a particular meaning, associating a different image with that music may reduce the enjoyment for that listener. Each image that accompanies music must allow each person to find their own meaning and emotional interpretation. An exception is program music. Program music by its very nature prohibits personal, alternative and multiple meanings because the composer allocates the meaning and emotion. From the very first time program music is heard, the particular meaning and/or emotion that the title suggests, will be associated with the music. This title can suggest a general or specific meaning and emotion.

Some music has an extremely precise meaning such as *Happy Birthday* and *Auld Lang Syne*. Opera music is another example where music has taken on specific meaning. In these cases the meaning is indisputable for many people and cannot be varied. However this meaning has occurred through context, through the music's association with lyrics and events. While songs always allocate a meaning, songs are not normally part of the instrumental music concert unless the voice is being used as an instrument where the words are meaningless. This discussion applies to instrumental music.

Even though many people believe that music has meaning, there are many who believe it has no meaning. The composer, Ivor Stravinsky believed that music does not and can not express mood or emotion, or natural phenomenon; that any apparent expressive quality is an illusion; and that music cannot express anything other than its own inherent properties[2]. The claim that music has no inherent meaning is supported by the variety of different interpretations of music by different people. Philip Glass states that many people have asked why his music is sad when he's such a happy person and his response has been that he didn't know his music was sad[3]. Australian composer, writer and broadcaster, Andrew Ford states that he has composed music that he believes to be positive and life affirming but that listeners have described as almost unbearably

[1] Meyer, L., *Emotion and Meaning in Music* (1956) 1.

[2] Stravinsky, I., *Chronicle of My Life*, Victor Gollancz (1936) 91-92.

[3] Glass, P., Book of Longing pre-concert talk 12 Oct 2008, Sydney Opera House.

sad; he believes that music is "in the ear of the beholder, varying from listener to listener and from listening to listening"[1].

The meaning of music is further complicated by education and experience. When we listen to music we listen through an internal filter created by our culture and experience, and this affects how we interpret the meaning[2]. In Western culture, such meanings include tones being characterised by physical elements such as light and dark, high and low, rough and smooth, or with certain characteristics linked such as 'large' associated with a 'low' tone[3]. That certain music is associated with certain ideas, experiences, emotions and cultures, is an important consideration in preparing images for music.

It is widely believed that music has meaning and creates an emotional response, and many people do find their own personal meaning in music and experience emotions when listening to music. Music can have apparent meaning because the narrative within music is created by the listener and its scope is vast[4]. Some listeners can clearly state what the music means to them, because for many people music readily takes on specific meaning[5]. A number of studies support the claim that music can cause a measurable emotional response[6]. Even so, music appears to have no inherent meaning across cultures and age groups[7]. Any attempt to decipher the meaning of music for an individual or group must be based on an understanding of that individual or group, and their cultural, experiential and educational influences.

For many, music creates a meaning that is beyond words. While it can be claimed that music has no inherent meaning that applies across all people and cultures, there are individuals for whom music has profound meaning even though this meaning may vary from person to person, group to group and across time and place. In other words asking what music means at a particular time and place is more appropriate than asking what music means; additionally music obtains meaning through context as the words, images and gestures that are part of the performance transfer their meaning to the music, this meaning obtained through context is one that the music itself does not initially have; this occurs because the music has

---

[1] Ford, A., *In Defence of Classical Music* (2005) 21.
[2] Feld, S., Communication, Music, and Speech about Music (1984) 6-8.
[3] Meyer, L., *Emotion and Meaning in Music* (1956) 48, 74, 259-261.
[4] Nattiez, J., *Music and Discourse: Toward a Semiology of Music* (1990) 51, 128.
[5] Walton, K., Listening with Imagination: Is Music Representational? (1994) 47.
[6] Juslin, P. & Västfjäll, D., Emotional Responses to Music: The Need to Consider Underlying Mechanisms (2008).
[7] Feld, S., Communication, Music, and Speech about Music (1984) 6-8.

the potential for meaning and will take on meaning at the slightest provocation[1].

Audiences are diverse, therefore different views about meaning in music are useful in determining the type of music-image associations that may enhance music and please the audience. This aspect, that different people put different connotations on the same music and possibly different meanings at different times and places, makes the addition of image to music both easy and difficult. Easy because of the flexibility it provides, difficult because creating one set of images to please an entire audience may be complex to achieve. However it is this pleasing the audience that is the primary goal, because without the audience the music concert does not exist.

The view that the music itself has no meaning, and that the listener allocates a personal meaning, suggests that the structure and form of the music may be used as the basis for the accompanying image. These views also suggest that the image itself should either be abstract, or open to different interpretations. This would allow listeners to allocate their own personal interpretation, or to put no interpretation on music and image, if for them music has no meaning.

Meaning and emotion in image

Art, along with religious ideologies, appears to have evolved between thirty thousand and sixty thousand years ago; these earliest images of animal cave paintings originated as part of ritual, first magical then religious and it is likely that their purpose was to add a magical component to the hunt[2]. Therefore we can say that from the dawn of human history, images have had meaning. However interpreting the meaning of image is more complex than it initially appears and depends on many factors including cultural influences. French critic, theorist and philosopher, Roland Barthes believes the image is neither real nor imaginary and whatever the image represents, and however it is presented, the same question is asked: *What is happening here?*; hence the image is a type of theatre that we view, absorb and understand; when it is over we remember but we are no longer the same "as in ancient drama, we have been initiated"[3].

Image is interpreted in three ways. The first is through any language associated with the image such as descriptions or explanations. The second is the literal meaning and occurs through how the objects within the im-

[1] Cook, N., *Analysing musical multimedia* (1998) 8, 22-3.

[2] Benjamin, W., *Illuminations* (1999) 217; Mithen, S., 1996:171-2, 190-198.

[3] Barthes, R., *The Responsibility of Forms* (1986) 150, 177.

age are read. Any object, for instance a tomato, requires recognition; you need to have seen a tomato to be able to recognise one. This literal meaning is given by the artist and is what the image represents. The third interpretation of the image and its meaning occurs through the decoding of the image and is prompted by the signs that are within the image such as the mix of colours and the arrangement of the objects. These occur through the artists and viewer's cultural and experiential filters. For instance, if an apple is part of an image, the way it is depicted by the artist will influence how it is interpreted by the viewer. If the apple is green and part of a bowl of fruit in the background, it will be interpreted very differently to a large, lush red apple with a bite taken out of it and dripping with juice. Therefore the interpretation of the image depends on the context, the way it is presented, and how the viewer interprets it.[1]

A similar view is stated by the art historian, Sir Ernst Gombrich. The image alone does not tell its story because the interpretation by the artist needs to be matched by that of the viewer; the correct reading of an image is governed by a number of factors, including the ability to decode the symbols within the image, and this relies on understanding artistic techniques and cultural symbols[2]. For instance if one of the figures in a painting is small and another large, the size of the figures may indicate perspective or, as in many past eras and cultures, it may indicate social status.

Symbols and metaphors pervade our lives, in language, advertising, entertainment, politics, religion, law, artworks, poetry and history; symbols can be everyday items such as a wedding ring, coloured traffic lights or a red rose, or can signify the inexplicable[3]. Even the composition of objects within an image can create symbolic meaning and this occurs with arrangements such as a door opening onto a street[4].

Photographs can be used as accompaniment for music. It might be thought that photographs are less open to interpretation than paintings and that photographs are clearer and easier to understand and interpret, but this is not necessarily the case. All photographs have multiple interpretations, including the press photograph, which is often thought to represent reality; photographs are susceptible to interpretation even though the interpreted meaning may not be immediately apparent[5]. A wide range of interpretation is clearly apparent in the art photography of

---

[1] Barthes, R., *The Responsibility of Forms* (1986) 5-8, 20-5, 31.

[2] Gombrich, E. H., *The Image and the Eye: Further studies in the psychology of pictorial representation*, Phaidon (1982) 142, 145, 147.

[3] Biedermann, H., *Dictionary of Symbolism*, FactsOnFile (1992) vii, ix.

[4] Barthes, R. *The Responsibility of Forms* (1886) 11.

[5] Barthes, R. *The Responsibility of Forms* (1886) 7.

Australian artist Bill Henson. People from outside the art community have described Henson's work as child pornography:

> "It's child exploitation, it's criminal activity and it should be prosecuted, both the photographer Bill Henson ... but also the gallery because these are clearly images that are sexually exploiting young children,"[1]

While the art world see the same works as having great artistic beauty and merit[2] with Australian critic Peter Craven stating they are rich in morality:

> "There is more moral power in a Bill Henson image of a naked girl, at the cusp of growing up -- more ability to make the eyes dazzle with a sense of the shock or poignancy of human life -- than there is [with] all our hand-wringing and fussing about the young"[3].

This difference of interpretation is not limited to photographs because when we look around us our imagination creates a large part of what we see. This also occurs when interpreting images, and it is difficult to determine what is given and what we supplement from memory. All images must be supplemented to be understood; no image can represent more than an aspect of its original and unless we know the codes and conventions needed to interpret the image, we have no means of concluding which aspect is being presented to us[4]. Additionally, our imagination fills in the details to make an image appear complete[5].

That we interpret our environment rather than accurately see it, is supported by the work of Professor Susan Greenfield at Oxford University, who believes our mental images of the world are only loosely based on reality. We don't have time to fully take in all the visual information around us that we need to comprehend, and the missing details are generated by the imagination[6]. Therefore the image produced to accompany music needs only to suggest, rather than spell out, and the imagination will fill in the details according to what the person wants to see, with each person's imagination filling out the details that are appropriate to their interpretation of the music.

---

[1] Controversial exhibition's opening night cancelled, *Sydney Morning Herald* May 22 (2008).

[2] Bibby, P. & Jensen, E., *Art obscenity charges*, Sydney Morning Herald, May 24 (2008).

[3] Craven, P., Sexuality or spirituality: it's a matter of taste, Sydney Morning Herald 24 May (2008).

[4] Gombrich, E. H., *Art and Illusion: A study in the psychology of pictorial representation*, Phaidon (1977) 204.

[5] Müller-Freienfels, R., On Visual Representation: The Meaning of Pictures and Symbols, *Aesthetics and Art Criticism* 7/2 (1948) 113.

[6] Greenfield, S., The Mind's Eye, *Brain Story* (2000).

Meaning of symbols in image

Image contains many symbols that we might not even be aware of, for instance colours, shapes and lines all create meaning. This can be observed in experiments where moving shapes were combined with music, and the shapes were attributed personalities, with a small circle perceived as weak and submissive whereas a large triangle was attributed as being aggressive[1]. Lines also have emotional meaning, and an example is that rising lines will seem either cheerful or agitating[2]. Colours have meaning even though these meanings are culturally based with colour research contradicting many common beliefs; colour associations are based on learning and vary from culture to culture[3]. Age is also a factor and young children do not associate colours as warm and cold, as reliably as adults, leading to the assumption that colour associations have a cultural rather than evolutionary or physiological basis[4]. However within an adult cultural group the meanings of images tend to be consistent and these meanings should be considered when creating image for music.

The Arrival and *The Red Tree*

The Australian Chamber Orchestra's 'The Red Tree' concert tour (2008) is an example of how two apparently similar formats of a music-image combination can create very different reactions in the same audience due to perceived differences in the meaning of music and image. The concert consisted of two items, *The Arrival* and *The Red Tree*, both of which have already been discussed in some detail. Both items used images from picture books by Shaun Tan, however, music for *The Red Tree* was specifically composed, while the music used in *The Arrival* was the Shostakovich *String Quartet No. 15 opus 144*.

The images used in *The Arrival* were of a poor family where the man leaves to find a more prosperous life and after many difficulties establishes a new and happier life for himself and family. These images were accompanied by music, which is slow, majestic, introspective, intellectual and beautiful, but is at the same time morbid and relates to death, and the fifth movement has the title 'Funeral March'. Even if the music had not been previously heard, the titles of the music may have created internal images before the performance and these internal images of a funeral may have been reinforced by the music itself.

[1] Marshall, S. & Cohen, A., Effects of Musical Soundtracks on Attitudes toward Animated Geometric Figures, (1988) 96, 100.

[2] Pickford, R., *Psychology and Visual Aesthetics* (1972) 22,32.

[3] Fehrman, K. & Fehrman, C., *Colour: The secret influence*, Prentice Hall (2004) 64-73,

[4] Morgan, G., Goodson, F., & Jones, T., Age Differences in the Associations between Felt Temperatures and Color Choices, *American Journal of Psychology*, 88/1 (1975) 125.

The images of a peasant seeking a better life and the music of a funeral have different meanings that are likely to create different emotions. For most people, the emotions involved in a struggle that ends in success, are very different to how they feel about death. The audience response was not as enthusiastic as normally occurs at an Australian Chamber Orchestra concert, nor was it as enthusiastic as for the following item.

The Red Tree followed after interval. The music was specifically composed for the images and therefore the audience had not previously heard the music and not previously associated any meaning with it. Composing music specifically for image normally results in the media being congruent, and this was the case with *The Red Tree* with meaning and emotions being as fully congruent as is possible with two different media. The audience response, as well as that of the critics, was noticeably more enthusiastic. These performances are an example of how perceived meanings of music and image can affect the audience's level of enjoyment of the music.

Conclusion

The meaning of images should be congruent with the meaning of the music they accompany, although this is complicated by the fact that music can mean different things to different people at different times. However this flexibility of interpretation of music may also make the combination easier provided the image is open to interpretation and the audience does not have a preconceived meaning for the music. Congruency of music and image can be assisted by ensuring music and images are not coded and therefore allow the audience to allocate their own meaning. Even so, the risk remains that only certain types of music will be accepted by an audience to take on specific meaning. These are either specifically composed music or program music where a title suggests a meaning.

Structure

The structure of the images should follow the structure of the music. Where the images are disjointed, music has the ability to enforce structure on the music-image combination.

Definition

The structure of music is the form of the music created by the arrangement of its components, such as motifs and phrases.

The structure of images is created by their sequence and how this sequence fits together. This is the sequence of scenes in film or the sequence of still images.

Note that the structure within an individual image is created by shape, line, texture, colour and space, which combine to create movement, balance, contrast and unity, but this is not the structure referred to here.

Structure of music

Music is highly structured and even improvised music displays structural regularity[1]. This structure is comprised of motifs, phrases and groups of bars that form movements and this music structure can be compared to that of a book with words, phrases and sentences of the book forming chapters. Like a good book, the music structure should have a beginning, middle and end. As occurs when a book is being read, the music structure unfolds over time. Different forms of music such as the sonata or the concerto will have different structures. Music has its own significance created through its structure and syntax[2]. It is the structure of the music that should be dominant in the music-image relationship, with the structure of the images following that of the music.

Structure and continuity

The structure of the music itself provides continuity to the music-image relationship[3] because music has the ability to enforce continuity[4]. However the ability of music to enforce continuity on image has its limits and any incongruency that creates conflict may cause these limits to be exceeded. Conflict may result in a change of the perceived structure of the music and may undermine the structure of the music. Timing, rhythm and emphasis can change the meaning of the spoken word; in the same way, the addition of image to music that results in a conflict can change the apparent timing and emphasis of the music, thereby changing its perceived structure[5].

Cuts and synchronisation are both able to create a focus that is contrary to the musical structure and can potentially undermine the structural relationship between music and image. While a single occurrence of an incongruent cut or sync point may not be noticeable, persistent and recur-

---

[1] Sloboda, J., Music Performance, in *The Psychology of Music* ed D. Deutsch, Academic (1982) 494.
[2] Gorbman, C., *Unheard Melodies* (1987) 2.
[3] Vernallis, C., *Experiencing Music Video* (2004) 21.
[4] Cook, N., *Analysing musical multimedia* (1998) 22.
[5] van Leeuwen, T., *Speech, Music, Sound* (1999) 137-141.

ring relationships in areas such as tempo or intensity create a cumulative pattern that will affect the music-image relationship[1].

Creating image structure based on music

Structure offers a means of creating congruency without the need to involve such things as perceived meaning and emotions, which may be different from one person to another[2]. As meanings and emotions that are acceptable to one person may not be acceptable to another, structure may be the most acceptable way to match the image to the music for the classical audience. A point of view in music philosophy that supports this concept is that music creates an experience in the listener. It is this listening experience, rather than the 'content' of the music that stimulates the imagination of the listener[3]. In other words when we see a painting of the ocean and think of the ocean, the painting has directly stimulated our thoughts. If we hear music and think of the ocean it is purely our imagination that has created the thoughts of the ocean. The music notes themselves have no connection with, nor do they represent the ocean.

Matching the structure of the music allows a match of the experience of the listener. While following the music structure would normally be considered poor form in films, films have different aims to concert. Image for the music concert is more closely aligned to image for the music-video. In music-video shots, the camera changes types of shots more freely because the shot decision is normally made according to the form of the music[4]. Therefore image shots created for the music concert can be more variable than those of cinema and can follow the structure of the music more closely.

How closely the structure should be followed can be determined by the type of music. Music may be categorised into two types, emotional and intellectual. An example of music that is often considered highly meaningful and emotional is that of Ludwig van Beethoven and the Romantics such as Frédéric Chopin and Robert Schumann. Images accompanying the music of the Romantic period could be those that include high symbolic meaning. However images for intellectual music should be very different. Intellectual music is considered music more for the sake of musical form. An example of intellectual music is J. S. Bach's work such as *The Well-Tempered Clavier*. During his lifetime much of Bach's work was considered difficult to understand, and 'mind' music. Even today his

---

[1] Johnson, W., Sound and Image: A Further Hearing (1989) 26.

[2] Eisenstein, S., *The Film Sense* (1947) 163-4.

[3] Walton, K., Listening with Imagination: Is Music Representational?, *Aesthetics and Art Criticism* 52/1, (1994) 60.

[4] Vernallis, C., *Experiencing Music Video* (2004) 36.

music is often described as intellectual, and mathematically based. Therefore the image to accompany it could be closely based on the structure of the music and be comprised of images that would have no apparent meaning or associations. Alternatively the images for this structured, intellectual and mathematical music could be images that are highly structured from a visual perspective, such as architectural images.

Structure and Congruency

Congruency between music and image is essential to maintain focus on the music and this includes congruency of structure. Even in emotional music where the images are more symbolic and the structure less dominant, there should be no incongruency of structure because it will cause conflict and distract from the music. In emotional music there need be only a loose relationship between the structure of the music and the structure of the images. At the same time, meaning and emotions of music are open to interpretation so from this perspective matching the structure may be more important than matching perceived meaning and emotions.

Numbers

Numbers (2005) by Kraftwerk is a highly structured song with the structure of the images matching that of the music. It is also an exciting use of non narrative patterns and repetition to achieve synchronisation. The lyrics consist only of numbers, which are sung in different languages including German, French, English and Japanese. The song is created almost entirely from percussion with no melody as such. The voice is used more as a percussion instrument and is not at all like a singing voice. Different tones are used within the various percussion sequences. The structure of *Numbers* could be considered a loose ternary form consisting of introduction–A–B–A–B–A–coda. There are two different types of major image patterns that match the two different structural patterns (A and B) of the music. Within each of the major patterns are sub patterns.

The song starts with the numbers from one to eight sung by an electronic voice in German. They are displayed as white digits on a black screen with a blue horizontal band of lighting running the length of the stage beneath the screen. These number sequences change to green and an instrumental part follows. The use of the colour green could be a play on the fact that green symbolizes nature and electronic numbers are far from natural, but green may also have been chosen because it is often the colour of digital displays.

The first A section is comprised of sequences of numbers in alternating patterns. The numbers flash individually or in a sequence on the screen, normally as digits but sometimes as words, in green or white on a black background, synchronised with the beat in time to the basic theme of the song. There are several sub patterns including the numbers being shown individually on the screen or several numbers sequentially. The group members are projected onto the screen as part of boxed sections or their faces are sometimes seen through the hollowed out centre of the numbers. Looking at the group through the centre of various numbers creates an interesting effect.

The first B section comprises hundreds of numbers displaying simultaneously flashing on and off, apparently synchronising with the fast music. There is no singing in the B section and the music is a very unusual and exciting sound, like trumpet bursts cut short. The hundreds of numbers flash on the screen apparently in time to the music, but there are only a few numbers that are actually in sync with the music. The eye focuses on those few that are synchronised with the beat and this creates the effect that the entire image is synchronised. The second pattern of this B section are groups of eight numbers flashing on and off together. The number sequence 'one two' sung quickly, is sometimes used as a bridge between parts and sections.

The second A section is brief and uses sub patterns that are similar to the first A section but with some variation. The second B section repeats the hundreds of numbers flashing on and off apparently synchronising with the music with its short trumpet-like bursts, followed by lines of numbers moving to the left across the entire back screen. The third A section is similar to the first. The coda is a different form to the A and B sections and is random numbers scattered across the screen accompanied by a voice that is more like a heavy breath than even an electronic voice sound. The scattered numbers of the coda are displayed in various colours of green, yellow and black on a white square, changing in size making them appear to move forwards and backwards.

Kraftwerk are always an integrated part of the image either by standing in front of the screen, or at times, are incorporated into the image. The entire song, even now, sounds progressive and more like a drum solo than a song. A drum pattern from *Numbers* was later used in a club record and became a worldwide club hit[1]. *Numbers* is a very unusual song. It is mostly percussion, is very repetitive, and the imagery consists only of numbers. Even so, it is as original and exciting now as when first re-

[1] Bussy, P., *Kraftwerk: Man, Machine and Music* (2005) 125-6.

leased in 1981 and "is perhaps the funkiest song Kraftwerk has ever made"[1].

Generated image

Visual images produced directly from the music, such as displays of wave forms and vibrations, are a common form of producing image to accompany the structure of the music. Mathematical algorithms that are run on a computer can also create various relationships between music and image. However, many of these creations of illustrated music can quickly become tiresome and predictable, and they do not affect people emotionally in the way the music normally does. Visuals can also be created to 'bounce along' with the music so that they look like the music feels. An even more interesting form can be created where they interact rather than form gridlocked patterns.[2]

Visual Music

Visual music, also called abstract animation, is imagery that is structured and presented in such a way that it is seen to change over time in much the same way as music is heard. It is normally comprised of a series of still or moving images. These images have no narrative nor are they representational. The images of visual music can be likened to absolute music that has no meaning.

Visual music may or may not be accompanied by music. Examples of visual music include the still images of Hans Richter's scroll painting, *Stalingrad* (1944) and Kandinsky's *Contrasting Sounds* (1923). A number of German experimental film makers including Walter Ruttmann, Viking Eggeling and Hans Richter pioneered moving images for visual music. However after the 1920s, most experimental filmmakers of visual music included music to support the visual rhythm[3].

Visual music starts from the premise that "the resolution of tension moves us through time"[4]. Visual music uses what it calls 'orchestration' to create image following the principles of music such as rhythm created by editing of visuals. It also creates repeating patterns by the use of counterpoint (that is similar to counterpoint in music) and harmony (which uses shapes and geometric forms changing over time). Visual music has structure in much the same way as music, and the type of imagery used

---

[1] Carney, E., Kraftwerk's Computer World, www.suite101.com (2008).

[2] Weidenaar, R., Live Music and Moving Images: Composing and Producing the Concert Video, *Perspectives of New Music* 24/2 (1986) 273-4.

[3] van Leeuwen, T., Rhythmic Structure of the Film Text (1985) 221.

[4] Evans, B., Foundations of a Visual Music, *Computer Music Journal*, 29/4 (2005) 11.

in visual music may be appropriate for use as accompaniment to the instrumental music concert.

Conclusion

The structural characteristics of music and image may be more important for the music-image combination than the perceived meaning and emotional response. Music, with the possible exception of program music, is able to take on different meanings depending on the context and the listener, so the meaning can change from time to time and person to person. Whereas each piece of music has its own structure defined by the composer and this structure remains more or less the same and dominates how the music is heard. The music structure can be undermined to some extent by images that generate strong responses that are considered incongruent with the music, such as occurred in the performance of *The Arrival* (2008). Other image forms that can undermine the music structure are cuts and changes that are fast, continuous, repeated, inappropriate and/or dramatic. Provided the music structure is not undermined, music can provide the structure to the music-image combination.

Genre-style, voice and text characteristics

The chapter discusses the relationship of the music genre and the image style, as well as the influence of voice and text on the music.

Genre-style

In the music concert, the genre of the music and the style of the image should match or at least be complementary to help maintain the focus on the music.

Definitions

The genre of music is created by the musical elements including melody, rhythm, harmony and form. These create a distinctive pattern that can be traced to an era or culture or possibly even a particular composer. Some well-known genres are baroque, romantic, jazz and rock.

The style of the image is determined by the artist's techniques and expressive qualities, and to a lesser extent, the subject of the artwork. When several artists have features in common, they are categorized as a group and some well known groups are: baroque, romanticism, impressionism, cubism, surrealism and minimalism.

Please note that while the words genre and style are normally interchangeable, here the word 'genre' refers to music and 'style' refers to image.

Matching genre and style

Matching music genre and image style is an important part of congruency in the music-image relationship. Congruency is not essential and a complementary or neutral relationship will not distract from the music, but incongruency will create conflict. Music and artworks have long been referred to with similar genre-style categories such as baroque, classical and impressionism. However, while these categories are associated with a particular time period, for the music-image relationship it is more relevant that they refer to a particular type of artwork or music, which has matching qualities because it is the relationship of the music-image characteristics that is important.

The impressionist art movement is associated with lightness and brightness as well as physical sensation and movement. Debussy's music is often referred to as impressionist with its qualities of harmony, fluidity, sensory impressions and an intangible atmosphere much like Turner's paintings. Romanticism in art is associated with the qualities of emotions, instincts, truth, freedom and revolution such as the paintings of the French revolution by Delacroix. Romantic music is associated with emotion, imagination, individualism, idealism and freedom of expression. Romantic composers and performers such as Liszt created passionate performances where they interpreted the music creating their own emotional 'truth' of performance. Baroque artworks are normally religious, spiritual and/or philosophical works with symbolic meanings often expressed through gestures, complex arrangements and intense emotions, with contrast achieved through light and dark. Baroque music is characterized by its religious or spiritual nature with contrast achieved through alternating loud-soft, fast-slow and high-low. Baroque composers aimed to create passion and awe in the listener. It is these matching qualities that are important in the music-image relationship rather than simply matching the period. The *Rembrandt's World* performance is an example of matching qualities in genre and style.

Rembrandt's World

The *Rembrandt's World* concert performed by the Brandenburg Ensemble in 2005, discussed previously, is an example of genre and style being used to create a congruent relationship. The concert included the art of Rembrandt, his peers, and artists who inspired him such as Titian and Rubens, with music of the era by composers from the Netherlands, London, Venice, Paris and Germany. Works included Biber's *Partita III from Harmonia Artificioso – Ariosa*, Pachelbel's *Canon and Gigue in D major*, and Albinoni's *Concerto à cinque in G Major.* There was no direct connection between the music and images but both were from the baroque era with matching qualities. Even though genre-style was the only congruent characteristic, it was strong enough to create partial congruency that tied the music and image together. As the other music-image characteristics, such as synchronization and structure, had neutral relationships, there was no incongruency to create conflict.

Complementary genre-style associations

While the era of the music and image provides a good indication of congruency, such as baroque music being associated with images of baroque paintings or architecture, more unusual combinations can be created provided the music and image is complementary. For instance, while the music of Johann Sebastian Bach is from the baroque era, it was not considered typical at the time and was considered highly intellectual and 'mind' music. Some of Bach's compositions for keyboard have a slightly minimalist feel. An option that might be considered to accompany this particular music of Bach are the paintings of Piet Mondrian before his works became completely abstract such as his *Evolution* series, *Rose in a Tumbler, Trees in Blossom* and *Trees*. Mondrian aimed to simplify his compositions and these earlier works were not yet geometric shapes but had strong symmetry and were considered somewhat austere. Another example of a complementary genre-style association to accompany Bach's music could be photographs of modern architecture such as the elegant, symmetrical glass pyramid structure that is the entry point to Louvre Museum in Paris.

Associating music and paintings

The relationship between music and art is more substantial than it might initially appear and it is common for particular artworks to be associated with particular music. For example, the work of Spanish artist El Greco has been identified with the Spanish song style cante jordo or cante bondo literally meaning 'a deep song'[1]. Research indicates it is not difficult to correctly identify artworks and music considered by the artist to be a match. In a series of experiments, individuals were generally able to match paintings by Swiss expressionist painter Paul Klee to the specific music that inspired the particular painting; while music knowledge assisted in this task, and female musically-trained students performed more accurately than other groups, even without music training people generally matched the correct music to each painting[2].

Conflicting genre and style

Incongruency of music genre and image style creates conflict and is a common technique used in films to emphasize a particular situation and to create focus on the image. This was done by composer Bernard Hermann in Alfred Hitchock's film *Psycho* (1960), where a classical style of music played on cello and violin was used for the terrifying bathroom scene. Incongruency of music and image was also used in Kubrick's *2001: A Space Odyssey* (1968) where classical music accompanied futuristic environments. The waltz *The Blue Danube* (1867) by Johann Strauss II was used in scenes in the journey from the Earth to the Space Station and the Moon. In *2001: A Space Odyssey,* the slow mini-

[1] Eisenstein, S., *The Film Sense* (1947) 105.

[2] Peretti, P., A Study of Student Correlations between Music and Six Paintings by Klee, *Research in Music Education*, 20/4 (1972) 503-4.

malist nature of the image and the music, being a well known piece from the repertoire, helped to reduce backgrounding of the music. Even so, a mismatch of genre and style is not appropriate in concert because it is likely that this incongruency will create conflict and focus audience attention on the image.

Luminous

The *Luminous* concert (2005) performed by the Australian Chamber Orchestra, used a video of the works of artist Bill Henson combined with a wide variety of songs and instrumental works. These ranged from classical through to pop classics. Also included were specifically created soundscapes to add coherence to this disparate group of works. The concert was comprised of: Paul Healy's soundscapes; Alfred Schnittke's *Trio Sonata* (1985); Benjamin Britten's *Corpus Christi Carol* (1933); Gabriel Yared's *Lullaby for Cain* (1999) from the soundtrack of *The Talented Mr Ripley*; Astor Piazzolla's *Oblivion* (1984); REM's (Peter Buck, Michael Mills and Michael Stipe) *I've Been High* (2001); George Crumb's *Black Angels* (1970): *God-Music*; Peteris Vasks' Violin Concerto *Distant Light* (1996-97); and Leoš Janáček's *On an Overgrown Path: 'Good Night'* (1901-08). This was a very unusual combination of composers and works.

Henson's artworks have been compared to paintings of the baroque, classical and romantic periods[1], and have been likened to the work of Caravaggio, Rubens and Titian[2]. Particularly, Henson's use of extremes of light and dark is often likened to baroque art. Henson's studies of young women have been likened to a merging of a Vermeer and Courbet[3]. As curators and critics compare Henson's artwork to those of the periods ranging from the Renaissance to Romanticism, it is likely that music from any of these periods would have been congruent. Benjamin Britten's *Corpus Christi Carol*, was such a piece. However from a genre-style perspective, most of the music was incongruous with the images.

Artistic Director, Richard Tognetti, stated that music of very different genres was chosen to reflect the extremes of light and dark in Henson's work[4]. This is a very loose connection. In Henson's work the light and dark are within a single work. To associate the extreme differences of light and dark in a single artwork, with extreme differences between various music compositions, requires a leap of the imagination. It is doubtful whether anyone in the audience would have recognised this

---

[1] Capon, E., Malouf, D. & Annear, J., in *Mnemosyne,* Art Gallery NSW, Scalo, (2005) 8-9, 12, 35.
[2] Smee, S., Touch of innocence, *Weekend Australian* [newspaper], January 22-23 (2005).
[3] O'Connell, C., Luminous, The Age [newspaper], 17 July (2005).
[4] Tognetti, R., Luminous documentary, *Sunday Arts,* ABC1 [television], 1 June (2008).

connection between music and image unless informed. Bill Henson was involved in the choice of the music so it is possible this selection is more a reflection of his taste, rather than music the audience would see as congruent with his artworks. While this widely different group of composers created an exciting and unusual concert, it was disjointed and to some extent less satisfying than it might have been had there been greater congruency within the music itself, as well as congruency between music and image.

Man Machine

Kraftwerk's *Man Machine* (2005) is based around the avant-garde concept of industrialisation and the improvements it would provide to society. The artwork for the original *Man Machine* cover is congruent with this industrialisation concept and the back cover contains what appears to be a portion of a drawing by Russian Constructivist and Suprematist, El Lissitzky, who was an architect, designer, typographer and artist. Lissitzky developed constructivist dynamic spatial effects and from this, extended the Suprematist art movement[1]. Suprematism was closely linked to Dadaism particularly by its anti-bourgeois aspirations. The Suprematist movement originated in Russia in 1915-1916 and the term 'suprematist' refers to the supremacy of this art movement over previous art movements. The artwork on the back cover appears to be from the eighth image in El Lissitzky's book *Of Two Squares* (1920). The animated graphics in the performance are a reference to various images in the book, particularly the ninth image, which shows shapes flying apart[2].

Lissitzky's aim was to create an impersonal art just as machines create impersonal products[3]. Kraftwerk also aims to remove their individual personalities from their music and present themselves as an industrial entity as their name suggests; 'Kraftwerk' means 'power plant' and in concerts the group has been introduced as a man-machine 'die Mensch-Machine, Kraftwerk'[4]. Another area of commonality was Lissitzky's belief that the barriers between the arts and the sciences no longer existed in a modern world[5]. This idea that there were no barriers between art and science was adopted by Kraftwerk with their celebration of the human-technology connection[6]. Kraftwerk consider their group as a machine and

---

[1] Simmen, J. & Kohlhoff, K., *Kaimir Malevich: Life and Work*, Konemann (1999) 54.

[2] The book images may be seen at http://www.ibiblio.org/eldritch/el/pro.html while the CD cover can be seen at www.amazon.com with a search for 'Kraftwerk Man Machine'

[3] Read, H., in *El Lissitzky: Life.Letters.Texts* (1968) 8.

[4] Bussy, P., *Kraftwerk: Man, Machine and Music* (2005) 28, 121.

[5] Levinger, E., Art and Mathematics in the Thought of El Lissitzky (1989) 227.

[6] Bussy, P., *Kraftwerk: Man, Machine and Music* (2005) 105.

group member Ralf Hütter states "The dynamism of the machines, the 'soul' of the machine, has always been a part of our music"[1].

The performance starts with the repeating lyrics 'man machine' and images of these words are built into architectural-like constructions that once formed, disappear to be immediately rebuilt. The constructions are typical of the graphic design of Lissitzky. The colour palette is black, red and white, which were the colours of the three phases of the Suprematist movement. The architectural-like constructions of words are followed by dynamic arrangements of lines and geometric shapes, comprised of red squares and white lines on a black background, followed by a red background with black shapes that fly apart. Later, various architectural-like combinations of red, black and white squares are constructed and deconstructed forming complex patterns reminiscent of changing city-scapes. All are references to various graphic images produced by Lissitzky.

Man Machine achieves congruency through a number of characteristics but most importantly through synchronisation (previously discussed) and genre-style. While there is no Suprematist music genre, if there were it would be difficult to image it being anything other than that created by Kraftwerk's *Man Machine*. This is an example of absolute congruency in the genre-style characteristic as well as congruency of the philosophy behind the music and image.

Voice and text

Written and spoken language, including lyrics, distract attention from the music and should not be used at the same time as the music. If the voice is used it should be as an instrument creating meaningless sounds that are not recognisable as language.

Definition

Voice refers to both the spoken word and song lyrics. Text refers to written words whether they are displayed separately or with included with images.

Dominance of voice

Filmmaker and composer, Michel Chion states "There are voices, and then everything else". Even when the voice is part of a jumble of sounds, it grabs the attention, such as the distant cry of a baby that immediately alerts its mother. The voice is like a solo instrument that dominates per-

[1] Interview in Paris 1991, in Bussy, P. *Kraftwerk: Man, Machine and Music* (2005) 104.

formance because the primary activity of the listener is to interpret the meaning of words. Other sounds such as music and noise are merely heard as accompaniment, and this vococentrism is a natural part of human listening. The voice dominates our perception in the natural world and it is a natural result of this phenomenon for humans to create a hierarchy of sound in which the voice dominates. This dominance of voice carries across into cinema where the voice structures sonic space just as the body structures visual space. In film the voice is given a privileged position over other sounds and is artificially enhanced to ensure comprehension of the words.[1]

This audio-visual film theory, that voice dominates other sounds and also images, is supported by research showing that when audio and visual information are congruent, narration 'drives' the processing of the visual information[2]. This dominance of the speaking voice can be applied in much the same way to singing, with the voice taking precedence over the musical instruments. This is normally recognised in opera by the loudness and complexity of the instrumental music being reduced during vocal segments, preventing conflict between the two mediums and allowing space for the voice. If lyrics are used with music then multimedia theory can be applied. Multimedia involves competing media and the theory states that each media needs space to exist within the multimedia configuration. This space is referred to as 'gaps' and these gaps allow each media to maintain its own individual integrity. The result of gaps is that the individual integrity of each media is achieved through interaction rather than hierarchy.[3]

Dominance of text

Where text is part of an image, or the spoken language accompanies an image as in video or film, there may be a linguistic message; this message, whether it is spoken or read, directs the reader to the various signifiers within the image, guides interpretation of the image and adds meaning to the image[4]. Thus to a large extent, the text dominates the interpretation of the image. Further evidence of the dominance of text and the mental resources it commands is shown by the difference in how we process visual imagery and visuals of the written word. Experiments indicate that visuals can be processed with little cognitive effort, that they require only a low level of attention when it involves only recognition of

---

[1] Chion, M., *Audio-Vision* (1994) 5-7; *The Voice of Cinema* (1999) 5-6.
[2] Grimes, T., Audio-Video Correspondence and Its Role in Attention and Memory (1990) 24.
[3] Cook, N., *Analysing musical multimedia* (1998) 103-107.
[4] Barthes, R., *The Responsibility of Forms* (1886) 29-30.

images[1]. This is not the case with the recognition of language. An important difference between image and speech is that we initially perceive a painting aesthetically then only afterwards analyse it; with speech, we analyse it first then perceive it[2]. In the same way that the language of speech must be first analysed and processed, so must the language of the written word be first analysed to be understood.

Adding to the dominance of the written language is our spontaneous reaction to read it. Reading is automatic; when we look at the written word we read it[3], a claim supported by research. This automatic reading of words appears to be an involuntary response regardless of whether we want to read the words or not; further, when we read the displayed words at the same time as hearing speech, unless they match exactly, the spoken words are ignored[4]. This suggests that other audio, such as music, may also be ignored during the reading process. It also suggests that if words are to be displayed during performance, only one or two words should be used and only intermittently, otherwise the music will be backgrounded.

Words change the meaning of music and image

Not only does the spoken word take precedence over other sounds, and the written word divert our attention from sound, but the words we hear and read change our perception of what we see. Words that accompany image can change the meaning of what we see and may change what we believe we see, such as when words direct attention to particular features of the image[5]. The result is that our interpretation of an image, and what we see within the image, may be different depending on how we are directed to look at the image. Studies of the brain show that we don't have time to fully absorb all the visual information needed at any given moment so whatever is missing is generated by the imagination, with the brain relying on information coming from memory as much as from vision; this means that our mental image of the world is only loosely based on reality[6]. Therefore, when we look at a particular feature of an image we fill in the other details from memory and imagination. The result is that our perception of the image will be different to what it would be if we were directed to look at a different feature. Any words that direct us to a particular feature of the image will change what we see. In the same

[1] Grimes, T., Audio-Video Correspondence and Its Role in Attention and Memory (1990) 23.

[2] Lévi-Strauss, C., *The raw and the cooked: Introduction to the Science of Mythology* (1970) 20.

[3] Grimes, T., Audio-Video Correspondence and Its Role in Attention and Memory (1990) 24.

[4] Reese, S. Multi-channel redundancy effects on television news learning, unpublished doctoral dissertation, in Grimes, Audio-Video Correspondence and Its Role in Attention and Memory (1990) 24.

[5] Chion, M., *Audio-Vision* (1994) 7.

[6] Greenfield, S., The Mind's Eye, *Brain Story* (2000).

way, words will direct us to a particular meaning and/or feature of the music, and will affect how we perceive that music. Both music and image are likely to bring the unconscious into play where we may absorb less obvious meanings without consciously realising it. Words, whether read or spoken, normally involve the conscious brain by immediately engaging the intellect.

Pre-concert talk

The pre-concert talk provides audiences with the opportunity to have a richer musical experience by focusing on those parts of the performance selected by the speaker as worthy of exploration. This might be a specific quality, instrument or section of the music. It might also include background information to the music, musician and period. The pre-concert talk also provides the opportunity to explain the rationale behind the programming. The comments are before, rather than during the performance, and won't distract from the focus on the music. Even so, it is likely the listener will hear the music differently, being attentive to the elements discussed, perhaps at the expense of other aspects of the performance. The pre-concert talk will create a different listening experience and may actually change what the listener hears and sees.

The Colour of Time

A variation on the pre-concert talk was the Sydney Symphony Orchestra's *The Colour of Time* (2008)[1]. This comprised discussions by American conductor David Robertson, examining the links between music and the visual arts. The event included the music *Prelude to the Afternoon of a Faun* by Claude Debussy, *Jeux* also by Debussy and *Chronochromie* by Olivier Messiaen. Visuals included projections of works by the impressionist artist Monet.

While this was described as a musical lecture, there seemed much more emphasis on the lecture component than the music. It was a frustrating event in that there were extended periods of talking without music. Other musical lectures, such as *Keys to Music* with Graham Abbott on Australian Broadcasting Corporation's Classic FM radio[2], normally make brief and succinct points about the music before the particular extract being discussed is played. However in *The Colour of Time* the music descriptions and the ideas often became lost in extended discussions. Given there were no text visuals to support the lecture, by the time the music was played, I had forgotten, or not gotten in the first place, the point be-

[1] Sydney Opera House, Friday 22 August (2008)

[2] Abbott, G., *Keys to Music* is a weekly radio program on ABC Classic FM that discusses various composers, musical concepts, genres and pieces of music.

ing made. This confused feeling transferred to the music, which seemed less interesting and less dynamic than when heard at other times.

I was not the only person unhappy with this performance. A woman in a nearby seat tried to have her ticket exchanged for another concert on the basis she had not been advised when she bought the ticket that this was a lecture rather than a concert and she did not want to attend a lecture. The event seemed a waste of resources in that a full orchestra sat idle for extended periods. Even with the projections of artworks by Monet, this was not a satisfying performance. An alternative format using brief discussions between each piece of music to highlight various aspects of the music-image combination would have made an enjoyable concert. However, as the event was publicised as a musical lecture, these comments might be considered as overly critical.

A Midsummer Night's Dream

A pre-concert talk at the performance of *A Midsummer Night's Dream* (2009)[1] by the Sydney Symphony Orchestra discussed a range of details including Mendelssohn's appreciation and interest in Shakespeare, as well as the appropriateness of the specifically composed music and the interaction of words and music. This provided a greater understanding and appreciation of the music and for many people would have increased pleasure of the performance.

The Red Tree

The Australian Chamber Orchestra's *The Red Tree* (2008), discussed previously, has two aspects relating to the dominance of language that show how words can be used to support music rather than background it. The first was the use of words displayed between movements. The picture titles from the book 'The Red Tree' were used in the performance as introductions to the music. These were displayed on the screen at the beginning and during the silence between movements. This is an ideal way of matching sound silence and image 'silence'.

The second way that the words were used to support the music was the type of singing and the sounds used as lyrics. Rather than being the typical song that often dominates a music performance, the singing was more like an additional instrument to the orchestra. The lyrics were mostly unintelligible to the audience because they were meaningless sounds that imitated words, or were mostly languages other than English. Only one of the seven movements was in English. This was one of the later movements and by the time this was heard it is likely the audience had

[1] Frindle, Y., Pre-concert talk, Sydney Opera House, 28 February (2009).

accepted the voice as music rather than as a communicator of language, and had stopped trying to interpret the words.

Unlike the typical song that often dominates a music performance, the singing was more like an additional instrument within the orchestra. This effect, that the voices seemed more an integral part of the orchestra, occurred for multiple reasons. The first was the chant-like nature of the singing. The second was that the words had no meaning or were in multiple languages, most of which could not be understood by most of the audience, and so were more like sounds than language. The third was that the singing was more like instrumental improvisation than a regular song and this probably occurred because the development of the music included improvisation sessions with the singers, even though they were children. The last reason the voices seemed part of the orchestra was due to the dissonant but resolving otherworldly melody. Therefore the unusual nature of the songs, being more like an instrument rather than language, resulted for the most part in the words not distracting attention from the music.

Book of Longing

The *Book of Longing* (2008) performance is an example of voice and text distracting from the music. This performance, as previously discussed, consisted of a series of songs composed by Philip Glass to accompany the poetry of Leonard Cohen. The musicians included Glass on keyboard. There were four singers: soprano, mezzo-soprano, tenor and bass-baritone. Voice recordings by Cohen were included, as were many of his drawings.

Multimedia presupposes that the mediums will interact and dominance will pass from one media to another and there would normally be some degree of conflict[1]. This occurred with *Book of Longing* where different media competed and became dominant at different times. For those interested in maintaining music dominance it was an example of how music cannot remain dominant in a multimedia performance, but at the same time the following criticisms could be considered unjustified given there was no intention for the music to remain dominant.

A black lattice construction held a projection screen along with drawings of varying sizes, with some drawings almost as large as the screen. During the performance, images were projected on the screen and these included Cohen's drawings, doodles, scribbling and words written in his own hand-writing. Even when the text was a single word it momentarily distracted from the music. Multiple words took time to read, especially

[1] Cook, N., *Analysing musical multimedia* (1998) 106.

being hand written rather than printed. As the music was my priority, I found the only way I could avoid reading the text and so avoid being distracted by it, was to not look at the screen. However the conscious action of doing this was itself a distraction. Those people who close their eyes to listen to music would not have had the problem, but I enjoy looking at the musicians and their expressions, so this created a dilemma in this visually integrated performance.

At times Leonard Cohen's voice boomed out from above, somewhat like God announcing the fate of expectant parishioners. This was a little startling but did not normally occur at the same time as the music. The singing was very much where the voice became dominant over the music. Glass had obviously composed the music for clear enunciation of the poetry to allow the meaning to be absorbed and understood. It was this clarity of the words that caused significant backgrounding of the music. Even though all media were congruent, and the music specifically written, *Book of Longing* is an example of music being backgrounded by voice and text. While I personally would have preferred the music to remain dominant throughout, the audience response was enthusiastic and my disappointment at the music being backgrounded at times was not shared.

Sinfonia Antartica

The *Sinfonia Antartica* concert (2007) is an example of the use of the spoken word where it does not background the music. As stated previously, Symphony No.7, *Sinfonia Antartica,* was originally written by Vaughan Williams to accompany the film *Scott of the Antarctic*. Extracts from Scott's diary were read during pauses between the movements of the music. This added a depth to the experience without backgrounding the music because voice and music each followed the other. Each allowed gaps for the other by not occurring at the same time and there was no conflict. Even though one media stopped before the other started, and this could seem disjointed under some circumstances, the single theme created continuity of performance.

Kraftwerk performances

Kraftwerk performances such as *Man Machine*, *Numbers* and *Tour de France* include lyrics and displayed text but these do not background the music. Kraftwerk use limited words, sometimes only the title of the song and this requires little attention to interpret and understand. Normally only one or two words will be displayed or sung at a time and these same words are repeated many times with both lyrics and text synchronised with the music. If words are required in the music concert, Kraftwerk performances provide an example of how they can be included without backgrounding the music.

Conclusion

The voice dominates all sound, and whether it is the spoken word or lyrics, language will grab attention from music. If the voice is used, it should create meaningless sounds or be simple words or phrases, which will have minimal impact on the music. Text displayed as words will also distract attention from the music because words are read and interpreted. If language, spoken or written, is used in the instrumental music concert, it should be limited to pauses between the music, or before or after the music. Activities such as the pre-concert talk or comments between pieces add value to the music-listening experience, but they must be separate from the music, otherwise the performance may become a multimedia event and the music may be backgrounded.

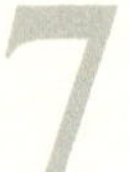

Integration and interpretation characteristics

This chapter discusses integration of the physical aspects of the instrumental music concert and how integration affects the music-image relationship. It also discusses the difference between interpretation and transformation. With interpretation, the music can enrich the performance while remaining true to the intentions of the composer. With transformation, something new emerges that may not be as originally intended.

Integration

In the instrumental music concert, the music and image should be integrated to maintain the integrity of, and focus on, the music. The integration encompasses all sound and visual aspects of the performance. The created image cannot be set apart from other visual aspects, as occurs in a picture gallery, and the musicians should be an integral part of the image.

Definition

Integration here means integration of the physical aspects of the performance, and how these physical aspects of people, instruments, equipment, media and environment work together to create an integrated concert.

Integration and congruency

All physical components of the concert should be integrated to create congruency, which will assist to focus audience attention on the music. If these performance components are not integrated they create incongruency, which distracts attention from the music.

Integration and the concert hall

Several major integration problems are created by the design of large concert halls, which are typically designed more for quantity of audience rather than quality of experience, with much of the audience being a great distance from the musicians. Another common problem is poor facilities for the projection of images. The average cinema integrates the audience into the entertainment to a much greater degree, by providing better and closer views.

Acoustics may be a problem with both venues. The shape of the cinema may lead to a reduction in the acoustic quality of the music. While in theory concert hall acoustics should be good, this is not necessarily the case due to the distance of the audience from the musicians and/or poor acoustic design. In some large concert halls it can at times be difficult to hear the quieter parts of performances. The Sydney Opera House Concert Hall is such an example with the acoustics being far below what is considered acceptable. This is no fault of the designer, Danish architect Jorn Utzon, who was continually hampered by Government interference and eventually resigned from the project. Many venues that are designed to have good acoustics must cater for speech as well as music, and as requirements for each are different, the music acoustics are to some extent compromised.

The sheer size of the concert hall is a major issue because it is important to clearly see musicians as well as hear their music. In classical music this visual aspect has been neglected over the last hundred years as discussed previously. While reduced ability to see the performance might have been acceptable in the twentieth century, film and the Internet have primed audiences to expect an intimate visual aspect to entertainment. In large venues where the music and musicians are distant, there is no intimacy and this can reduce audience involvement resulting in a lesser experience for the audience.

When we hear a sound we normally attempt to identify the source and this has been reinforced by film where the camera normally points to the person speaking or the sound source, or wanders until the search is resolved; this matches nature, where an object might not have a sound, but a sound is always produced by something imaginable; therefore, a sound that remains sourceless creates tension[1]. The result is that just as images create an instinctive need for accompanying sound[2], sound creates a need for accompanying image and it is natural to want to see the source of a sound. We may feel dissatisfied with performance if we cannot see the source of the music. However due to the size of the concert hall, a large part of the audience cannot clearly see the source of various sounds and are therefore unlikely to satisfy their natural response to seek out the specific sound source. From the viewpoint of understanding the music, seeing the source of the sound is more important for the less experienced in the audience who may not be able to differentiate between similar in-

[1] Altman, R., Moving Lips: Cinema as Ventriloquism, *Yale French Studies* 60 (1980) 71-74.

[2] Lindgren, E., *The art of the film* (1963) 137.

struments, but who may find it helpful and interesting to know which sound is coming from which instrument.

Seats at the front of the concert hall in music-image concerts may be a problem, not only because of the uncomfortable head position looking up at the screen, but also due to the placement of lighting. At the Australian Chamber Orchestra's *The Red Tree* concert (2008) at least one person needed to change their seat due to a poorly directed light. This occurred when a lamp that was used to illuminate the score for one of the musicians pointed directly at the audience and was a nuisance for a number of people. Something similar occurred with the lighting at the Philip Glass *Book of Longing* (2008). At times, some of the overhead stage lights pointed directly at the audience at the front, making it difficult to look at the stage when these particular lights were on. It appeared this was due to an attempt to light the singers at the front of the stage but keep lighting away from the screen displaying the projected images. Lighting that points at the audience and the physical discomfort it creates is unacceptable.

Integrating the screen into the setting

Music and image are very different in many ways and some of these differences make the music-image combination challenging. Sound has no boundaries whereas image is within a defined space and as such is framed. Framing is more obvious in the concert environment where the orchestra, even if on stage, are part of the same continuous space as the audience. The flatness of projected image in a three-dimensional environment impedes its credibility, whereas music surrounds us, and surrounds us with harmony, texture and instrumental colour that further enhance the quality of fullness[1]. The projection of images in a concert hall often involves framing created by a screen hovering high above the heads of the musicians, where it sits clearly bounded from all else. This is unlike films where the boundaries of the screen are not apparent due to darkness. A large screen high above the musicians is ugly, impractical and reminiscent of home slides or a school lecture. Many of the audience in the large concert hall do not have a clear view of such a screen and some have almost no view at all. For those at the front it involves an uncomfortable head position.

The Philip Glass *Book of Longing* (2008) used a very different approach to the screen that was thoughtful and well designed. As previously discussed, this performance comprised a series of songs accompanying the poetry, text and images by Leonard Cohen. The projection screen was

[1] Kalinak, K., *Settling the score* (1992) 44.

within a black lattice construction and surrounded by other framed black and white images in an arrangement and was partially behind the musicians rather than high above. Due to this arrangement, the few times the screen was blank it looked more like a section of a Piet Mondrian abstract painting than an empty screen. Performers often blocked parts of the images but this enhanced the concert rather than detracted from it.

Kraftwerk resolved the issue very differently. The imagery for their 2004 tour was shown on three massive screens, which were black when not in use. These screens covered almost the entire back of the stage except for a horizontal band from hip height down to the floor. This band was coloured according to the colour palette of the images. The group stood in front of and partially obscured the images but this added to the total visual presentation.

In *Luminous* (2005), the screen was the typical concert hall approach to image with screen hovering high above the musicians. Henson recognised the problem of music and image needing gaps where each needs to give the other space. To address this, the images were stopped at various times. Hence the screen was often blank. Given the images had already focussed attention on the screen, audience attention tended to remain there for a period expecting the images to return and then needed to regularly return in the expectation of further images. This regular checking to see whether the images had restarted kept bringing audience attention to the blank screen. Rather than eliminating the images, Henson's images were replaced by an image of a prominent, empty square. This huge white square was ugly and incongruous with the music, even though the lights were partially dimmed. This problem would have been reduced if the screen had been partially behind the musicians. When it was not used, it could have just become a neutral background to the orchestra and it would have been immediately apparent when the image projection restarted. This would be a problem for the musicians if front projection was used.

In a documentary about *Luminous*[1], the setting appeared much darker with the result that the screen appeared much less prominent, so this problem may have been recognised and addressed at subsequent concerts. Even so, in the documentary the screen still hovered high above the orchestra. Another alternative is to project a dark ambient image, such as a vague pattern, onto the screen. This serves two purposes: it darkens the screen so it is not as obvious; and, it alleviates the need to keep looking back because if much brighter images are projected, the dramatic change

[1] Luminous documentary *Sunday Arts*, ABC television, 1 June (2008).

in brightness levels should attract the audience attention immediately back to the screen.

Integration of music and image: gaps

Integration of sound and image requires that each allows space for the other. This can be achieved by each media leaving gaps for the other as previously described. Gaps can range from gross physical gaps, such as sound level, through to subtle gaps within a single piece of music. For example, stopping or lowering the sound level of the orchestra during opera, so it does not overwhelm a solo voice, creates a gap on the gross level. Ensuring that the melody and harmony of voice and orchestra are compatible creates a gap at the subtle level. This can be achieved by techniques such as a reduction in the complexity of each or one part.

Any medium that is used with music must allow space for the music otherwise the combination becomes overly dense. As previously stated Bill Henson in the *Luminous* (2005) performance recognised the issue of each media allowing space for the other and chose to withhold images at particular times, but the way this was physically achieved (leaving the screen blank) created other problems. An overly dense combination of media does not normally occur when media are created specifically for each other because they are written with 'pre-compositional gap-making'[1] where each media allows space for the other. This explains, at least in part, why performances work well where the music is composed specifically for the image such as *The Red Tree* (2008).

A problem that occurred with *The Arrival* (2008) was that there was no pre-compositional gap-making. Both the Shostakovich music and the Shaun Tan book were created as complete within themselves and the image creator did not allow for the density of the combination. This was especially noticeable at the beginning with the face-after-face images and the speed at which they were shown. These faces were the visual equivalent of loudness in music and they allowed no space for the music. Even though the program description of *The Arrival* stated that it inspired memory "urging us to fill in the silent gaps, animating them with the addition of our own storyline" in fact the gaps referred to here are gaps of meaning that created ambiguity, and not density gaps that allowed space for each media.

The combined force of this strong music and strong image was much like relentless wave after wave in a large ocean swell, and the lack of congruency made these waves turbulent. While stunning, it was at the same

[1] Cook, N., *Analysing musical multimedia* (1998) 105, 141.

time difficult to absorb, at least for some of the audience, due to the denseness of the combination. A musician or avid classical music listener very familiar with the particular music might find the dense combination exciting, whereas the average listener is likely to be challenged. The degree of effort required to focus on both music and image might not meet the expectation for a relaxing and pleasurable evening at a concert. The likely outcome of this dense music-image combination is that the audience will focus on the image at the expense of the music.

Integration of silence and image

Silence is an important part of sound. Silence can be expressive, such as in film where a soundless facial movement may explain the plot or add tension[1]. "Silence is necessary to music but is not part of music. Music leans on it"[2]. The result is that it may be difficult to achieve congruency of music and image during silence. Visual art exists as matter in space and while space is boundless, visual art is a special type of limited space[3]. Music is not bounded by space. This results in sound being able to fade out and disappear completely, thus silence appears natural. Not so with images where fading to nothing does not result in there being nothing to look at. Two-dimensional image is bounded by a screen and when the image stops, the screen remains unless there is complete darkness. Therefore stopping the image when the music stops does not achieve congruence because the blank screen continues to be seen and a blank screen is neither natural nor congruent with silence. With even a moderate amount of light, the blank screen normally remains as a large white framed object.

Stopping the image and leaving the screen blank is similar to what happened with music in films in the first half of the twentieth century. The music stopped abruptly in early film to allow conversation, and this created a strange effect that focused attention on the music, or lack of it[4]. Exactly the same thing happens when the image stops in the music-image combination. It focuses attention on the lack of image and on the blank screen. In film, you can't interrupt the auditory flow and have a few moments of silence because the spectator would think there was a technical problem and attention would be drawn to the silence; in film, silence is replaced with ambient silence, the sounds that are normally heard in a natural environment[5]. It is much the same with music, you can't have a

---

[1] Balazs, B., Theory of the Film: Sound, in *Film Sound: Theory and Practice*, Columbia (1985) 119.
[2] Bresson, R., *Notes on Cinematography*, Urizen (1977) 71.
[3] Crosby, S., *Helen Gardner's Art Through the Ages*, Harcourt (1959) 3, 6.
[4] Chion, M., *Audio-Vision* (1994) 54.
[5] Chion, M., *Audio-Vision* (1994) 57.

blank screen when the music stops because the blankness will immediately become obvious.

Silence is not neutral, it is the opposite of just heard sound and it creates contrast[1]. If badly handled, that contrast can be incongruent so silence should be integrated. To address the issue of an unnatural silence being created when music stops, to allow speech in film, the sound became more constant but at the same time more indistinct[2]. The same solution can be applied to the music concert. The image needs to be more constant but more indistinct. It must become ambient. Ambient image might be a gradual process of blurring or fading image until it becomes indistinct but it should not disappear. Alternatively it may be a gradual subduing of the colours. A dark colour may be displayed on a screen; however creating a dark environment, as occurs in a cinema, is impractical in a live concert.

Alternatively the image could be replaced with words that are meaningful and part of the performance. The displaying of text during pauses in the music was used by the Australian Chamber Orchestra in their performance of *The Red Tree* (2008), with the words from the book used as introductions to each movement of the music. Displaying text during pauses in the music is an excellent method of matching sound silence and visual silence and creating a congruent music-image relationship. Whatever the solution is, it must be less attention grabbing than a blank screen.

Integration of performer and image

As previously discussed, one of the issues of image in concert is that its two-dimensional projections onto a framed screen sets it apart from the sound and orchestra, making it a separate media experience. The technique of mixing image and artists was used by Pink Floyd in the 1960s. The images were projected onto the musicians, but this is not practical for musicians using sheet music. Floor to ceiling rear projections, with the musicians in front of the images, ameliorate this separate media experience. Rear projection is often used in ballet.

Before Tchaikovsky, composers wrote ballet music that was used with little regard to whether it was appropriate to the meaning of the ballet at a particular time. Much the same thing often happens now with VJing where videos are projected that have little or nothing in common with the music. When Tchaikovsky agreed to write ballet music, his genius ensured that the music was congruent with the story and the choreography.

[1] Chion, M., *Audio-Vision* (1994) 57.
[2] Chion, M., *Audio-Vision* (1994) 54.

Ballet companies have been integrating music and visual forms ever since, and more recently dancers and image. In the ballet *Wild Swans* (2003)[1], images were projected over the entire back of the stage with the dancers in front forming part of the image. The ballet was based on the Hans Christian Andersen story of the same name. The story tells of Princess Eliza who worked to reverse the spell that turned her eleven brothers into swans. The visual component consisted of dancers, their costumes, stage sets and visual projections. This merging of projected image and dancers created a visually rich three-dimensional experience.

Integrating musicians into the image has many advantages. Extreme close-ups of musicians are often used when filming concerts. While it might be acceptable for male pop groups to be strained and sweaty during performance, it is unlikely the classical audience would enjoy this look. It is not even considered appropriate throughout the pop industry. Pop stars such as Madonna and Kylie Minogue, when they appear on stage and in music videos, do not appear strained or dripping with perspiration. Merging musicians with the images reduces the focus on the musician and allows more freedom to concentrate on their playing. This issue, of not obtaining the best result by giving the performer too many activities at one time, is recognised in film. In many films, the voices to be used in the final version of the film are not recorded during shooting. The actors themselves record their voices in a studio while watching the film after it has been assembled. This is a slow labour intensive process so it appears that directors believe it is important to allow actors to concentrate on one aspect of performance at a time.

Integration of performers and image in the instrumental music concert can be achieved using a rear projection screen and placing the musicians in front of the image. While there are other considerations such as colour palette, integration of musician and images should not be difficult to achieve. This format has been successfully used by Kraftwerk and for the Philip Glass *Book of Longing*, as previously discussed.

Integration within images

The integration of image to image should not be an issue because music provides continuity to image[2]. An exception might be colour, which is the first thing noticed visually, and which creates an immediate impres-

[1] Wild Swans was created for the Australian Ballet by choreographer Meryl Tankard. The work was based on the story by Hans Christian Andersen, is a mix of dance and photographic and video illuminations created to a commissioned score for orchestra and soprano voice, by composer Elena Kats-Chernin, with the images created by visual artist Regis Lansac. It was premiered in April 2003 at the Sydney Opera House (Australia Dancing, 2003).

[2] Vernallis, C., *Experiencing Music Video* (2004) 21.

sion[1]. The colour palette of the entire performance should be considered because continuity of colour from one image to the next is important for integration. In *The Red Tree* (2008) pictures were sometimes interspersed with moving patterns. To ensure that the abstract patterns were part of an integrated whole, colours and textures from the same source ('The Red Tree' book) were used. This continuity of colour integrated the pictures and patterns from one image to the next. The overall colour palette, including performers, should also be considered. The Philip Glass *Book of Longing* coordinated the colour palette for the entire performance and this included the clothing of the musicians, even though at a first glance, it appeared an ad hoc combination. In *The Necks* (2008) concert, previously discussed, the second half of the performance was accompanied by continually changing images projected onto a screen high above the performers, and while the rate of change was not fast, the actual change process was abrupt and created a flash effect much like a home slide show. In this case the music was unable to unify the images and the result was unprofessional and difficult to watch.

Integration of setting

The physical environment, including the stage and anything that surrounds it, is always considered in theatre, opera and ballet. In films, the look of the venue is not an issue because it cannot be seen in the darkness. This aspect of the classical music concert is usually completely ignored, and the setting can be quite ugly as in the Sydney Opera House Concert Hall where audience sit behind the orchestra. For those in front, the actions and faces of the audience behind the orchestra can be distracting and certainly do not add any value to or understanding of the music.

The Australian Brandenburg Orchestra considers the visual aspect of the concert hall and works hard to achieve fully integrated performances. They often use a coloured curtain behind the orchestra, one or more large displays of flowers, and at times statues have graced the baroque organ. In *Rembrandt's World* (2005) in Sydney, a few simple props gave the impression of a romantic garden in which the speakers, who discussed the music and images between pieces, sat looking at the chamber music performance. This created the feeling of being back in the period.

A music video of a live performance of singer-songwriter-musician Norah Jones live at the House of Blues in New Orleans[2] showed the stage set with Persian style rugs, stylish lamps on the keyboards, a coloured curtain behind the group, and an effective prop to one side created

---

[1] Fehrman, K. & Fehrman, C., *Study Guide: Color: The Secret Influence*, Prentice Hall (2000) 85.

[2] *Norah Jones Live in New Orleans* [DVD], on 24 August 2002, Blue Note (2003).

from louvre doors with lighting behind. These props added interest and gave depth to the scene, and were unobtrusive but effective in creating a visual accompaniment that was congruent with the music. Similar types of imagery would be easy to project behind musicians.

André Rieu's performance of Bach's *Suite No. 3 Air*[1] is not one of his usual extravaganzas but a more sombre interpretation as befits the music. The performance started with the flames of a log fire in an iron grate. The location appeared to be an old monastery. The architecture, with vaulted roof, timber beams and stone walls, was integral to the performance. Musicians stood on steps leading out of the room from a carved wooden door into a corridor. Close-ups showed performers expressions and hand movements, with fade-ins and the glow of the fire adding softness and warmth. The musician at the top of the stairs was surrounded by bright light as if from a religious vision. A simple ceramic vase was placed on a wooden stand. The view moved slowly around the room from musician to musician, all with serene expressions. The baroque-style environment supported and enhanced Bach's elegant music. Props and imagery from the era of the music could enhance any performance creating congruency of environment and music.

A Midsummer Night's Dream

The Sydney Symphony Orchestra's performance in 2009 of Felix Mendelssohn's *A Midsummer Night's Dream* was a rare opportunity to experience an authentic rendition of the work, which Mendelssohn intended as an integrated production of music and Shakespeare's drama. While Mendelssohn composed the overture at age seventeen, the performance presented by the Sydney Symphony was commissioned by Friedrich Wilhelm IV for the Prussian court in Potsdam, with its public premiere following in Berlin. In English this type of composition is known as 'incidental music', although the term downplays the magic, beauty and sophistication of Mendelssohn's *Midsummer Night's Dream*.[2]

The performance was unusual in many ways. The costumes were minimalist, with actors in black suits and black dresses, similar to those of the musicians. However the fairies had a mass of tiny lights on their black clothes, with the Fairy Queen's lights twinkling as she entered and exited the stage. Music was integral to the performance. The 'flower' that was squeezed to obtain a potion that creates love at first sight, was a musical instrument, as were the ears of an ass that were endowed on the unsuspecting Snug.

---

[1] Rieu, A., *Australia Bound* [promotional DVD], track 6, (2007).

[2] Frindle, Y., Pre-concert talk, Sydney Opera House, 28 February (2009). Yvonne Frindle is Publications Editor & Music Presentation Manager, Sydney Symphony Orchestra.

Music and drama were equally prominent and musicians and actors shared the same space, with actors weaving through the orchestra. Each group acknowledged and interacted with the other, as occurred when an actor borrowed a musical instrument leaving the musician empty handed. The distraught Helena complained bitterly of her situation to the conductor, the acclaimed Vladimir Ashkenazy, and his nod of agreement created much amusement in the audience. At another time the Fairy King turned to Ashkenazy with the words "I *am* invisible" and the conductor gestured in response. These small nuances added a freshness and liveliness to the performance.

The conductor, orchestra, choir and musical instruments as well as the music itself were all integral to the performance, with musical instruments used as props. Where music and speech occurred concurrently, there was ample gapping created by the music composition, for both to be clearly heard and understood. This gapping of music and image, even though it is to be expected to some extent with specifically written program music, emphasized Mendelssohn's understanding of the play and his brilliance in being able to combine both, in much the same way as he would different music lines within the same piece of music. *A Midsummer Night's Dream* was an integrated performance over all areas where neither medium competed with the other, and the delight of the audience was part of the entertainment. Musicians, actors, props, audience and music were all lightly enmeshed to create an unusual but delightful event.

Conclusion

In the music-image relationship, integration is a form of congruency that assists in focusing attention on the music. Integration of all aspects of a performance is an important part of theatre, ballet and opera and there is no reason to think that the music concert should be any different.

Interpretation

Interpretation occurs in the music-image combination, where the whole is greater than the sum of the parts and where the music is enriched by the image but where this combination remains true to the original features of the music and the intention of the composer.

Definitions

Interpretation in music is where the performer creates a distinctive personal rendering of the music while remaining faithful to the composer's intention. Interpretation in the music-image combination is the process that occurs when music and image create a combination where both work together to create a richer experience without undermining the composer's intention for the music.

Transformation in the music-image combination occurs where something new emerges and a new meaning is created[1].

Authentic performance and interpretation

It can be claimed that adding image to music will change the music and this is true, but in previous eras every performance of music was different and it was expected that each performer would interpret the music. Throughout most of Western classical music history, interpretation, improvisation and innovation were an important part of performance. Each musician presented the work differently with the possibility that each individual performance by the same musician was different. The idea that music must sound the same at every performance became fashionable in the twentieth century and probably had its origins in music recording.

Interpretation, improvisation and innovation were a necessary part of musicianship in the past and this is obvious from manuscripts of the medieval eras, which did not show the exact notes but indicated only the shape of the melody, acting as a reminder for music previously learned[2]. In baroque music, the figured bass, a type of shorthand score, was used to indicate the composer's intentions. Musicians were responsible for filling out the composition by adding ornamentation including trills, passing notes, slides, melodies, harmonies and arpeggios[3]. Improvising on the organ, which Johann Sebastian Bach was admired for, was a major part of organ performance from its inception and this has continued through to the present[4].

In the classic era, Wolfgang Amadeus Mozart was known more for improvising than composing[5]. His scores are described by internationally acclaimed pianist Alfred Brendel, as being incomplete and needing to be filled in[6]. In the Romantic era, performances used improvisation as a bridge to link one composed piece to the next; Clara Schumann when pressed, documented some of these improvisations but protested it was

---

1 Cook, N., *Analysing musical multimedia* (1998) 82-86.
2 Brown, H., Performing Practice. I Western, *Grove Music Online* (2007).
3 Sadie, S. & Latham, A., *The Cambridge Music Guide* (1996) 142.
4 Bailey, D., *Improvisation: its nature and practice in music*, Da Capo (1993) 29.
5 Levin, R,. *Improvising Mozart* [presentation], Cambridge, 12 December (2001).
6 Benson, B., *The improvisation of Musical Dialogue: A Phenomenology of Music*, Cambridge (2003) 83.

difficult because they changed for each performance[1]. Romantic era performers freely interpreted scores and Franz Liszt took this to extremes. His interpretations of Frédéric Chopin's music apparently annoyed Chopin who is said to have snapped at Liszt to play what was written[2].

Today, period orchestras study performance practice and figured bass to enable them to create an authentic performance that includes improvisation. The Australian Brandenburg Orchestra states that each musician's improvisations are entirely their own however they must sound integral to the original work with the aim being to produce a seamless tapestry of music[3]. It is traditional for musicians to interpret and therefore subtly enhance the score and this important aspect of performance is sometimes forgotten. These types of changes initiated by the musician are normally considered appropriate even in a classical piece from the repertoire. Australian violinist and National Living Treasure Richard Tognetti, is acclaimed for his innovative interpretations of classical music.

Just as important as the question of authenticity of classical music when it is changed by interpretation, is the realization that the mere act of watching a musician changes how we hear the music. For instance, experiments show that a musician's facial expressions and body movements can change such things as the level of pitch heard by the listener[4]. Changes resulting from interpretation and from looking at the expressions and gestures of musicians are an important part of music performance that enlivens often heard music. Pre-twentieth century music performance traditions meant that music at each performance was different. Additionally, just watching musicians changes what we hear. It is therefore reasonable to argue that changes introduced by adding image are a form of interpretation of the music. For the music to remain authentic, these changes should appear to be a natural addition to the original music, and be faithful to the intentions of the composer.

Added value

The amount and type of change that image introduces to the music is an important consideration. The theory of *Added Value*[5], in referring to film, states that sound enriches image with meanings and emotions in such a way that it appears these meanings and emotions were in the image to

---

[1] Goertzen, V., Setting the Stage: Clara Schumann's Preludes, *In the Course of Performance. Studies in the World of Music Improvisation*, ed Nettl, Chicago (1998) 237.

[2] Schoenberg, H., *The lives of the great composers* (1971) 173.

[3] Beck, J., personal communication, 6 July (2006). James Beck is cellist and librarian for the Australian Brandenburg Orchestra.

[4] Thompson, W., Graham, P. & Russo, F., Seeing music performance (2005) 203-4.

[5] Chion, M., *Audio-Vision* (1994) 5, 21-2.

begin with, and are a natural part of the image. This theory also states that the added value concept works reciprocally so it can be equally applied to music, where image can add value to music and enrich it. This is one of the objectives when adding image to the music concert, for the image to enrich the music.

In film, the juxtaposition of two separate shots is not a simple combination, but the creation of a new concept[1], and the same may occur in the music-image combination where something new emerges. However this should not occur in the music concert. The image should not change the music to the extent that something new emerges. If something new does emerge, a transformation has occurred and this moves beyond interpretation. There is a limit as to how much music can be changed while remaining true to its original intentions. This might not be an issue with pop music, but it is important in classical music because the classical audience normally expects an authentic performance that remains faithful to the composer's intentions. The following diagram shows the performance as it changes from the original concept, through to enrichment of the music by interpretation and finally transformation where something new emerges.

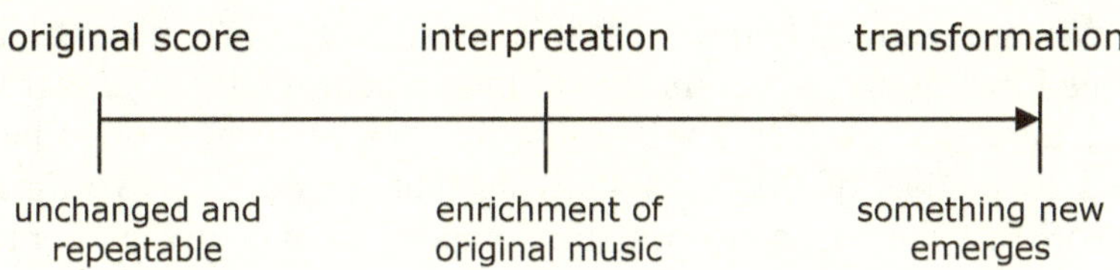

Figure 19 Changes created by the performance of music

The audio-visual illusion

Cognitive psychology experiments support the theory of *Added Value*. These experiments show that when the brain processes music and image at the same time, it may literally change the individual's perception of external reality[2]. This concept, that changing the sound changes the image and vice versa, is part of Associationism, a school of psychology, where mental experiences are associated with sensory experiences[3]. Research as early as the 1940s showed that the mere act of opening and

[1] Eisenstein, S., *The Film Sense* (1947) 4-7.
[2] Cohen, A., Film Music: Perspectives from Cognitive Psychology (2000) 265, 366, 369.
[3] Cohen, A., Associationism and musical soundtrack phenomena (1993) 163.

closing the eyes can affect the perception of the location of a sound[1] and the effect, that hearing changes what we see and seeing changes what we hear, is also claimed by many music listeners who state they hear better with their eyes closed. Therefore the visual aspect, whether it is the musicians themselves, the environment, or any added imagery, always changes how music is heard.

There are several different but related results from cognitive psychology experiments relevant to the music-image combination. The first, as already mentioned, shows that when image and music are combined, depending on the congruency of the match, our perception of reality is likely to be a construct, which is an illusion that does not match reality. A second observation is that it appears a music-image combination encourages the suspension of disbelief, resulting in events that are not real, being more readily accepted as real. A third observation is that music combined with image can heighten the listener's sense of reality making an event seem more real than reality itself. Therefore, even though the perception created by combining music and image may be an illusion, the addition of music heightens reality and at the same time suspends disbelief, making the audience more likely to see and believe the illusion.[2]

In summary, the music-image combination may be a construct that is an illusion. We are ready to believe that this constructed illusion is real, and in fact this illusion may seem more real than actual reality. The fact that we create a version of events that is not real might seem strange but is supported by studies of the brain showing that we do not have time to fully absorb all the visual information needed at any given moment. Whatever is missing is generated by the imagination, with the brain relying on information coming from memory as much as from vision; this means that our mental image of the world is only loosely based on reality[3]. This idea, that reality is in fact self-created is taken further by an even more surprising claim. The brain is said to be a dreaming machine that creates images that are then turned into reality by the information coming through the senses; the result is that our waking state and dreaming state may be very close and possibly exactly the same[4]. This implies that each person creates a different reality that is their own and not necessarily related to what is actually happening.

---

[1] Ryan, T. & Schehr, F., The Influence of Eye Movement and Position on Auditory Localization, *American Journal of Psychology*, 54/2 (1941) 251.

[2] Cohen, A., Film Music: Perspectives from Cognitive Psychology (2000) 265, 366, 369.

[3] Greenfield, S., The Mind's Eye, *Brain Story* (2000).

[4] Llinas, R., Prof. of Neuroscience at New York University, in Greenfield, The Mind's Eye (2000).

The possible creation of illusion by the music-image combination may also be explained by music requiring more mental activity than image or speech and it is possible that this increased mental activity required for music, heightens our sense of reality[1]. This heightened sense of reality may explain why listeners experience a strong emotional reaction to music and are often convinced that music has meaning even though different people may not agree on what the meaning actually is. It may also explain why people find music inspirational and enjoy listening to it as background, in that it may heighten the sense of reality of life itself.

Integration versus transformation

The added value of image causes music to acquire qualities that the music doesn't have by itself[2]. If the addition of image results in enrichment of the music, then this is interpretation and this level of change follows a longstanding music tradition. If the level of change results in something new emerging with the music taking on a new meaning, then it is transformation. Whether music falls into the category of interpretation or transformation, is likely to depend on the level of congruency, and whether there is any incongruency in the characteristics of the music-image combination.

The addition of image to music, if done imaginatively, can deepen the experience of the music, as the attributes of one media transfer to the other. Whether the result is the emergence of something new depends on a number of factors. For this new meaning to occur the music-image combination must have some congruent properties at both an obvious level and a deeper less obvious level. This needs to be a limited overlap of attributes, where the characteristics neither completely overlap, nor totally diverge. It is this limited overlap that creates a new meaning. The addition of image to music can construct something new, a creation that is not the addition of both mediums but a transformation, where each media contextualizes and clarifies the other adding emergent qualities. This is not a simple mixing or averaging of combined effects of the music and image but an 'emergent' property.[3]

If there is no overlap of attributes then the relationship is full incongruency and it is likely the music-image combination will not make sense. Emergence requires a limited overlap of attributes (a form of partial congruency) but partial congruency is not enough. The concept of

[1] Cohen, A., Film Music: Perspectives from Cognitive Psychology (2000) 366.
[2] Cook, N., *Analysing musical multimedia* (1998) 67.
[3] Cook, N., *Analysing musical multimedia* (1998) 69, 73-74, 82-86.

emergence is from multimedia theory[1] where contest (referred to here as incongruency) is a normal part of the multimedia relationship. For something new to emerge a level of incongruency needs to be added to the partial congruency. The combination of partial congruency and incongruency is partial incongruency, but partial incongruency will be just as detrimental as full incongruency to music dominance. The combination of partial congruency and incongruency may result in the emergence of something new but at the same time it is likely that the music will be backgrounded. The following diagram shows the music-image continuum where the result changes from interpretation to transformation where there is partial congruency with the addition of incongruency.

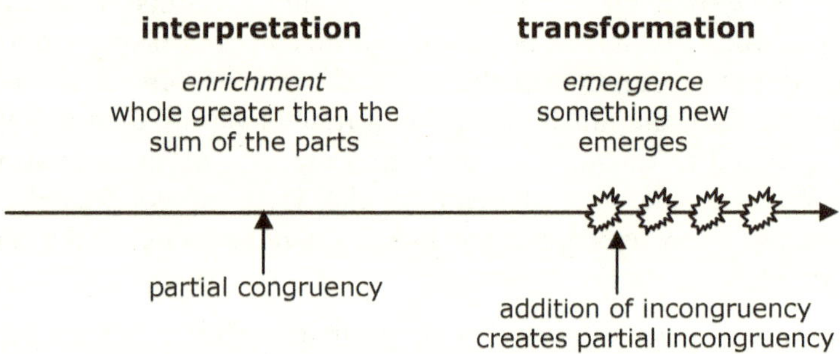

Figure 20 Interpretation versus transformation

While image in the music concert is meant to enhance rather than transform the music, there may be reasons to push the boundaries of interpretation and one of these is familiarity fatigue. To some extent the more often we hear a piece of music and the better we know it, the more we enjoy it because it's more meaningful; on the other hand listeners tire of music that becomes overly familiar[2]. Introducing changes that border on transformation may be both useful and acceptable with music that is extremely well known and frequently performed.

The decision as to whether the transference of attributes from image to music results in interpretation or transformation is an artistic decision. There are several aspects to be considered. One is whether, in the original music, the potential for these new attributes is already there in the music but not noticed until the images draw attention to them; another factor is whether the combination of music and image make the apparent

[1] Cook, N., *Analysing musical multimedia* (1998) 69, 73-74, 82-86.

[2] Meyer, L., *Music, the Arts and Ideas*, University of Chicago Press (1970) 46, 49.

meaning of the music clearer and more coherent[1]. The decision on whether the changes introduced by the image are interpretation or transformation also applies to where musicians introduce their own changes, which may go further than would be normally acceptable as interpretation.

In making this decision on how far to push the interpretation, the reaction of the audience is a major consideration. It is the illusion created by the music-image combination, and the willingness to believe it, which will result in audience acceptance of the changes created by the images. If these changes are too far removed from the composer's intention for the music they will normally cause rejection of the combination and this was the case, to some extent, with the performance of *The Arrival* (2008). The composer's intention was for the music to represent the mystery and reverence of death, whereas the images were of a poor peasant looking for and eventually finding a better life, in a science fiction-like world. As a music critic observed, the marriage of the pictures from Tan's book 'The Arrival' with the Shostakovich *String Quartet No. 15* "misfired chiefly because the projected images often seemed to have no reflection in the musical content. Where the Russian composer's score comprises six Adagio movements of varying weight, the illustrated story of one man's movement from home to the city and back again only seemed to fit the aural content fitfully"[2].

Unpredictability of the music-image combination

The way the senses interact and the results of their interaction are complex. It is widely accepted that vision dominates sound and this dominance continues even when sound is more intense than image; visual dominance becomes overwhelming when there is a conflict between image and sound[3]. Visual dominance may become so pronounced that vision may completely block other senses[4]. Classical film theory assumes that meaning comes from image while music plays only a secondary role of reinforcing or altering that which is already present[5], and it is normally considered, whether correct or not, that music will project the content of image but not that image will project the content of music[6].

While research supports the belief that shows vision controls attention when competing against other senses, it also shows that in a high arousal

[1] Cook, N., *Analysing musical multimedia* (1998) 73-4.
[2] O'Connell, C., Visual feast, young choir in fine voice (2008).
[3] Colavita, F. & Weisberg, D., A further investigation of visual dominance (1979) 345, 347.
[4] Posner, M., Nissen, M. & Klein, R., Visual dominance (1976) 170.
[5] Kalinak, K., *Settling the score* (1992) 29.
[6] Cook, N., *Analysing musical multimedia* (1998) 100.

state, visual dominance is reduced and then sound may become dominant[1]. The sense of touch, also appears to mediate visual information, at least to some extent[2]. The human auditory and nervous systems are "exquisitely tuned for music"[3] and though vision carries more information, we can hear a fast sequence of tones but a similarly fast sequence of images becomes blurred[4]. It is this complexity of the sensory systems and their interactions that makes the results of the music-image combination unpredictable. This was observed by acclaimed Russian filmmaker, Sergei Eisenstein, who found that the combination of music and image often created unpredictable results[5] even though both mediums project their own meaning when separate[6]. These unpredictable results may lead to transformation where something new emerges and this is not normally the aim of the music concert.

The Red Tree

The Australian Chamber Orchestra's performance of *The Red Tree* (2008) is an example where the music-image combination borders on transformation while staying faithful to the intentions of the music. This is a somewhat artificial observation given that the music was written specifically for the images. *The Red Tree* performance is described as a "combination of music, image and voice enticingly complex, chaotic and beautiful"[7]. As good as Tan's book is, for me, reading the book without the music after seeing the performance was to some extent disappointing. It is likely that the music without the images would create the same response. The music created for *The Red Tree* performance is a special type of program music where, being created for the image, a transformation can occur while at the same time, the music remains faithful to the composer's intention, which was for the music and image to form a congruent combination. *The Red Tree* is a truly integrated performance, where judging by the critical acclaim and audience response, it could be claimed the whole was greater than the sum of the parts.

Pocket Calculator

Kraftwerk's *Pocket Calculator* (2005) was described earlier in apparent synchronisation and is also an example of interpretation that verges on

---

[1] Shapiro, K., Egerman, K. & Klein, R., Effects of arousal on human visual dominance (1984) 547, 552.

[2] Easton, R. & Falz, M., Finger pressure during tracking of curved contours: Implications for a visual dominance phenomenon, *Perception & Psychophysics* 24/2 (1978) 153.

[3] Sacks, O., *Musicophilia*, Picador (2007) xi.

[4] Scholes, P., Colour and Music (1970) 207.

[5] Eisenstein, S., *The Film Sense* (1947) 159.

[6] Cohen, A., Film Music: Perspectives from Cognitive Psychology (2000) 369.

[7] Botticelli, L., The Red Tree (2008).

transformation, but where the illusion remains faithful to the intention of the music. *Pocket Calculator* is particularly applicable to the concept that the attributes of one media transfer to the other, especially because few things could be considered less interesting than watching a finger pressing calculator buttons. This playful song includes sounds from Casio and Texas calculators[1].

As the song starts, an image of a calculator appears and an animated hand moves across the calculator pressing buttons. This imagery has two different types of transformation. The first type of transformation is that of perceiving movements, which are not actually there. The eye perceives more slowly than the ear and image cannot match the tempo of sound, so sound will determine what is seen; if the image is too fast to be clearly comprehended, sound may lead us to see movements that don't exist or to miss movements that do exist[2]. In *Pocket Calculator*, once the hand moves to hover over the correct position above the appropriate button, it does not move. However, when the sound of the button is heard we 'see' the finger moving down to press it. It is the sound that makes us 'see' the movement. The transference of attributes between music and image has two results. The first is the apparent movement of the finger in sync with the sound of the button being pressed. The second type of transference of attributes occurs when the button pressing actions are made interesting by the liveliness of the music.

A second type of transformation occurs when the live images of individual group members are displayed on the calculator buttons, which are either pink or green. These colours remain even when the group members are displayed on the buttons resulting in pink and green faces. The images of the group on the calculator buttons completely change the impact of the song, so instead of the performance being under the control of the group, it appears the group is under the control of the calculator. This exemplifies and focuses on Kraftwerk's aim of being an integrated man-machine.

Conclusion

If the whole is to be greater than the sum of the parts, and the addition of image is to create a richer musical experience, then some level of perceived change is necessary. If the music and image match exactly, then it is likely that no change will occur and there will be a risk that the combination will be uninteresting or comical. If music and image include incongruency, transformation is likely to occur where something new

---

[1] Bussy, P., *Kraftwerk: Man, Machine and Music* (2005) 115.

[2] Chion, M., *Audio-Vision* (1994) 11-12, 15.

emerges and this may result in multimedia. Multimedia presupposes that the mediums will interact and dominance will pass from one media to another and there would normally be some degree of conflict[1]. The exception to this may be music written specifically for the image. A successful music-image combination includes interpretation that enriches the music but retains the music as the dominant medium, or at least at an equal level where the music is not backgrounded.

Not all music will be suitable for added image so when combining image and music, it should be taken as given that the music will be changed and these questions should be asked:

1. *Is it appropriate to add image and therefore change this particular music?*
2. *To what extent are the properties of the image compatible with the music?*
3. *To what extent will the addition of image change the music and will the audience find this acceptable?*
4. *Will the addition of image enhance the audience's pleasure of the music?*

[1] Cook, N., *Analysing musical multimedia* (1998) 106.

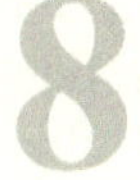

Changing and developing technologies

This chapter discusses the aims and issues involved in adding image to music, the lessons that can be learned from early cinema, the importance of a visual component in concert, the use of holography, why the music concert should not be a multimedia event, the importance of being willing to take risks in adding image to music, and why it is important to ensure the instrumental music concert continues as a viable form of entertainment.

Aims in adding image to music

A number of orchestras have more recently introduced image into the instrumental music concert in an effort to attract a wider audience[1]. The practice is still in its infancy and a greater understanding of the music-image relationship is necessary to ensure that performances achieve their objectives. The addition of image can invigorate the instrumental music concert for a media-inundated public who have grown accustomed to an intimate form of image that is not available to the majority of the concert hall audience. To increase audience size, the music-image combination needs to achieve a balance that will interest new audiences, while at the same time satisfying those music lovers who are interested only, or primarily in the music.

The aim of adding image to the instrumental music concert should be to enhance the music. Image can put back a visual component that should at least to some extent, replace the loss of contact between musician and audience that has occurred through large concert halls. It can also lessen the pressure of showmanship on performers and allow more time and energy for musicianship. The addition of image should not create a multi-media extravaganza, as often occurs with pop concerts, because this would be unlikely to please the serious music listener even though it may attract a younger audience.

Achieving a music-image relationship that foregrounds the music or at least does not background it, involves a number of issues. Particularly important are congruency and narrative. Incongruency between music

[1] Wilson, R. personal communication, 28 March (2007). Raff Wilson is Artistic Administration Manager, Sydney Symphony Orchestra.

and image is likely to undermine the audience focus on the music, and this may also occur with certain types of narrative. Congruency, particularly partial congruency, assists in foregrounding the music. Narrative that is strong, ambiguous and/or humorous is likely to background the music. Narratives that are open, loose and apparent reduce the effect of backgrounding and may help to foreground the music.

An issue that must be addressed is that music, once heard, is likely to be associated with each listener's own personal meaning, and the addition of image may alienate listeners whose own internal imagery is different to that of the added imagery. A conflict between personal and added imagery is less likely to occur with program music, where from the first hearing, the meaning and imagery in the listener's mind is based on the title allocated by the composer. Music specifically composed for image is a special type of program music and this may be the most successful type of music in music-image concert performances. Where music has been specifically created to accompany particular images, congruency is ensured and an example of this was the performance of *The Red Tree* (2008).

Adding image to music that has a well established tradition is more difficult, as was discussed with *The Arrival* (2008). Images from the picture book 'The Arrival', about a peasant seeking and achieving a better life, were added to the Shostakovich *String Quartet No. 15 opus 144,* which is known as a funeral march. The result was an audience and critical response that was less enthusiastic than normally occurs at an Australian Chamber Orchestra performance. Even if music has no particular association but is well known, such as Bach's *Brandenburg* concertos, many music listeners will have established their own meaning and associations and may be unhappy with images that undermine their own personal meanings and emotions connected with the music.

The theories in this book claim that partial congruency of music-image characteristics, without any incongruency, is the most effective combination to maintain focus on the music. While narrative is one of these music-image characteristics, it has an additional feature that influences the music-image combination, and this is plot. Whether the narrative is congruent or not, certain types of narrative are likely to background the music and the most effective forms to maintain focus on the music are likely to be: open, apparent, loose and non narrative. While these theories are well supported with evidence from other fields they are by no means proven and more work is needed to establish whether they apply across different types of music-image situations.

Lessons from early cinema

There were many issues that needed to be addressed when the silent film emerged as a new form of entertainment. Silent film was not actually silent because it was accompanied by live music. Initially this accompanying music was ad hoc, at the discretion of the musicians, but was eventually replaced by appropriate scores. When this occurred, clichéd mood music became the standard accompaniment for film. Once the speaking film was introduced, the live music ceased, and the use of music became more subtle. Even so, film today is often criticised for over use of background music.[1]

Today the addition of image to much live pop music can be compared to the beginnings of cinema. Just as unrelated music was initially added to silent films, today video jockeys often add unrelated image to music. The stage that followed in film, the addition of clichéd music, will hopefully not occur with the music concert. The addition of congruent clichéd image would not be an improvement over unrelated images. The issue in film, of background music often being over used, will probably occur with the use of image in the music concert. Over use of images occurred at the beginning of *The Arrival* (2008) with too many images of faces creating an intellectual overload. This overload was further increased by the complexity and drama of the Shostakovich music. A lack of images may also create problems. In early cinema the music stopped abruptly to allow dialogue[2]. The equivalent occurred in *Luminous* (2005) where Bill Henson recognised the need for breathing space between media, and displayed images intermittently. This resulted in a large, blank, white, ugly screen that needed to be regularly checked to see if the images had restarted.

The image in music performance has the potential to suffer from the same synchronisation difficulties as occurred with live music accompanying the silent film. Synchronisation of music and film remained a problem until sound was recorded as part of the film[3]. Synchronisation of image with the live concert is a challenge, which can be ameliorated by various techniques including perceived and continuous synchronisation. Another issue that is similar to film is the level of quality of the accompanying media. In film, the appropriateness of the music is more important than the quality of the music because overly prominent music will call attention to itself at a cost to the film, and well known music can

---

[1] Lindgren, E., *The art of the film* (1963) 134-8.

[2] Chion, M., *Audio-Vision* (1994) 54.

[3] Lindgren, E., *The art of the film* (1963) 138.

be a distraction[1]. In much the same way, the appropriateness of the images in the concert is more important than the quality of the images, and well known images may be a distraction from the music. At the same time it should be remembered that it appears the addition of image compensates for poor sound quality but the addition of sound does not compensate for the loss of visual quality[2].

Looking at the problems of adding music to early film may assist in avoiding a repetition of similar problems when adding image to music. This is essential given the sophistication of today's audiences. The complexity of creating image that foregrounds the music, or at least does not background it, requires experienced filmmakers and/or graphic designers who understand the music-image relationship and how each media influences the other.

French composer, Alexandre Desplat, when discussing his score for the movie *The Curious Case of Benjamin Button* (2008), made a number of comments on the appropriateness of music in film. These sentiments apply equally to the addition of image to the instrumental music concert. Desplat stated "less is more ... it shouldn't show off ... it can shine and be intricate ... it shouldn't be overwhelming ... it can be simple ... it can be subdued ... and still be very strong ... to do this is simple but difficult"[3].

Importance of visual component in concert

Live music can be considered to be perceived or consumed because it is experienced far more as part of spectacle than situations where the musicians are hidden from view; even in the instrumental classical concert, the musicians are positioned to be viewed and the concert hall is designed for viewing[4]. However for that part of the audience who watch the musicians at a great distance, as occurs in large concert halls, the more subtle gestures and expressions are not visible. The events where large audiences in large spaces work well are normally outdoor venues where there is social interaction and projections of the artists. The outdoor performance of *On a Beautiful Scottish Evening,* with Edinburgh Castle in the background, projected video images of the musicians and singers onto a large screen behind the orchestra as they performed[5]. While this projection showing the musicians may have been repetitive and unimagi-

---

[1] Lindgren, E., *The art of the film* (1963) 139.

[2] Iwamiya, S., Interaction Between Auditory and Visual Processing When Listening to Music in an Audio Visual Context, (1994) 152.

[3] Desplat, A., *The Curious Case of Benjamin Button* [DVD], 2009.

[4] Durant, A., *Conditions of music*, London: Macmillan (1984) 86.

[5] Caledon and The Scottish Fiddle Orchestra, *On a Beautiful Scottish Evening* [DVD], (2005).

native, it did provide a sense of being close to the orchestra. Indoor pop concerts where multiple screens show close-ups of performers also provide intimate views of the artists. The importance of a visual component is confirmed with audiences and musicians being unhappy with electronically created music where there is little to look at[1]. However more is needed than just showing close-ups of performers. Classical music is often demanding and most musicians need to focus on musicianship rather than showmanship. Incorporating musicians into the image provides a visual component for the audience without placing an undue burden on the musicians.

Recorded music was originally responsible for a reduction in live performances, but the recording industry is now in decline[2]. Recorded music is now mostly background music. At the same time, direct broadcasts and recordings of live performances cannot be compared to and cannot replace live performances. While broadcasts and recordings have strengths and weaknesses, it is far from clear that their strengths balance their weaknesses and these weaknesses include the de-humanising, decontextualizing and abstracting of music; studio performances should not be considered interchangeable with live performances as they offer a different atmosphere and promote different values[3]. Recorded music is in fact not a reproduction but merely an approximation of a live performance and only live performance can offer the full and satisfying musical experience that balances the expected with the unexpected[4].

Music is no longer an elite activity heard only in formal settings such as opera houses and concert halls; it has penetrated into every part of day to day activities and is heard by large numbers of people in informal settings such as the home, car and office[5]. Regardless, live performances will continue because the audience excitement during live concert is the 'sharp end' of musical performance[6]. While the excitement of live performance is indisputable, a clearer understanding of the music-image relationship is needed to achieve the balance required to attract a wider audience, while meeting the expectations of the current instrumental music enthusiast, to maintain the music as the primary art form in concert.

---

[1] Morgan, R., *Twentieth-Century Music: A History of Musical Style in Modern Europe and America*, Norton (1991) 470

[2] Lebrecht, N., Sunday Arts [interview], ABC1 television, screened 7 October (2007); Smith, E., Sales of Music, Long in Decline, Plunge Sharply, *Wall Street Journal*, 21 March (2007).

[3] Davies, S., *Musical Works and Performances: A Philosophical Exploration*, Oxford (2001) 317,339-340.

[4] Dunsby, J., Performance (2007).

[5] Konečni, V., Social Interaction and Musical Preference, *Psychology of Music*, D Deutsch ed, Academic Press (1982) 498-9.

[6] Dunsby, J., Performance (2007).

With the twenty-first century expectation for image and multimedia, the music concert must adapt to compete with the ever increasing number of entertainment options available to the public. It is time to invigorate the live performance by incorporating image because "the addition of image can create a new or deeper experience of the music"[1].

Hologram technology

Instead of replacing large concert halls with smaller venues, the use of holograms offers an alternative to provide a more intimate relationship between musician and audience in large spaces. Holograms also solve the problem of two-dimensional projections onto a framed screen, which sets the images apart from a three-dimensional sound and orchestra. From this perspective, the current music-image performance is not an integrated experience but a separated media experience. Floor to ceiling rear projections, as used by Kraftwerk and which are often used in ballet, such as the *Wild Swans* (2003) performance, ameliorate the problem to some extent, but hologram projection would substantially resolve it.

Hologram technology is now being used commercially, with CNN broadcasting holograms of reporters during the coverage of the USA election between Republican John McCain and Democrat Barack Obama[2]. Within five years, as technology development makes holograms cheaper and more accessible, it is likely holograms will be able to replace the flat screen currently used in concert halls. It is predicted that over the next few years high quality realistic holograms will be available inexpensively and these holograms will have the capability to respond to changes in light and the viewer's direction[3]. Holograms could be projected to various places in the concert hall, and would provide a feeling of audience involvement and closeness that occurs in small venues. A semi-transparent hologram suspended in the air would work well with much instrumental music, as it would be more like an artwork. This is not to suggest that creating imagery with holograms is a simple matter of pointing a camera at a musician. It requires experienced filmmakers who can blend live musicians with imagery and achieve a quality result.

The 2003 MTV Europe Video Music Awards performance of *Aero Dynamik* by Kraftwerk suggest how future holograms might be used. This was filmed live and included on the *Minimum–Maximum* DVD. It is unclear if any imagery was added to the video after the event but this is

---

[1] Cook, N., *Analysing musical multimedia* (1998) 74.

[2] CNN debuts hologram reporters, *Sydney Morning Herald*, 5 November (2008).

[3] Bland, E., Future 6D holograms interact with light, *News in Science*, ABC [web site] (2008).

irrelevant. The DVD shows transparent blocks and columns of luminous green images scattered throughout the concert space. These are comprised of moving text, lines, patterns and circuit boards. The transparent blocks are suspended above the audience while the columns extend from floor to ceiling. The result is a dynamic visual accompaniment to the music that does not distract from or background the music.

In the instrumental concert, holograms of the orchestra could be combined with such things as the music score. If the images were semi-transparent, or slightly blurred, there would not be the usual problem with close-ups on screen, where every imperfection and bead of sweat can be seen. Even so, the images would be clear enough to see facial expressions and gestures and to allow the audience to feel the intimacy of a close performance. Ghost-like projections of different musicians in different places would not look out of place but create an effect focusing attention on the musicians, their playing and their music. When the live concert creates these types of visuals, and hopefully holography technology will allow it in the near future, then image in concert will have come of age.

Multimedia

It could be claimed that any music-image combination is multimedia and the dictionary meaning is normally something to the effect of involving several media and entertainment. If this were the case, ballet and opera would be considered multimedia although they are not normally thought of as such. There is a more appropriate definition of multimedia.

Multimedia presupposes that the mediums will interact, dominance will pass from one media to another, that conflict will occur and something new will emerge. There are three models of multimedia that are based on the perceived interaction of media, which are: conformance, complementation and contest. The first, conformance, occurs with a close match of music and image. This is rare in multimedia because conformance is more a simple joining together of different art forms and multimedia is normally more complex. Complementation is where music and image contrast and/or one media adds what is missing to the other media. Complementation may border on conflict but in fact it does not conflict. Complementation might also occur less than expected because multimedia is often more about contest. The third mode, contest, occurs where music and image appear in conflict. It might at first appear the overall multimedia relationship is based mainly on conflict but this is a superficial view and closer analysis distinguishes that all three relationships exist even if conformance and complementation are a minor part. In summary, multimedia presupposes that the mediums will interact and dominance will pass from one media to another and something new will emerge.[1]

In the music-image relationship in concert, the music and image are not meant to interact. The likely outcome of interaction is a focus on the image or at best the music-image combination. The music and image should match or be complementary. However a complementary relationship in the music-image concert is not quite the same as that defined in the multimedia models. In the multimedia models a complementary relationship can 'teeter' on the verge of conflict[2]. In the music-image combination for the music concert, a complementary relationship means the music and images clearly support each other and do not border on the verge of incongruency. For the music concert, each media should complement the other to make the combination perfect.

In the music-image combination for concert it is likely that the image will often need to be sacrificed to maintain the dominance of the music. For an audience interested in general entertainment rather than specifically listening to the music, multimedia may be more appropriate.

Innovation in the music concert

The music-image performances of the Australian Chamber Orchestra have been discussed extensively and this is due to the orchestra's innovation and willingness to take risks. The Australian Chamber Orchestra has been leading edge in the introduction of image to classical music, and this has been especially difficult given that music-image concert theory is in its infancy. While a number of their performances have been criticised in this book, even these performances have been of exceptional quality and contain new and intriguing ideas. Others who attended these concerts may consider some of the reviews here harsh, and they may well be, but these reviews were written from the perspective of achieving a perfect music-image result. It is to the credit of the Australian Chamber Orchestra that a high level of quality is achieved while implementing new concepts. It is only through the willingness to take risks and experiment with something new that the emerging field of music and image in concert will develop.

---

[1] Cook, N., *Analysing musical multimedia* (1998) vii-ix, 98-106,112-120.

[2] Cook, N., *Analysing musical multimedia* (1998) 120.

Last word

"Music is a fundamental human resource which has played in the past, and may well play again, a vital role in the survival and development of humanity"[1]. While some aspects of society might be considered as superfluous for day-to-day survival, it is not so with music. Music could be compared to child's play, which might also seem non-essential to life itself. In the last decade evidence has emerged that play is valuable from an evolutionary perspective because it is essential for development of social, intellectual and physical skills; there is also evidence that play deprivation leads to both intentional and unintentional violence against others[2].

Music is an important part of society, and cultures without music do not exist; so while music may not be essential to an individual, it may be essential to a society[3]. Music may well have a similar role as that of play in building social structure and cohesion, so it is important to maintain all types of music. If it is necessary to add image to keep the instrumental music concert alive and introduce it to a wider audience we should do so. However, adding image to music should be carried out from a knowledgeable base. The ideas offered here provide a starting point for instrumental concert music-image theory where image does not background the music, with the possibility that it may be used to foreground the music.

---

[1] Sloboda, J., *The musical mind: the cognitive psychology of music* (1985) 268.

[2] Brown, S., Through the lens of play, & Concepts of childhood and play, *ReVision*, 17/4 (1995) 4-12 & 35-42; Play as an organizing principle in *Animal Play*, M. Bekoff & J. A. Byers eds, (1998) 247-248.

[3] Sloboda, J., *The musical mind: the cognitive psychology of music* (1985) 267.

Glossary

Added Value: Chion's theory where one sensory perception influences another and transforms it, resulting in us not seeing the same thing when we are listening, and not hearing the same thing when we are seeing.[1]

Ambiguous narrative: The narrative is unclear and demands the viewer decipher the information to find the correct interpretation; often occurs in mysteries and art films.

Apparent narrative: A brief, superficial story that skims over the details but has a beginning and an ending and the feeling of time passing; is often used in music-videos.

Apparent synchronisation: There appears to be synchronisation but actually there is none. There are two types: a) sound creates apparent visual movement where there is an expectation of movement but none actually occurs; b) the synchronisation occurs within a window of time that appears synchronised but when measured precisely is not.

Characteristic: The characteristics of the music-image relationship that are considered important for the addition of image to the instrumental music concert; these are: narrative, synchronisation, rhythm, tempo-pace, meaning, emotion, structure, continuity, genre-style. Voice, text (written words), integration (of the performance components) and the musical interpretation by the musician or conductor, are a slightly different form of characteristic as they influence the music-image relationship rather than actually being part of it.

Complementary relationship: A music-image relationship which forms a 'balanced whole' where one media adds what is missing in the other media; and/or one media contrasts with the other as occurs with complementary colours; there is no conflict between the music and image which co-exist without detracting from each other.

Complex narrative: A narrative that requires focused concentration to be understood due to its complexity.

Congruency: A relationship where the characteristics of the image match the music, and vice versa; where they are perceived as corresponding and being in a general state of agreement, as far as this can be achieved with different media.

---

[1] Chion, M., *Audio-Vision* (1994) 5.

Continuous synchronisation: The music and image occur in parallel over a period of time with nothing out of sync; this may be in the form of waxing and waning in unison, and/or they may start and end on a sync point.

Element: See music elements; and image elements.

Full congruency: A match of each image characteristic to the equivalent music characteristics within the music-image relationship.

Humorous narrative: A narrative that tells a humorous story such as is created in cartoons and comedies.

Incongruency: A conflict between music and image caused by any type conflict within any music-image characteristic. The conflict may occur across one or more characteristics.

Instrumental music concert: A performance where it is intended that the music remains dominant or at least maintains the same level of dominance as other media, and where at no stage in the performance is the music backgrounded by other media.

Intensified continuity: A film industry term which applies to scenes created from the continued use of rapid cuts and close-ups. It is a technique used by some B-grade filmmakers and is intended to create shock and suspense with moment-to-moment anticipation that glues the viewer to the screen.[1]

Image element: Line, shape, mass, texture and colour.

Image rhythm: In film, image rhythm is created by change, movement and cuts. In a series of still images it is created by changing the image.

Loose narrative: Loosely linked themes as often occur in music-videos but with no traditional storyline.

Media: Music, speech and image individually or collectively.

Mickey-mousing: A very close synchronisation of music and image which can easily and unintentionally slip into cartoon mode[2]. It can also refer to the duplication of action by music or dialogue which may in film be considered a weakness.

Multimedia: Where multiple media interact and dominance passes from one media to another.

Music element: Pitch, timbre, harmonics, loudness and rhythm.

---

[1] Bordwell, D., Intensified Continuity: Visual Style in Contemporary American Film (2002) 14, 16-17, 22, 24

[2] Chion, M., *Audio-Vision* (1994) 54.

Music-image characteristic: See characteristic.

Music rhythm: Rhythm in music is the grouping of separate sounds into structured patterns and these patterns may be the result of the interaction of pitch, intensity, timbre, texture, harmony and duration[1]. While strictly speaking pulse (beat) and metre are separate to rhythm, here the term 'rhythm' includes all three temporal modes: rhythm, pulse and metre.

Narrative: A story that communicates particular events that occur over time. Narrative may be created through the spoken word, written down as text, or documented using visual media.

Neutral congruency: A music-image relationship where the characteristics of the music and image are complementary. They do not match the music but nor do they conflict.

Neutral synchronisation: There is no synchronisation but nothing is out of sync.

Newstring music: Original music that combines elements from classical, jazz and varying types of popular music, and is played on a combination of modern and classical instruments. It most frequently includes the violin and a modern percussion instrument or electronic percussion device. It has a fluid but recognisable structure and includes improvisation. It is not to be compared with easy listening music that takes removes the harmonic complexity and dissonance from classical music. Newstring would normally increase harmonic complexity and dissonance. Term coined by the author in 2007 to describe the music of groups such as the Australian group CODA and the Haitian-American violinist and band leader, Daniel Bernard Roumain, DBR.

Non Narrative: A series of disconnected images that can be comprised of two types of images. The first type of image is where individual images have meaning but even if these images are all on the same topic, there is no storyline relating them to each other. The second is where the images themselves have no intended meaning, such as patterns and colours.

Open narrative: The narrative is open to accept many different overlays allowing the viewer to construct their own meaning but (importantly) the narrative does not demand to be deciphered.

Pace: The speed of image change, which in films is often created by cutting scenes but can be created by movement. With still image the pace is

[1] Cooper, G. & Meyer, L., *The Rhythmic Structure of Music*, (1963) 1.

determined by the rate the images are changed. Note that for clarity, 'tempo' is used for music and 'pace' refers to image.

Partial congruency: A music-image relationship comprised of a combination of congruent characteristics and neutral characteristics.

Partial incongruency: A music-image relationship comprised of a combination of incongruent characteristics and neutral characteristics. Even if only one characteristic is incongruent it will distract from the music. Partial incongruency is necessary for the multimedia concept of 'emergence' where a limited overlap of attributes can create a new meaning. See Cook's models of multimedia.[1]

Program music: Music specifically composed to represent or accompany a theme or narrative. Program music was popular in the Romantic period. While opera and song could be considered program music, the term is normally only used for instrumental music. It is also used here to refer to music specifically written to accompany images.

Program music narrative: Narrative that has already been suggested by the title(s) allocated by the composer. It can also be the narrative in music written specifically to accompany another art form.

Rhythm: See Music rhythm; Image rhythm.

Strong narrative: A strong traditional style story that dominates all else, as normally occurs in dramas, thrillers and mysteries.

Synchresis: An unlikely combination of sound and image which become associated because of synchronisation. Term coined by Michel Chion[2].

Synchronisation: A regular process of recurring accents of music and image that appear to occur at the same time. An accent in music may be made using tone, loudness or beat. An accent in image may occur through movement or change.

Tempo: The rate of speed that the music is performed. Traditionally, it is indicated by the Italian markings such as 'largo', 'andante', and 'presto'. Since the nineteenth century, tempo has also been indicated by a metronome marking. Note that for clarity, 'tempo' is used for music and 'pace' refers to image.

---

[1] Cook, N., *Analysing musical multimedia* (1998) 69, 73-74, 82-86, 98-106.

[2] Chion, M., *Audio-Vision* (1994) 63.

Suggested reading and viewing

Audio-Vision by Michel Chion

Chion's wide ranging ideas form the basis of an all encompassing audio-visual theory, and his book[1], even though based around films, is essential reading to understand the music-image relationship. This book has been brilliantly translated by Professor Claudia Gorbman, and even though originally written in French, the English version is extremely coherent, readable and easy to understand.

Analysing Musical Multimedia by Nicholas Cook

Cook's multimedia models discussed in his book[2] provide valuable insights into the music-image relationship and provide an understanding of how media interact and the result of their interaction.

Experiencing Music Video by Carol Vernallis

Vernallis' book[3] provides a wealth of ideas and examples on how music and image can be combined to create specific effects. The book has a comprehensive index which allows readers to home in on their areas of interest. However as the intention of the book is to discuss the music-video, care needs to be taken in its application to the music concert and the ideas should be checked against the theories in this book to ensure they are appropriate for concert. Even so, the Vernallis book provides many useful ideas and is a must for all image creators.

Minimum–Maximum by Kraftwerk [DVD]

The 2004 World Tour by the German avant-garde group Kraftwerk, which has been captured on DVD[4] and shows examples of how the theories discussed in this book can be applied. These music-image combinations show how music can be accompanied by image which is minimalist, congruent and interesting, and at the same time maintains the focus on the music. The images used have evolved over time with some dating back to the seventies; even so the imagery is "still light years ahead of anyone else"[5]. Kraftwerk appear to have an instinctive understanding how to use image to focus on the music.

---

[1] Chion, M., *Audio-Vision* (1994).

[2] Cook, N., *Analysing musical multimedia,* (1998).

[3] Vernallis, C., *Experiencing Music Video* (2004).

[4] Kraftwerk, *Minimum-Maximum* DVD (2005).

[5] Reed M., (2004) Kraftwerk, http://www.mark-reed.net/[review of concert performed at Royal Festival Hall, London, on 18 March 2004].

Bibliography

Alessandrini, Paul, Kraftwerk, *Rock & Folk* 118 (Nov. 1976).

Allen, George D., Speech Rhythm: its relation to performance universals and articulartory timing, *Journal of phonetics* 3 (1975) 75-86.

Alperson, Philip, The Instrumentality of Music, *Aesthetics and Art Criticism* 66/1 (2008).

Altman, Rick, Moving Lips: Cinema as Ventriloquism, *Yale French Studies* 60, Cinema/Sound (1980) 67-79.

Annear, Judy, in *Mnemosyne* [Bill Henson exhibition catalogue], Art Gallery of NSW, Zurich: Scalo (2005).

Bailey, Derek, *Improvisation : its nature and practice in music*, New York: Da Capo (1993).

Balazs, Bela, Theory of the Film: Sound, *Film Sound: Theory and Practice*, E Weiss & J Belton (eds), New York: Columbia University Press (1985).

Barthes, Roland, *Image Music Text*, London: Fontana Press, HarperCollins (1977).

Barthes, Roland, *The Responsibility of Forms: Critical Essays on Music, Art and Representation*, Oxford: Basil Blackwell (1986).

Benjamin, Walter, *Illuminations* ; edited and with an introduction by Hannah Arendt, translated by Harry Zohn, London: Pimlico (1999).

Benson, Bruce Ellis, *The improvisation of Musical Dialogue: A Phenomenology of Music*, Cambridge University Press (2003).

Bibby, Paul & Jensen, Erik, Art obscenity charges, *Sydney Morning Herald*, May 24 (2008).

Biedermann, Hans, *Dictionary of Symbolism*, translated from German by James Hulbert, New York: FactsOnFile (1992).

Björnberg, Alf, Structural Relationships of Music and Images in Music Video, *Popular Music* 13/1 (1994).

Björnberg, Alf, Video. 2. Structure, *Gove Music Online* ed L. Macy (2008) http://www.grovemusic.com accessed 10 Feb 2008.

Bland, Eric, Future 6D holograms interact with light, *News in Science*, Australian Broadcasting Corporation (2008) http://www.abc.net.au/science/articles/2008/09/09/2359903.htm accessed 20 February 2009.

Bolivar, Valerie J., Cohen, Annabel J., & Fentress, John C., Semantic and Formal Congruency in Music and Motion, *Psychomusicology* 13 Spring/Fall (1994) 28-59.

Boltz, Marilyn, Schulkind, Matthew & Kantra, Suzanne, Effects of background music on the remembering of filmed events, *Memory and Cognition* 19/6 (1991) 593-606.

Bordwell, David & Thompson, Kristin, *Film art: an introduction*, New York: McGraw Hill (2004).

Bordwell, David, Intensified Continuity: Visual Style in Contemporary American Film, *Film Quarterly* 55/3 (Spring, 2002) 16-28.

Botticelli, Lisa-Maree, *The Red Tree Concert Reviews* [online] (2008) http://www.aco.com.au/?url=/redtree-reviews accessed 12 Sep 2008.

Bresson, Robert, *Notes on Cinematography*, translated from French by Jonathan Griffin, New York: Urizen Books (1977).

Brown, Howard M., Performing Practice. I Western. 1 General, *Grove Music Online* ed. L. Macy, http://www.grovemusic.com accessed 5 May 2007.

Brown, Stuart L., Concepts of childhood and play, *ReVision*, 17/4 (1995) 35-42.

Brown, Stuart L., Through the lens of play, *ReVision*, 17/4 (1995) 4-12.

Brown, Stuart L., Play as an organizing principle: clinical evidence and personal observations, *Animal Play: Evolutionary, Comparative and Ecological Perspectives,* M. Bekoff & J. A. Byers eds, Cambridge University Press (1998) 243-258.

Bruner, Jerome, The Narrative Construction of Reality, *Critical Inquiry*, 18/1 (1991) 1-21.

Buck, Tony, in Who's Necksed?, *Timeout Sydney*, (2008) http://www.timeoutsydney.com.au/music/classicaljazz/the-necks.aspx accessed 4 June 2008.

Buck, Tony, in The Necks, *Sydney Morning Herald,* 24 May (2008).

Bussy, Pascal, *Kraftwerk: Man, Machine and Music*, London: SAF (2005).

Calvert, Gemma A., Brammer, Michael J. & Iversen, Susan D., 'Crossmodal identification', *Trends in Cognitive Sciences* 2/7 (1998) 247-253.

Capon, Edmund, in *Mnemosyne* [Bill Henson exhibition catalogue], Art Gallery of NSW, Zurich: Scalo (2005).

Carney, Emily, Kraftwerk's Computer World, *suite101.com* (2008) http://electro-music.suite101.com/article.cfm/kraftwerks_computer_world accessed 26 December 2008.

Chion, Michel, *Audio-Vision: Sound on Screen*, New York: Columbia University Press (1994).

Chion, Michel, *The Voice in Cinema*, Edited and translated by Claudia Gorbman, New York: Columbia University Press (1999).

Clark, Eric F., Structure and Expression in Rhythmic Performance, *Musical Structure and Cognition*, eds Howell, P., Cross I. & West, R., London: Academic Press (1985).

Cohen, Annabel J., Associationsim and musical soundtrack phenomena, *Contemporary Music Review* 9 Issue 1 & 2 (1993) 163-178.

Cohen, Annabel J., Film Music: Perspectives from Cognitive Psychology, *Music and Cinema*, Buhler, James, Flinn, Caryl & Neumeyer, David, eds, Hanover: Wesleyan University Press (2000).

Cohen, Annabel J., Music Cognition and the Cognitive Psychology of Film Structure, *Canadian Psychology* 43/4 (2002) 215–232.

Colavita, Francis B. & Weisberg, Daniel, A further investigation of visual dominance, *Perception & Psychophysics* 25/4 (1979).

Cook, Nicholas, *Analysing musical multimedia*, New York: Oxford University Press (1998).

Cooper, Grosvenor & Meyer, Leonard B., *The Rhythmic Structure of Music*, University of Chicago Press (1963).

Craven, Peter, Sexuality or spirituality: it's a matter of tastė, *Sydney Morning Herald*, 24 May (2008).

Crosby, Sumner McK, *Helen Gardner's Art Through the Ages*, 4th ed, New York: Harcourt, Brace & Co (1959).

Davison, Jane W., Visual Perception of Performance Manner in the Movements of Solo Musicians, *Psychology of Music* 21 (1993) 103-113.

Davies, Stephen, Representation in Music, *Aesthetic Education*, 27/1 (1993) 16-22.

Davies, Stephen, *Musical Works and Performances: A Philosophical Exploration*, Oxford University Press (2001).

Dunsby, Jonathan, Performance, *Grove Music Online*, ed L. Macy (2007) http://www.grovemusic.com
accessed 5 May 2008.

Durant, Alan, *Conditions of music*, London: Macmillan (1984).

Easton, Randolph D. & Falz, Michelle, Finger pressure during tracking of curved contours: Implications for a visual dominance phenomenon, *Perception & Psychophysics*, 24/2 (1978) 145-153.

Eisenstein, Sergei M., *The Film Sense*, New York : Harcourt, Brace & World (1947).

Eisenstein, Sergei M., *Film Form: Essays in Film Theory*, New York : Harcourt, Brace and World (1949).

English, Horace B., "Fantasia" and the Psychology of Music, *Aesthetics and Art Criticism*, 2/7 (1942-3) 27-31.

Evans, Brian, Foundations of a Visual Music, *Computer Music Journal*, 29/4 Winter (2005) 11-24.

Farah, Martha J., Director, Center for Cognitive Neuroscience, University of Pennsylvania in Greenfield, The Mind's Eye, *Brain Story* (2000).

Fehrman, Kenneth R. & Fehrman, Cherie, *Color: The secret influence*, New Jersey: Prentice Hall (2004).

Fehrman, Kenneth R. & Fehrman, Cherie, *Study Guide: Color: The Secret Influence*, New Jersey: Prentice Hall (2000).

Feld, Steven, Communication, Music, and Speech about Music, *Yearbook for Traditional Music* 16 (1984) 1-18.

Föllmer, Golo & Gerlach, Julia, Audiovisions: Music as an Intermedia Art Form, *Media Art Net* (2004)
http://www.medienkunstnetz.de/themes/image-sound_relations/audiovisions/
accessed 13 February 2008.

Ford, Andrew, *In Defence of Classical Music*, Sydney: ABC Books (2005).

Geringer, John M, Cassidy, Jane W & Byo, James L, Effects of Music with Video on Responses of Nonmusic Majors: An Exploratory Study, *Research in Music Education* 44/3 (1996) 240-251.

Goertzen, Valerie Woodring, Setting the Stage: Clara Schumann's Preludes, *In the Course of Performance: Studies in the World of Music Improvisation*, ed Bruno Nettl, London: University of Chicago Press (1998).

Gombrich, Ernst Hans Josef, *Art and Illusion: A study in the psychology of pictorial representation*, London: Phaidon Press (1977).

Gombrich, Ernst Hans Josef, *Four Theories of Artistic Expression*, Manchester University (1996).

Gombrich, Ernst Hans Josef, *The Image and the Eye: Further studies in the psychology of pictorial representation*, London: Phaidon Press (1982).

Gorbman, Claudia, *Unheard Melodies: Narrative Film Music*, London: British Film Institute (1987).

Gorbman, Claudia, Aesthetics and Rhetoric, *American Music*, 22/1 Spring (2004) 14-26.

Gray, Louise, The Classic Kraftwerk, *New Internationalist* 314 (1999)
http://www.newint.org/issue314/reviews.htm
accessed 3 February 2008.

Greenfield, Susan, The Mind's Eye, *Brain Story*, BBC Television (2000).

Grimes, Tom, Audio-video correspondence and its role in attention and memory, *Educational Technology Research and Development*, 38/3 (1990) 15-25.

Hagström, Andréas, *Neon lights - Signs of Düsseldorf* (2004-5)
http://www.valand.gu.se/dm/students/andreas/kw_skivor/neon/neonlight.html
accessed 22 February 2009

Hennion, Antoine, The Production of Success: An Anti-Musicology of the Pop Song, *Popular Music* 3 Producers and Markets (1983) 159-193.

Hershman, Daniel P., Rhythmic Factors in Tonality, *Psychomusicology* 14 (1995) 4-19.

Hindson, Matthew, The Future of Classical Music, *2MBS FM Fine Music* [magazine], May (2005).

Hocking, Rachel & Letts, Richard, *International classical music audience attendance trends 1990-2005*, Music Council of Australia (2008).

Iliffe, A. H., A study of preferences in feminine beauty, *British Journal of Psychology*, 51 (1960).

Iwamiya, Shin-ichiro, Interaction Between Auditory and Visual Processing When Listening to Music in an Audio Visual Context: 1. Matching 2. Audio Quality, *Psychomusicology* 13 (1994) 133-153.

Johnson, William, Sound and Image: A Further Hearing, *Film Quarterly* 43/1 Autumn (1989) 24-35.

Johnson, William, The Liberation of Echo: A New Hearing for Film Sound, *Film Quarterly* 38/4 (1985) 2-12.

Jones, Steve, Cohesive But Not Coherent: Music Videos, *Popular Music and Society* 12/4 (1988) 15-29.

Juslin, Patrik N. & Västfjäll, Daniel, Emotional Responses to Music: The Need to Consider Underlying Mechanisms, *Behavioral and Brain Sciences* 31/5 (Oct 2008) 559-575.

Kahneman, Daniel, *Attention and effort*, New Jersey: Prentice-Hall (1973).

Kalinak, Kathryn, *Settling the score: music and the classical Hollywood film*, University of Wisconsin (1992).

Kamien, Roger, *Music an Appreciation*, Boston: McGraw Hill (2000).

Kassabian, Anahid, *Hearing Film: Tracking Identification in Contemporary Hollywood Film Music*, New York: Routledge (2001).

Kassabian, Anahid, The Sound of a New Film Form, *Popular Music and Film*, I. Inglis ed, Wallflower Press (2003).

Katz, Steven D., *Film directing shot by shot: visualizing from concept to screen*, Studio City, CA: Michael Wiese Productions in conjunction with Focal Press (1991).

Kidd, Gary, Boltz, Marilyn & Jones, Mari Riess, Some Effects of Rhythmic Context on Melody Recognition, *American Journal of Psychology*, 97/2 Summer (1984) 153-173.

Kinder, Marsha, Music Video and the Spectator: Television, Ideology and Dream, *Film Quarterly* 38/1 (1984) 2-15.

Konečni, Vladimir J., Social Interaction and Musical Preference, *The Psychology of Music*, D. Deutsch ed, New York: Academic Press (1982).

Koopman, Constantijn, Essay Review of Gender and Aesthetics, *Action, Criticism & Theory for Music Education* [online journal] 5/1 January (2006).

Kozma, Robert B., Learning with Media, *Review of Educational Research* 61/2 (1991) 179-211.

LaBerge, David, Attentional Processing in Music Listening: A Cognitive Neuroscience Approach, *Psychomusicology* 14 Spring/Fall (1995) 20-34.

Langer, Susanne, *Philosophy in a new key: a study in the symbolism of reason, rite, and art*, Cambridge: Harvard University Press (1960).

Lebrecht, Norman, *Sunday Arts* [interview], ABC1 television screened 7 October (2007).

Lehiste, Ilse, Rhythmic units and syntactic units in production and perception, *Acoustical Society of America*, 54/5 (1973) 1228-1234.

Levin, Robert, *Improvising Mozart*, presentation at American Academy of Arts and Sciences, Cambridge, Massachusetts, 12th December (2001). www.amacad.org/publications/bulletin/winter2002/levin.pdf accessed 17 July 2006

Levinger, Esther, Art and Mathematics in the Thought of El Lissitzky: His Relationship to Suprematism and Constructivism Art and Mathematics in the Thought of El Lissitzky: His Relationship to Suprematism and Constructivism, *Leonardo Music Journal*, 22/2 (1989) 227-236.

Lévi-Strauss, Claude, *The raw and the cooked: Introduction to the Science of Mythology*, London: Jonathan Cape (1970).

Lindgren, Ernest, *The art of the film*, 2d ed, New York: Macmillan (1963).

Lindner, Daniel & Hynaan, Michael T., Perceived structure of abstract paintings as a function of structure of music listened to on initial viewing, *Bulletin of the Psychonomic Society* 25/1 (1987) 44-46.

Lipscomb, Scott D. & Kendall, Roger A., Perceptual Judgement of the Relationship between Musical and Visual Components in Film, *Psychomusicology*, 13 (1994) 60-98.

Malouf, David, in *Mnemosyne* [Bill Henson exhibition catalogue], Art Gallery of NSW, Zurich: Scalo (2005).

Manning, Toby, *The Rough Guide to Pink Floyd*, London: Rough Guides (2006).

Marks, Lawrence E., *The unity of the senses: interrelations among the modalities*, New York: Academic Press (1978).

Marks, Martin, Music, Drama, Warner Brothers: The Cases of Casablanca and The Maltese Falcon, *Michigan quarterly review*, XXXV/1, (1996) 112-142
http://hdl.handle.net/2027/spo.act2080.0035.001:15 accessed 31 Aug 2008.

Marschalek, Douglas G., What Eye Movement Research Tells Us about Perceptual Behavior of Children and Adults: Implications for the Visual Arts, *Studies in Art Education* 27/3 Spring (1986) 123-130.

Marshall, Sandra K., & Cohen, Annabel J., Effects of Musical Soundtracks on Attitudes toward Animated Geometric Figures, *Music Perception* 6/1 (1988) 95-112.

Martinec, Radan, Rhythm in Multimodal Texts, *Leonardo* 33/4 (2000) 289-297.

Martynov, Ivan Ivanovich, *Dmitri Shostakovich, the man and his work*, translated from Russian by T. Guralsky, New York: Philosophical Library (1947).

Mason, Nick, *Inside Out: A Personal History of Pink Floyd*, San Francisco: Chronicle Books (2004).

Mathison, Laura, A Potent Mix, *The Red Tree Concert Reviews* [online] (2008) http://www.aco.com.au/?url=/redtree-reviews accessed 12 September 2008.

McBurney, Gerard, *Shostakovich, Dmitri: String Quartet No.15 in Eb minor op. 144* [Repertoire Note] Boosey & Hawkes (2008) http://www.boosey.com/cr/music/Dmitri-Shostakovich-String-Quartet-No-15-in-Eb-minor/2880 accessed 12 September 2008.

McGurk, Harry & MacDonald, John, 'Hearing lips and seeing voices', *Nature* 264 (1976) 746 - 748.

Metz, Christian & Gurrieri, Georgia, Aural Objects, *Yale French Studies* 60 (1980) 24-32.

Meyer, Leonard B., *Emotion and Meaning in Music*, University of Chicago Press (1956).

Meyer, Leonard B., *Music, the Arts and Ideas*, University of Chicago Press (1970).

Miles, Barry, *Pink Floyd: The Early Years,* London: Omnibus Press (2006).

Miller, Benjamin O., Time Perception in Musical Meter Perception, *Psychomusicology*, 12, (1993) 124-153.

Mithen, Steven, *The prehistory of the mind: a search for the origins of art, religion and science,* London: Phoenix (1996).

Morgan, George A., Goodson, Felix E. & Jones, Thomas, Age Differences in the Associations between Felt Temperatures and Color Choices, *American Journal of Psychology*, 88/1 (1975) 125-130.

Morgan, Robert P. *Twentieth-Century Music: A History of Musical Style in Modern Europe and America*, New York: W. W. Norton (1991).

Müller-Freienfels, Richard, On Visual Representation: The Meaning of Pictures and Symbols, *Aesthetics and Art Criticism* 7/2 (1948) 112-121.

Nattiez, Jean-Jacques, *Music and Discourse: Toward a Semiology of Music*, New Jersey : Princeton University Press (1990).

Nicolson, Mairi, *Weekend Life*, ABC Classic FM radio, 30th August (2008).

Nielsen, *Television's Popularity is Still Growing*, Nielsen Media Research (2006).

O'Connell, Clive, Visual feast, young choir in fine voice, *The Age* [newspaper] 17 July (2008).

Orpen, Valerie, *Film Editing: the Art of the Expressive*, London: Wallflower (2003).

Peretti, Peter, A Study of Student Correlations between Music and Six Paintings by Klee, *Research in Music Education*, 20/4 Winter (1972) 501-504.

Pickford, R.W., *Psychology and Visual Aesthetics,* London: Hutchinson Educational (1972).

Posner, Michael I., Nissen, Mary J. & Klein, Raymond M., Visual dominance: an information-processing account of its origins and significance, *Psychological Review* 83/2 (1976) 158-9,170.

Rantzen, Andy, Audio Visual Synthesis, *Soundtoys*, (2005) http://www.soundtoys.net/journals/audio-visual-synthesis accessed 11 February 2008.

Read, Herbert, in *El Lissitzky: Life.Letters.Text*, ed S. Lissitzky-Küppers, London: Thames and Hudson (1968).

Reed, Mark, Kraftwerk [review] mark-read.net (2004) http://www.mark-reed.net/
accessed 1/2/2008

Ryan, T.A. & Schehr, Frances, The Influence of Eye Movement and Position on Auditory Localization, *American Journal of Psychology*, 54/2 (April 1941) 243-252.

Sacks, Oliver, *Musicophilia*, London: Picador (2007).

Sadie, Stanley & Latham, Alison, *The Cambridge Music Guide*, Cambridge University Press (1996).

Said, Edward, *Musical Elaborations*, New York: Columbia University Press (1991).

Schoenberg, Harold C., *The lives of the great composers*, London: Davis-Poynter (1971).

Scholes, Percy A., Colour and Music, *Oxford Companion to Music*, Oxford University Press (1970).

Sebastian Smee, Touch of innocence, Weekend Australian, January 22-23, (2005).

Shapiro, Kimron L., Egerman, Barbaba & Klein, Raymond M., Effects of arousal on human visual dominance, Perception & Psychophysics, 35/6 (1984) 547-552.

Simmen, Jeannot & Kohlhoff, Kkolja, *Kaimir Malevich: Life and Work*, Cologne: Konemann (1999).

Sink, Patricia E., Effects of Rhythmic and Melodic Alterations and Selected Musical Experiences on Rhythmic Processing, *Research in Music Education*, 32/3 Autumn (1984) 177-193.

Sink, Patricia E., Effects of Rhythmic and Melodic Alterations on Rhythmic Perception, *Research in Music Education* 31/2 Summer (1983) 101-113.

Sloboda, John A., Music Performance, *The Psychology of Music,* ed D. Deutsch, New York: Academic Press (1982).

Sloboda, John A., *The musical mind: the cognitive psychology of music*, Oxford: Clarendon Press (1985).

Smith, Ethan, Sales of Music, Long in Decline, Plunge Sharply, *The Wall Street Journal*, 21 March (2007).

Sternthal, Brian & Craig, C Samuel, Humor in Advertising, *Journal of Marketing*, 37/4 October (1973) 12-18.

Stockhammer, Jonathan, *Morning Interview*, ABC Classic FM radio, 7th March (2008).

Stravinsky, Igor, *Chronicle of My Life,* London: Victor Gollancz (1936).

Sutton, Mike, Much Ado About Nothing, *DVD Times* (2008) http://www.dvdtimes.co.uk/reviews/region2/muchadoaboutnothing.html accessed 31 October 2008.

Sydney Morning Herald, CNN debuts hologram reporters, 5 November (2008) http://www.smh.com.au/news/home/technology/cnn-debuts-hologram-reporters/2008/11/05/1225560913200.html accessed 20 November 2008.

Szabo, Adam, ACO Shines in The Red Tree, *The Red Tree Concert Reviews* [online] (2008) http://www.aco.com.au/?url=/redtree-reviews accessed 12 September 2008.

Thompson, William, Graham, Phil, & Russo, Frank Seeing music performance: Visual influences on perception and experience, *Semiotica* 156/1-4 (2005).

Thompson, William F., Russo, Frank & Quinto, Lena, Audio-visual integration of emotional cues in song (2008) unpublished.

Tuttle, Raymond, Dmitri Shostakovich: String Quartet #15, *Classical Net* (2003) http://www.classical.net/music/recs/reviews/e/ecm01755a.php accessed 12 September 2008.

van Leeuwen, Theo, Rhythmic Structure of the Film Text, in *Discourse and communication: new approaches to the analysis of mass media discourse and communication*, ed T. A. van Dijk, Berlin: Walter de Gruyter (1985).

van Leeuwen, Theo, *Speech, Music, Sound*, London: MacMillan (1999).

Vernallis, Carol, *Experiencing Music Video: Aesthetics and Cultural Context,* New York: Columbia University Press (2004).

Vitouch, Oliver, Sovdat, Sandra & Holler, Norman, Audio-vision: Visual input drives perceived music tempo, *9th International Conference on Music Perception and Cognition*, Alma Mater Studiorum University of Bologna, August 22-26 (2006).

Walton, Kendall, Listening with Imagination: Is Music Representational?, *Aesthetics and Art Criticism* 52/1, The Philosophy of Music, Winter (1994) 47-61.

Weber, William, Concert (ii), *Grove Music Online*, ed L. Macy (2007) http://www.grovemusic.com accessed 17 April 2008.

Weidenaar, Reynold, Live Music and Moving Images: Composing and Producing the Concert Video, *Perspectives of New Music* 24/2 (1986) 270-279.

Wilson, Raff, Artistic Administration Manager Sydney Symphony Orchestra, personal communication, 28 March (2007).

Woods, Peter, Coping at School through Humour, *British Journal of Sociology of Education* 4/2 (1983) 111-124.

Young, Kay & Saver, Jeffrey L., The Neurology of Narrative, *SubStance* 30, No. 1/2, Issue 94/95: Special Issue: On the Origin of Fictions: Interdisciplinary Perspectives (2001) 72-84.

Index

www.ingramcontent.com/pod-product-compliance
Lightning Source LLC
LaVergne TN
LVHW090942080826
845145LV00003B/854